HIDDEN ®

Philadelphia & the Amish Country

HIDDEN®

Philadelphia & the Amish Country

Including Lancaster, Brandywine and Bucks County

Patricia Kime

Ulysses Press®
BERKELEY, CALIFORNIA

Published by:
ULYSSES PRESS
P.O. Box 3440
Berkeley, CA 94703
www.ulyssespress.com

ISSN 1555-466X
ISBN 1-56975-530-2

Printed in Canada by Transcontinental Printing

10 9 8 7 6 5 4 3 2 1

MANAGING EDITOR: Claire Chun
EDITOR: Lily Chou
COPYEDITOR: Barbara Schultz
EDITORIAL ASSOCIATES: Kathryn Brooks, Leona Benten
TYPESETTING: Lisa Kester, Matt Orendorff
CARTOGRAPHY: Pease Press
COVER PHOTOGRAPHY: © Gettyimages.com

Distributed by Publishers Group West

For my fellow vagabonds:
Carl, Dean, Stephen and Jenny

Write to us!

If in your travels you discover a spot that captures the spirit of Philadelphia and the Amish Country, or if you live in the region and have a favorite place to share, or if you just feel like expressing your views, write to us and we'll pass your note along to the author.

We can't guarantee that the author will add your personal find to the next edition, but if the writer does use the suggestion, we'll acknowledge you in the credits and send you a free copy of the new edition.

ULYSSES PRESS
P.O. Box 3440
Berkeley, CA 94703
E-mail: readermail@ulyssespress.com

What's Hidden?

At different points throughout this book, you'll find special listings marked with this symbol:

◀ HIDDEN

This means that you have come upon a place off the beaten tourist track, a spot that will carry you a step closer to the local people and natural environment of Philadelphia and the Amish Country.

The goal of this guide is to lead you beyond the realm of everyday tourist facilities. While we include traditional sightseeing listings and popular attractions, we also offer alternative sights and adventure activities. Instead of filling this guide with reviews of standard hotels and chain restaurants, we concentrate on one-of-a-kind places and locally owned establishments.

Our authors seek out locales that are popular with residents but usually overlooked by visitors. Some are more hidden than others (and are marked accordingly), but all the listings in this book are intended to help you discover the true nature of Philadelphia and the Amish Country and put you on the path of adventure.

Contents

Maps

OUTDOOR ADVENTURE SYMBOLS

The following symbols accompany national, state and regional park listings, as well as beach descriptions throughout the text.

⛺	Camping	🏊	Swimming
🥾	Hiking	🛶	Canoeing or Kayaking
🚲	Biking	🛥️	Boating
🐎	Horseback Riding	🚤	Boat Ramps
⛷️	Cross-country Skiing	🎣	Fishing

ONE

The City of Brotherly Love

Perhaps you haven't toured Philadelphia since you were a child, or you have kids and want them to follow the Founding Fathers' footsteps. Maybe you have a business trip scheduled to William Penn's "green countrie towne," or you've never visited and are curious. Whatever your reasons for wanting to visit Philadelphia, be glad you waited until now.

Comedian W. C. Fields seldom let a monologue slide without verbally thrashing his hometown, and for years there was much here to malign. The city that held such treasures as the Liberty Bell, Independence Hall and the Philadelphia Museum of Art suffered blight as well as an inferiority complex, comparing itself with the U.S. culture capital of New York City, just 90 miles north, or the Capital City of Washington, DC, to the south.

But thanks to a decade-long urban renewal effort, Philadelphia is ascending. The nation's birthplace has become more than a repository of history—it's a destination for enjoying the arts, sports, dining, shopping, relaxation, adventure and more. In Philadelphia's own backyard lie world-class museums, the nation's richest tales and some of the East Coast's edgiest restaurants, bars and boutiques. In the downtown area, known as Center City, gleaming office towers have replaced crumbling facades and unkempt streets have been swept clean. Along the historic routes, streets have been reinvented with helpful signs and compelling walking tours. And throughout the city, new museums, cultural centers, state-of-the-art sports arenas and world-class restaurants are contributing to this civic renaissance.

Wake in Philadelphia on a crisp fall day and you'll find Philadelphians sweeping their cobblestone streets, throwing open shop doors and shining their brass—from the portholes of a four-masted barque on the Delaware River to tiered chandeliers hanging in Independence Hall. Market stall owners in South Philadelphia stock their wares with produce, meats and cheeses, while across town, university rowers warm up in the morning mist on the Schuylkill River. Joggers hit the trails in Fairmount Park, one of the nation's largest urban parks, and visitors pick up their timed tickets to enter Independence Hall and the new Liberty Bell Center.

From the time William Penn landed on the Delaware's shore in 1682, Philadelphia has drawn people of all races, religions and ethnic heritages. Penn, a Quaker, advocated religious tolerance, diversity and peace, and this spirit lives on in his city today. With a population of nearly 1.5 million, Philadelphia is the East Coast's second largest city and the fifth largest in the nation; an additional 3.8 million residents live within the greater metropolitan area—the Delaware Valley region. The Delaware Valley includes the Pennsylvania counties of Bucks, Montgomery, Chester and Delaware and reaches eastward across the Delaware River to the New Jersey counties of Burlington, Camden and Gloucester.

Until 1830, Philadelphia was the largest city in the United States, serving as the U.S. capital from 1790 to 1800. Later, it was an early railroad center, bearing the nation's largest steam locomotive works and the headquarters for the Pennsylvania Railroad, once the largest public corporation in the world. Philadelphia's population peaked in 1960 at more than 2 million and has been in decline since. In the '60s and '70s, much of the city's middle class fled to the suburbs, leaving a city spiraling into decay. At Philadelphia's civic lowpoint—likely the bombing of a radical group's home in 1985 by city police—Philadelphia was an uninviting, undesirable place that intimidated visitors and turned off potential investors.

But no longer is this the case. In the 1990s, then-mayor Edward Rendell set out to fix Philadelphia's image problem by righting some of its fiscal issues and cleaning up neighborhoods. By attracting businesses and making the tourist areas more appealing, he helped restore pride among city residents. Philadelphia has become a destination for more than its 18th-century history—it is celebrated for its thriving downtown, commerce, public and private art collections, sports teams, music, parks and more.

Changes in the city's historic areas in the last decade include the opening of the Liberty Bell Center and the National Constitution Center, a 160,000-square-foot interactive museum dedicated to the U.S. Constitution. The City Tavern, a meeting place for city folk of the Colonial era, has been rebuilt and revived as a dining destination. Costumed Colonists now stroll among tourists in the city's historic district, ready to answer questions and lend an air of days gone by. In the neighborhoods, residents and business owners have accepted new walking tour signs and enjoy business brought in from visitors. Sure, tourists can still get snubbed at Geno's Steaks or Pat's King of Steaks in South Philadelphia if they don't order their cheesesteak sandwiches fast enough, but on the whole, Philadelphians are willing

Text continued on page 6.

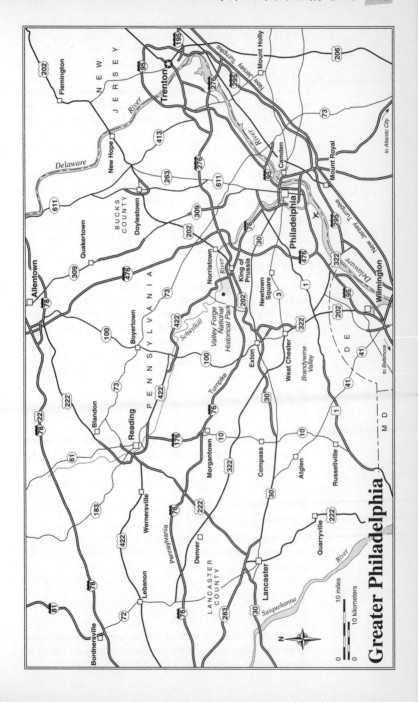

Greater Philadelphia

Philadelphia Sampler

If you only have a long weekend to visit Philadelphia, the following tour hits the highlights. Consider planning your getaway for Friday through Sunday because most museums and activities are closed Monday.

Day 1
- Get a timed ticket at the **Independence Visitor Center** (page 48) for an early afternoon tour of Independence Hall. Then orient yourself by taking a commercial tour.

- Return to your starting point and head to the **National Constitution Center** (page 49). Afterwards, dash across the street to check out Benjamin Franklin's grave in **Christ Church Burial Ground** (page 62).

- Pause for lunch. For sit-down fare, try Philadelphia restaurant guru Stephen Starr's take on comfort food at **Jones** (page 57), or grab a quick bite at the **Bourse** (page 57). You could even join the lunch wagon line and enjoy everything from hot dogs and Philly cheesesteaks to egg rolls and soft pretzels.

- Walk through **Independence Hall** (page 50), where it all started. Imagine being sequestered in this building in mid-July without central air conditioning. Yes, Washington really did sit in that chair and stand on that floor, along with Thomas Jefferson and James Madison. More than 200 years later, their great vision endures.

- Cross the street and view the **Liberty Bell** (page 50). This icon to American freedom was one of the first to symbolize freedom for all people, regardless of race, color or creed.

- Stroll east on Chestnut to visit the **Second Bank of the United States** (page 52). The portrait gallery inside features many fine likenesses of the founding fathers.

- Depending on your interests, head to **Franklin Court** (page 63), the **Betsy Ross House** (page 64), **Christ Church** (page 63) or **Elfreth's Alley** (page 64).

- Drink and dine at one of many eateries in Old City or 2nd Street. If you're still in a Colonial mood, hopefully you've made reservations at the **City Tavern** (page 58).

- If it's the first Friday of the month, consider taking in the art galleries at Old City to top off your evening or take in a movie at the **Ritz Theatres** (page 82) near City Tavern.

Day 2
- Head to Center City (Chapter Four) and start your day with a tour of the magnificent **Masonic Temple** (page 85), across the street from City Hall.

- Stroll over to the **PSFS Building** (page 88)—now a Loew's hotel—and walk through the nation's first Modernist-International skyscraper. Check out the Cartier clocks near the elevators. Take a ride to 33rd floor for the view. It's okay, you don't have to be a guest; Loew's is proud of their renovations.

- Head to **Wanamaker's** (page 88) to enjoy the noon concert on Lord and Taylor's 100-year-old organ.

- Eat lunch at the veritable smorgasbord of **Reading Terminal Market** (page 86). Save room for dessert—cannoli—at Termini Bros. Bakery in the market's southwest corner.

- Head to **Rittenhouse Square** (page 103) and the surrounding streets for a relaxing afternoon of window shopping, afternoon drinks or ice cream at Ben and Jerry's.

- Consider a meal at one of the Rittenhouse area steakhouses or **Sansom Street Oyster House** (page 110). Then enjoy a nightcap at **McGillin's** (page 98), the oldest pub in Philly, or **Monk's Café** (page 114), a popular spot for a variety of Belgian ales.

Day 3
- Every Philadelphian knows the city's best-kept secret: on Sundays, the **Philadelphia Museum of Art** (page 117) is "pay as you wish." It opens at 10 a.m.; allow at least two hours.

- Have lunch at the museum since there's not much selection this side of the Benjamin Franklin Parkway.

- If the weather's nice, head to Lloyd Hall, 1 Boathouse Row, behind the museum, and rent bikes to tour Kelly Drive and Fairmount Park. If you have kids in tow, head across the river to the **Philadelphia Zoo** (page 126).

- If the weather is unpleasant, you have several choices: the **Franklin Institute** (page 118) appeals to those interested in science; **Eastern State Penitentiary** (page 122) is for anyone who enjoys the macabre; and the **Rodin Museum** (page 120) is for those who haven't gotten enough art at the art museum.

- Complete your visit by dining at a local favorite, the **Valley Green Inn** (page 131), or, for simpler fare, head to **Jim's Steaks** (page 81) or the dueling **Pat's King of Steaks** or **Geno's Steaks** (page 143) for your cheesesteak fix. You won't get them like this at home.

to help, guide and direct guests toward finding out what's special about their town.

Stroll past City Hall during the work week and you'll experience a metropolis on the upswing. At lunchtime, suited office workers and construction hands line up at lunch wagons for hoagies and the ubiquitous cheesesteak. Others catch a smoke, chat and watch a game of chess, shadowed by large sculptures or artwork

Music is a large part of Philadelphia's heritage, dating back to Ben Franklin's invention of the glass-blown "armonica," an instrument that plays music in a method similar to running one's finger around the edge of a wine glass. Philadelphia has produced such influential musicians as Grover Washington, Jr., John Coltrane, Mario Lanza and Marian Anderson. The Chamber Music Society, the Philadelphia Orchestra and Philly Pops play for one type of audience, while major pop acts entertains a different crowd at the Wachovia Center and the Spectrum. Outdoor summer concerts are common in city parks, and clubs at night fill with the sounds of rock, jazz and soul. Classical music fans won't want to miss a performance by Tempesta di Mare, Philadelphia's baroque orchestra. For the performing arts, the city is home to the Pennsylvania Ballet, dance troupes from local universities and modern dance companies PhilaDANCO and Zero Moving Dance Company. In addition, Philadelphia houses the oldest continuous English-speaking theater in use, the Walnut Street Theatre, as well as dozens of smaller stages throughout the city and suburbs.

In terms of commerce, Philadelphia houses the national headquarters of several major corporations, including GlaxoSmithKline Pharmaceuticals, Aramark food services, petroleum giant Sunoco, insurance companies CIGNA and Lincoln Financial Group and

MULTICULTURAL MIX

Philadelphia is a panoply of neighborhoods, and it's as common to hear Russian and Armenian spoken here as it is to catch Italian, Spanish and Korean. In addition, Philadelphia's history is intertwined with that of African Americans; the city's population is more than 40 percent black, and it boasts a wealth of black-history sites, many hidden in neighborhoods. A stroll down a Philadelphia street can reveal places where W. E. B. DuBois penned The Philadelphia Negro or unveil the high school where Wilt Chamberlain and Will Smith studied. Jazz, hip-hop and funk flow in Center City nightclubs while African-American culture is celebrated at Temple University, with one of the largest privately owned compilations of black-heritage memorabilia, and at the African American Museum in Philadelphia, the largest museum of its kind in the United States.

cable provider Comcast. Comcast has signed on to open a new headquarters building, the Comcast Center, in 2007; when complete, it will be the tallest skyscraper between New York City and Chicago.

Touring Philadelphia is a mostly urban experience, but the city also has a wealth of parks and outdoor recreation activities. A few well-mapped bike paths wend through the city parks and along the Schuylkill River. Along the waterfront, just four city blocks from City Hall, wildflowers bloom while blue herons soar beside the busy interstate. Canoeing, kayaking and rowing are popular along both the Schuylkill and Delaware rivers.

Hidden Philadelphia will guide you through this historic, attractive city. It will walk you through Philadelphia's "must-sees," but also lead you to those unique, lesser-known spots that capture the city's essence. We will take you along the narrow roads of neighboring counties as well. You'll find restaurants, inns, sights and stores grouped by region, and we'll help you locate the historical sites, recreational opportunities and activities that demonstrate Philadelphia's significance to America, 300 years ago and today. You may find that a weekend or week is not enough to explore all the Delaware Valley region has to offer. But never fear, Philadelphia's doors are always open.

The city that encompasses what's called the United States' "most historic square mile" actually spans 129 square miles and boasts a number of attractions. Philadelphia's

Where to Go

museums and intellectual organizations rank among the world's best. The Philadelphia Museum of Art and its affiliate Rodin Museum are national treasures, containing more than 300,000 objets d'art. The Pennsylvania Academy of the Fine Arts, the country's first art school, houses more than 1700 paintings and 300 sculptures. The city also is home to numerous private galleries and studios. And both on and off the beaten path, city buildings have become palettes themselves, boasting 2400 indoor and outdoor murals—the most of any U.S. city.

The city's assortment of galleries and museums appeal to the curious of all ages. The Please Touch Museum, the Franklin Institute and the Academy of Natural Sciences—a must-see for dinosaur fans—feature numerous exhibits for the younger set, while places like the Mütter Museum, a collection of medical oddities at the College of Physicians of Philadelphia, and the University of Pennsylvania Museum of Archaeology and Anthropology, appeal to adolescents and an older crowd.

In Philadelphia and its neighborhoods, you'll find history at nearly every turn, in the centuries-old buildings designed by well-known architects, at the homes of the founding fathers and less familiar yet groundbreaking Americans, and among the trove of artifacts housed at the city's repositories. You'll also experience a city of diversity, of colorful neighborhoods that remain closely tied to their ethnic apron strings—a salad bowl of communities rather than a mixing bowl.

Center City is less than an hour's drive to the vineyards of a burgeoning Pennsylvania wine industry as well as the famous Revolutionary War sites of Trenton, Valley Forge and Brandywine. And its streets lie less than two hours from the bucolic roadways of Pennsylvania's Amish Country.

Mummer string bands hold free concerts from May through September at the Mummers Museum.

To truly appreciate the beauty of eastern Pennsylvania, a trip out to the nearby countryside, less than 20 miles away in some parts, is a necessity. Bucks, Lancaster, Delaware and Chester counties have fought to preserve their rural character, and the day-tripper or weekend hiker will find ample opportunity to ramble through fertile farmland, vineyards and woodlands or check out streams, rivers or creeks by canoe or kayak. Each county has its own distinct flavor, with Lancaster being famous for its Pennsylvania Dutch heritage and large Amish population; Bucks for its grand agricultural estates, antiquing and famous residents; and the Delaware–Chester counties area, usually referred to as the Brandywine Valley, for its mansions, gardens and historic battlefields.

When to Go

SEASONS

The Eastern Seaboard is known for its breadth of seasons, and Philadelphia, located 60 miles inland, experiences all four in intensity. Winters can be unforgivable—remember Valley Forge? George Washington's frozen encampment of 1777 is just 24 miles from City Hall. Average snowfall in Philadelphia is 20.8 inches and temperatures in winter run an average of 33 degrees. Sometimes the city experiences unexpected days of bright sunshine and bearable temperatures, up to 50 degrees in winter, but visitors shouldn't bank it. The trick to touring Philadelphia in the cold is to bundle up. Gloves, hats and scarves are necessary for outdoor events such as parades and football games. Stadium bleachers and parade risers provide some degree of warmth at the peak of the day, but once the sun disappears, either behind clouds, buildings or stadium seats, temperatures plummet, so it's best to be prepared. A good pair of boots, a warm coat and a decent pair of gloves will allow visitors to enjoy some of the city's celebrated sites in the winter, when crowds are fewer.

In summer, Philadelphia can be insufferable as well; days and nights are often hot and muggy, with average temperatures in June, July and August at 84 degrees and humidity running as high as 78 percent most mornings. Rain showers usually offer little relief—a brief thunderstorm often adds even more humidity to the air. But again, humidity shouldn't deter one from visiting the city. Philadelphia's top tourist sites, restaurants and public transportation modes are climate controlled. Plan to arrive at opening time in the morning, catch a few sights and then turn indoors for lunch and a museum tour during the heat of the afternoon.

Spring and fall are undoubtedly the region's best seasons. In springtime, days are cool and sunny with an undercurrent of summer warmth. Fall brings crisp, dry, warm days and cool clear nights with low humidity. Precipitation can occur in any season, and average rainfall in Philly is 41 inches—four more inches than the average rainfall of supposedly sodden Seattle. An umbrella is a handy accoutrement at any time during the year, and if you forget yours, area shops will gladly sell you one (the National Constitution Center has an eye-catching, albeit expensive, one printed with the Preamble).

Weather for the surrounding counties of Lancaster, Delaware and Bucks is similar to what you'll find in the city, only temperatures run a few degrees cooler than downtown. Snowfall often is heavier to the north and west of the city, so if you plan to visit any of the three counties during winter, check forecasts before venturing out. In Bucks County, the average snowfall is 25 inches a year, while in Lancaster County, average snowfall runs 31 inches per year.

CALENDAR OF EVENTS

If there's a major holiday on the calendar, Philadelphia celebrates it, usually with a parade, or at least with a festival. Philadelphians will brave all types of weather and temperatures to watch a good parade, and the city's finest—the Mummers Parade—kicks off the year with pageantry on the grandest of scales. There's at least one major event a month. The following is a sampling of the most popular.

JANUARY

Citywide The **Mummers Parade** is a spectacle of feathers, paint, wigs and satin, with roughly 15,000 men from 44 different brigades and string bands celebrating the New Year. Revelers strut down Broad Street for ten city blocks, "ending" at City Hall (the truth is, this is a party that lasts all day). The city observes **Martin Luther King, Jr.'s birthday** on January 16 with a day of service; nearly 250,000 volunteers perform a variety of projects honoring King's memory.

Benjamin Franklin Parkway & Fairmount Park Benjamin Franklin's **birthday** is also celebrated throughout the city, most notably at the Franklin Institute, with scientific demonstrations and a birthday cake.

FEBRUARY   **Citywide** This month celebrates the city's diversity. **Black History Month** activities are scheduled throughout the region. With **Mardi Gras** celebrations in flux in New Orleans, rowdy Philadelphians would like to assume some of the partying load; South Street is at its wildest on Fat Tuesday.

Historic Philadelphia The African American Museum in Philadelphia offers a round-up calendar of **Black History Month** events.

Center City The **Chinese New Year** is marked with a parade and fireworks; the Chinese Cultural and Community Center and Chinatown restaurants offer traditional ten-course, fixed-price banquets.

MARCH   **Citywide** For gourmands, the **Book and Cook Festival and Fair** mixes cookbook authors and the city's finest chefs in a weeks-long tribute to food.

Center City The Pennsylvania Convention Center blooms in early March with the **Philadelphia Flower Show**, the nation's largest and most prestigious, featuring acres of exhibits, arrangements and shopping.

Benjamin Franklin Parkway & Fairmount Park The **St. Patrick's Day Parade**, held along the Benjamin Franklin Parkway on the Sunday closest to March 17, features more than 100 floats and 10,000 marchers.

Philadelphia's Neighborhoods The former mill town of Manayunk celebrates **Manayunk in Bloom** with an Easter Egg Scramble and other spring celebrations.

APRIL   **Citywide** **Philadelphia Open House** tours are held weekends during the spring.

Center City **Pennsylvania Hospital**, the nation's oldest, hosts tours of its beautiful botanical garden, which was planned in 1774 but not planted until 1976.

Benjamin Franklin Parkway & Fairmount Park Throughout April and May, **Fairmount Park** hosts tours with special trolley rides.

Philadelphia's Neighborhoods Morris Arboretum hosts the **Japanese Cherry Blossom Celebration**. The **Philadelphia Antiques Show**, a benefit for the University of Pennsylvania Health System, features lectures, dinners, tours and sale of museum-quality antiques. Baseball season kicks off with the **Phillies** taking the field at Citizens Bank Park. The American-Swedish Historical Museum hosts **Valborsgmassoafton** in late April, a traditional festival featuring a bonfire and concert to shoo away winter spirits. The **Penn Relays**, the world's oldest and largest track-and-field meet, is held the last weekend of the month at the University of Pennsylvania's Franklin Field.

Citywide   Philadelphians mark Israel's independence with the
Israel Day Parade, held the second or third Sunday of the month;
the parade route runs from the Benjamin Franklin Parkway to
the front of the Philadelphia Museum of Art, and features a day-
long bazaar of Judaica, food vendors and more. The **Dad Vail
Regatta**, the largest collegiate rowing event in the country, and
the **Stotesbury Cup Regatta**, the nation's oldest and largest high-
school rowing event, are held the second and third weekends of
the month on the Schuylkill River.

Historic Philadelphia   On Memorial Day weekend, the city
fires its opening salvo of summer with **Jam on the River**, a two-
day music fest at Penn's Landing featuring some big-named
artists of jazz, funk and rock.

Center City   During the third week of May, **Rittenhouse
Square** blooms as a flower market, with a two-day sale of plants,
flowers and food, including lemon candy sticks and gingerbread.

Philadelphia's Neighborhoods   The **Philadelphia International
Children's Festival**, held at University of Pennsylvania's Annen-
berg Center for the Performing Arts, boasts live shows, crafts,
art, comedy and music.

Bucks County   In Doylestown, the **Mercer Museum Folk Fest**
pays tribute to folk music. Later in the month, the Moravian
Pottery and Tile Works, also in Doylestown, hosts its **Tile
Festival**, with sales of both historic and new decorative tiles.

Brandywine Valley   Starting Memorial Day weekend, Longwood Gardens hosts the **Summer Festival of the Fountains** with
daytime and evening choreographed fountain shows. For a memorable family outing, the **Devon Horse Show** near Berwyn features equestrian events and a country fair with food, rides and
games.

MAY

Citywide   More than a half million spectators watch the world's
top cyclists in the **Wachovia USPRO Cycling Championship**, usually scheduled for the first Sunday in June.

Historic Philadelphia   For history enthusiasts, the nation's oldest residential street throws open its doors one weekend in June
for tours and a Colonial craft fair and other events—**Elfreth's
Alley Fete Days** offer a once-a-year peek—at least a permissible
one—into these 300-year-old private homes. The **Head House
Square Craft Fair** runs weekends from Memorial Day through
nearly Halloween, featuring local artists at one of the country's
oldest markets. **Candlelight tours of Society Hill** are available
Saturday evenings, June through October. **Flag Day**, June 14, is
celebrated with much fanfare at Betsy Ross' house.

Center City   Rittenhouse Square hosts its own **fine arts festival**
the first Thursday through Sunday of June; more than 100 local
painters, sculptors and printmakers turn out for this juried exhibit.

JUNE

JULY   **Citywide** Philadelphians fete the Fourth of July like no one else: **Sunoco Welcome America!** is a weeklong tribute to independence, featuring parades, big-name concerts, fireworks, and the annual presentation of the prestigious Philadelphia Liberty Medal, whose recipients have included Nelson Mandela and Lech Walesa. Free music events are held throughout the city during the summer months: weekdays at noon, corporate types and tourists alike enjoy rock concerts at JFK Plaza, also known as LOVE Park.

Historic Philadelphia At **Penn's Landing,** bands both big and small put on shows on the pier and shoreline.

Benjamin Franklin Parkway & Fairmount Park At **Mann's Music Center** in Fairmount Park, fans can bring a picnic and watch free concerts. On July 14, France's freedom is marked at **Eastern State Penitentiary**, where commoners seek revenge on costumed monarchs, including Marie Antoinette, at a re-enactment of the storming of the Bastille.

Lancaster County The weeklong **Kutztown Festival** celebrates Pennsylvania's German heritage with a re-enactment of a hanging, cake walks, farm demonstrations, auctions, food, crafts and other events. And while most corn mazes aren't open until autumn, Lancaster County's **Amazing Maize Maze** kicks off its season in July.

AUGUST   **Lancaster County** The **Pennsylvania Renaissance Faire** in Cornwall re-creates a 16th-century English village with hundreds of Tudor structures, stages, actors and shows.

Brandywine Valley Grab your Birkenstocks and head to Schwenksville for the nearly half-century-old **Philadelphia Folk Festival,** a weekend tribute to grassroots folk music, crafts, storytelling and activism.

SEPTEMBER **Citywide** Two of Philadelphia's finest teams, the **Philadelphia Orchestra** and the **Philadelphia Eagles,** kick off their fall seasons in September.

Center City Sculpture, photography, glass and paintings from more than 50 galleries is displayed at the **Rittenhouse Square Fine Art Show** the second weekend in September. The Puerto Rican heritage parade and festival, **Festival Puertorriqueno Fildelfia,** offers food, music and performances for and about the city's Puerto Rican population.

Philadelphia's Neighborhoods The **Steuben Gala and Parade** celebrates the city's German heritage in the neighborhood of Mayfair.

Bucks County Polka 'til you pop at the **Polish American Festival,** held at the National Shrine of Our Lady of Czestochowa; music, food, dance performances, rides, shopping and a grand sweepstakes are enough to stay busy at this grand church in historic Doylestown.

Citywide   The city hosts two parades in October: the **Pulaski**   **OCTOBER**
Day Parade, a tribute to Polish culture and heritage, and the
Columbus Day Parade, acknowledging Christopher Columbus'
trek to the New World. Throughout the city, art studios open
their doors for tours, an effort that coincides with the **USArtists**
exhibition at 103rd Engineers Armory, which draws hundreds of
American painters, sculptors and artisans.
Benjamin Franklin Parkway & Fairmount Park   Halloween is
especially frightening at the already scary Eastern State
Penitentiary, which makes a particularly ghoulish and macabre
setting for a haunted house.

Citywide   The city sparkles as winter approaches. The **Philadel-**   **NOVEMBER**
phia Marathon is run the Sunday before Thanksgiving, starting
and ending at the Philadelphia Museum of Art, twisting through
the streets of Center City and Fairmount Park. The nation's oldest **Thanksgiving Day Parade** features elaborate floats and live
music, heralding the arrival of Santa Claus for the season and
kicking off the city's holiday celebrations.
Center City   American contemporary crafts figure prominently
in the **Philadelphia Museum of Art Craft Show**, held at the
Pennsylvania Convention Center.
Philadelphia's Neighborhoods   The nation's largest **African**
American Art Show runs concurrently with the craft show, usually the second weekend of November, at Temple University's
Liacouras Center.

Citywide   The annual gridiron battle between the U.S. Military   **DECEMBER**
Academy and the U.S. Naval Academy, the **Army-Navy Game**,
takes place the first weekend of December in Philadelphia, chosen as the site more than 100 years ago because the city lies
roughly halfway between West Point, NY, and Annapolis, MD.
As the holidays approach, the city hosts many activities focusing
on Christmas, Hanukkah and Kwanzaa.
Historic Philadelphia   Near Independence Hall, Mikveh Israel
displays a 25-foot menorah for Hanukkah, while Kwanzaa is
marked by events at the African American Museum in Philadelphia.
Center City   A Christmas tree is lit in the City Hall courtyard.
At the Wannamaker building (a Lord and Taylor department
store), concerts are held daily on one of the largest organs in the
world. Market Place East, a former department store at 701
Market Street, hosts a **Colonial Christmas village**.
Benjamin Franklin Parkway & Fairmount Park   The mansions
of Fairmount Park host **Yuletide House Tours**, as do those in

Germantown and Chestnut Hill. At night, they can be appreciated by candlelight as well.

Philadelphia's Neighborhoods   Kitsch reigns in South Philadelphia, where families show their holiday spirit by investing heavily in lights, glowing Santas, light-up nativity scenes, reindeer and more. The **Santa Lucia Festival** at Gloria Dei Church features song, prayers and an Advent wreath lighting in the city's oldest church structure.

Bucks County   The New Hope & Ivyland Railroad offers holiday-themed rides on their vintage trains; children can drink hot chocolate and eat cookies while meeting with Santa Claus or riding on the Polar Express. For a unique historical twist to the season, check out the **re-enactment of George Washington crossing the Delaware** at Washington Crossing Historic Park (the event has been canceled several times due to rough water, not because of the faint-heartedness of the participants).

▾▾▾▾▾▾▾▾▾▾▾▾▾
Before You Go

VISITORS CENTERS

The **Philadelphia Convention & Visitors Bureau** publishes a handy semiannual visitors guide and sponsors an informative website. It can also serve as a resources while you're in town. ~ 1700 Market Street, Suite 3000; 215-965-7676, 800-537-7676; www.pcvb.org.

The **Greater Philadelphia Tourism Marketing Corporation** runs an exceptional website on all things Philadelphia. ~ 30 South 17th Street, Suite 1710; 215-599-0776; www.gophila.com.

A visitor's first stop in Philadelphia should be the **Independence Visitor Center**, conveniently located across the street from the city's two top tourist draws, the Liberty Bell and Independence Hall. Here, visitors can plan their trips; National Park Service rangers offer advice on the city's historic sites while travel specialists can assist with reservations, tickets and transportation. Self-guided computer kiosks offer a range of trip-planning programs for Philadelphia and the outlying areas, including Bucks, Chester, Delaware and Montgomery counties. A "Share the Heritage" guide addresses the city's ethnic legacies, including historic African-American, Latino, Asian-American and American Indian sites and restaurants. ~ 6th and Market streets; 215-965-7676, 800-537-7676; www.independencevisitorcenter.com.

Neighboring counties also have their own visitors centers and publish their own guides. You'll find information on those centers in their corresponding chapters.

PACKING

As with any metropolitan city, Philadelphia enjoys a sense of style, dressing in neat casual for daytime and upping the ante for dining, theater or clubbing. The weather dictates how much clothing you'll need. In spring and fall, layers are a necessity. Comfortable cotton pants or skirts, good walking shoes, short-sleeve shirts and a light sweater or sweatshirt are well-suited for touring; dressier slacks and skirts are appropriate for dining. The city has several fine restaurants; if you are planning a memorable dinner or romantic evening, a coat and tie or dress should be included in your suitcase. During winter, it's wise to bring along a decent pair of boots or shoes with a firm tread that can help you maneuver through ice, salt, water and slush. A hat, gloves and warm coat are essential, as are the warmest sweaters and pants in your wardrobe.

Spring and fall can be unpredictable, so it's best to bring items to layer, including medium and lightweight slacks and shirts, sweaters and a light jacket. Be sure to take that jacket or coat when venturing out at night; evenings can get chilly after sundown. For summer, dress for extreme heat. Pack light clothing, cotton or linen shorts, lightweight T-shirts, polos or short-sleeved shirts, comfortable walking shoes and cotton socks. An umbrella should be brought along during any season, as precipitation can occur anytime. And don't forget your camera and copy of *Hidden Philadelphia*!

LODGING

Philadelphia offers a range of lodging for any style or budget. City hotels tend to fill in the summer and prices are higher at that time, but nearly any part of the year finds this city's hotels occupied, as it's a business traveler and convention destination as well. As Philadelphia becomes more attractive to visitors, hotel rates on the weekends are not dropping like they used to. The best deals in the city can be found in January, February and mid- to late August and during some, but not all, weekends.

Philadelphia's outlying areas are thick with unique inns and historic lodges, many featuring fireplaces, libraries, warm brandy and a helpful innkeeper.

In the countryside, prices are lower at hotels and inns during the week; Bucks and Lancaster counties, as well as Brandywine, are getaway sites for the entire mid-Atlantic region, so it's best to book ahead if you intend to stay there on the weekend.

Philadelphia has a wide selection of lodging choices, ranging from luxury lodgings that include a Mobil four-star hotel to small boutique hotels, chain franchises and B&Bs in 200-year-old homes. Whatever your price range, you're likely to find something appropriate in the individual chapters of this book. Be sure to ask about special packages and discounts when making reservations.

The hotels in this book are organized by region and classified by price. The listings are for double occupancy during the high season, so if you seek low-season bargains, be sure to inquire about them. Also remember to inquire about American Automobile Association (AAA) discounts if you're a member, or about special rates for military or government personnel, if this applies. The discount rates are usually restricted to those traveling on orders, but sometimes hotels will honor military rates even if you're traveling for pleasure. It's worth a try.

In this Hidden guide, *budget* facilities are generally less than $60 per night and are clean and basic. Hotels that fall into this category are mostly chain hotels in the suburbs. *Moderate*-priced accommodations are between $60 and $120, offering slightly more amenities than budget hotels and more personal service. *Deluxe* means you should expect to spend at least $120 to $175 per night and receive extras for it, such as a cozy room in a bed and breakfast or a standard room at a well-suited hotel or resort. You're likely to find more amenities at this price, including spacious common rooms, pleasant guest rooms, a restaurant and amenities such as an exercise room or pool. *Ultra-deluxe* properties, priced above $175, feature the extras you'd expect from a space in this price range, such as fine service, whirlpool baths, exercise rooms and pools, concierge, 24-hour service and gourmet dining.

If you want a specific amenity or view, be sure to ask for it when making reservations. And to save money, consider staying at one of the city's many B&Bs. Most are moderately priced, well-appointed and rates include breakfast. However, most B&Bs don't allow children under age 12, so check with the innkeeper before making reservations if you plan to travel with children.

In Philadelphia, expect to pay a 13 percent tax on your bill for lodging. Also, if you're driving, be sure to inquire about parking. Many hotels expect patrons to pay for daily valet parking or park in area garages—an inconvenience that can add between $12 and $20 a day onto your bill.

DINING Philadelphia is a food town, home to some of the nation's hottest restaurants. In fact, *Condé Nast Traveler* readers have voted Philadelphia the "Best Restaurant City in America" and diners will find choices ranging from the well-known and Mobil five-star-rated Le Bec Fin and other top-rated dining rooms to neigh-

FIRST THINGS FIRST

Philadelphia is known as a city of "firsts." Its buildings played host to the drafting and signing of the Declaration of Independence and the Constitution. Its streets served as a laboratory for Benjamin Franklin. Its schools contributed to the development of modern medicine and today's judicial system. Other firsts include the nation's first botanic garden, brick house, Episcopal church, African Methodist Episcopal church, mint, art museum and hospital.

borhood bring-your-own-booze restaurants, family-style diners and street vendors. The available choices appeal to nearly every palate; there are seafood and steak houses as well as Chinese, Japanese, Italian, Indian and Moroccan eateries. There's even a Malaysian restaurant, one of a few in the country. A growing phenomena throughout the city are BYO restaurants. Because Pennsylvania has unique restrictions regarding the sale and distribution of liquor licenses, many small neighborhood restaurants are BYOB, allowing the proprietor to concentrate on serving quality food while the customer gets the benefit of not paying mark-ups on alcohol. Be sure to find out about corkage fees before you bring your own wine, however.

In this book, restaurants are categorized geographically, with each entry describing the type of cuisine, general decor and price range. The restaurants listed offer lunch and dinner unless otherwise noted. Dinner entrées at *budget* restaurants usually cost under $10. The ambiance is casual, service is speedy—maybe even walk-up-window fast—and the crowd local. *Moderate*-price restaurants range between $10 to $18 for dinner entrées and offer casual surroundings and a varied menu. *Deluxe* establishments charge between $18 and $25 for their entrées; menus are thorough and well-prepared, decor is upscale and service attentive. In *ultra-deluxe* dining rooms, entrées begin at $25 and dining, hopefully, is an experience in itself. Expect an attentive waitstaff, a beautiful setting and an artistically prepared meals.

If you'd like to try some of Philadelphia's finest restaurants but are on a budget, consider making a lunch reservation at the restaurant of your choice. The menus may differ slightly from the dinner menu, but the food is prepared with the same care for about half the price, in some cases. In Philadelphia, diners are charged a 7 percent tax. Expect to tip between 15 to 20 percent as well.

An interesting note about restaurant service here, which might take visitors (especially Southerners and those from the Midwest) by surprise: While the waitstaff at most restaurants is friendly and service-oriented, some servers can be snobby, bordering on snarky, as if they're doing you a favor. Maybe this is an urban thing. But if you find this to be the case, don't suffer through it; say something, either directly to the server or to a manager. The Zagat 2005 guide reported that Philadelphians are the nation's biggest tippers, averaging 19.2 percent. Just make sure your waiter or waitress deserves it.

We've made every effort to include places with established reputations for good eating. As with any dining experience, especially in the budget to moderately priced restaurant range, service may vary. But using this guide, you should expect a decent meal in a clean setting with timely service.

TRAVELING WITH CHILDREN Philadelphia is tailor-made for children. American children learn about Philadelphia's historical sites nearly as soon as they enter kindergarten, and the city has made every effort to pique their interests. The museums, shops and festivals offer activities for children as well as special games and information geared toward their learning levels. Several Philadelphia draws (including the Franklin Institute, the Please Touch Museum and the Academy of Natural Sciences) were created primarily for youngsters, and if you have kids in tow, you'll want them on your must-see list.

For lodging, Philadelphia has hotels with amenities that appeal to children, such as indoor pools or children's activities. Some accommodations offer suite-type rooms and continental breakfasts—choices that allow children to camp out on a sleep sofa in a room separate from their parents and eat in the morning before touring that day. If you need a cot or crib, remember to arrange it when making a reservation. And if you plan to stay in a historic inn or bed and breakfast, be sure to inquire about their age policies; many B&Bs do not accept children under the age of 12.

When traveling with youngsters, take along the extras you need, although Philadelphia has plenty of shops for items you may have left behind. When touring, carry water and snacks and maybe even a book or game to keep youngsters occupied if they must stand in line for any reason. Always allow plenty of time to get from one place to another. Philadelphia's most historic sites are in close proximity to one another, but to reach other interesting kid-friendly destinations such as Penn's Landing and Camden, NJ, sites, you'll have a long walk or quick shuttle ride.

Also, be sure to carry along a first-aid kit that includes adhesive bandages, antiseptic cream, anti-itch lotion, diarrhea medication, cold medication and an antihistamine. And don't forget any personal medications. For late spring, summer and early fall, carry sunscreen and insect repellent. If you have left something behind at home, ask your hotel clerk to point you toward the nearest late-night pharmacy. The city has many. If you plan to travel outside the city, be sure to take along your first-aid kit as well as the sunblock, repellant and hats. The Philadelphia countryside, especially the woodlands, are the habitat for a variety of pests, including mosquitoes and ticks.

Philadelphia has a number of publications geared toward parents, and these free magazines can help guide you through the scheduled activities designed for children. These weekly publications can usually be picked up at information kiosks in attractions or at area visitors centers.

WOMEN TRAVELING ALONE Perhaps you're on a business trip to Philadelphia and have some spare time, or perhaps you'd prefer to gear your vacation to your own tastes, interests and pace. Regardless of the reason you are

Cheesesteaks & Pretzels

On nearly every street corner in Philadelphia, there's a wagon selling cheesesteak sandwiches. These filling favorites consist of chopped beef and fried onions slathered in a cheese product and are served on a soft, 12-inch Italian roll. Outsiders may be horrified at the thought of putting Cheez Whiz on a sandwich, but for many Philadelphians, no other type of dairy product belongs on a cheesesteak. Luckily, Philadelphia cheesesteak vendors have adapted their venerable recipe and now offer the choice of Cheez Whiz, provolone or American; some even offer mozzarella, lettuce and tomato. You may turn out to be a fan, but if you're not, don't despair—many Philadelphians can't digest it, either.

Philadelphians don't mess around when ordering their cheesesteaks, and they don't have much tolerance for indecision. It's best to practice your order before you get in line. First, decide what you want and get out your cash. Cheesesteaks are basically three ingredients plus onions: thinly sliced steak, cheese and an Italian roll. There are three choices of cheese: Cheez Whiz, American and provolone. Brevity is required when ordering, so Philadelphians start by saying what type of cheese they'd prefer and whether they want onions—wit' or wit-out. An order for an original cheesesteak of Cheez Whiz and onions would be "Whiz wit." A cheesesteak with provolone but no onions would be "Provolone wit-out." Other additions can include hot peppers, lettuce and tomato. Simply add those to the end of your order: "Provolone wit. Hot peppers."

Do not order Swiss, like Senator John Kerry did at Pat's King of Steaks while on the 2004 campaign trail. He was not sent to the back of the line but he did receive instruction on proper ingredients. His final order? Whiz wit. Lettuce. Tomato.

In the cases of cheesesteaks and hoagies (called submarine sandwiches, grinders or heroes elsewhere in the United States), the quality of the bread is key to a great meal, and many Philadelphia sandwich shops rely on fresh-baked breads from Amoroso's Baking Company in West Philly or Sarcone's Bakery in South Philly.

Another Philadelphia favorite is the soft pretzel. Found at street corner wagons as commonly as cheesesteaks, soft pretzels are best served hot and sprinkled with coarse salt. They also must be knotted, not stamped, into shape. Philadelphians eat them slathered in yellow mustard. Delicious, completely extraneous calories. Yum.

traveling alone, independent travel can be one of the most enlightening ways to see a place, yet it requires caution. Single travelers—especially women—are more vulnerable to crime and additional precautions must be taken to ensure you don't become a victim.

Before making a reservation at a hotel, ask for references from friends or coworkers on its location and reputation. If researching a property on the internet, don't be fooled by photos or claims of location. Try to find lodging in main tourist areas instead of the outskirts of town. Bed-and-breakfast inns are often a safe lodging bet as many of them are owner- or innkeeper-occupied, and you're seldom truly alone when there.

When venturing out, know where you're going and how to get there. Keep all valuables hidden and hold purses tightly while walking. Avoid late-night treks in Philadelphia. If you attend the theater or a late movie, consider taking a taxi back to your hotel or walking alongside others for as long as possible. If you find yourself alone, hold your head up and walk confidently toward a safe or busy area. If you notice someone is following you, don't look away or act timid. Face the person, stare long enough to make sure he or she knows you've seen them, and continue walking briskly. If you have a cell phone, get it out—you won't want to use it so that it distracts you, but you will want anyone to know that you have the ability to call emergency services if necessary.

It goes without saying, but never tell anyone you're traveling alone. Use all locks available in your hotel room and draw the curtains in the evening. If your room is located near an exit door, a stairwell or on the first floor, consider asking to be moved to a safer location.

Travel is on the rise for women going it alone, and the thought of becoming a victim shouldn't deter you from seeking adventure. Stay alert, use common sense and trust your instincts. If you don't carry a cell phone, carry change for a pay phone in case of an emergency or just dial 9-1-1. **Women Organized Against Rape**, a Philadelphia non-profit, runs a 24-hour crisis line. ~ 215-985-3333; www.woar.org.

GAY & LESBIAN TRAVELERS

Philadelphia played host to some of the first gay and lesbian civil rights' marches in the 1960s. Today, it is very much a gay-friendly destination, marketing itself as a place to "Get Your History Straight and Your Nightlife Gay." Center City is the hub of Philadelphia's gayborhoods, specifically Washington Square West, or "WashWest." The largest concentration of gay-owned and gay-friendly businesses are found between 11th and Broad streets, from Walnut to Pine.

The **Greater Philadelphia Tourism Marketing Corporation** offers information on hotels, restaurants, gay-owned businesses and events, as well as on the **Philadelphia Freedom Package**, a hotel package that includes accommodations, breakfast and information on the city's gay-friendly spots. ~ 30 South 17th Street, Suite 1710; 215-599-0776; www.gophila.com/gay.

For more information, the **Philadelphia Gay News** can be viewed online. It offers articles and a calendar of events. ~ 505 South 4th Street; 215-625-8501; www.epgn.com.

The **William Way Community Center** serves as a resource for information on gay services and events and offers cultural and social programs, classes and recreational opportunities. ~ 1315 Spruce Street; 215-732-2220.

Older travelers will find Philadelphia hospitable and easy to navigate, with its compact historic district and traversable streets. Spring and fall are the best seasons for seniors to visit as the weather is moderate. Most museums and attractions offer senior discounts; for more information, inquire at the **Independence Visitors Center**. ~ 6th and Market streets; 215-965-7676, 800-537-7676; www.independencevisitorcenter.com

SENIOR TRAVELERS

Should you need to discuss concerns or inquire about information available to seniors, the **Mayor's Commission on Services to the Aging** is part of City Hall. ~ 1401 Arch Street; 215-686-8499.

The **American Association of Retired Persons** (AARP), offers membership to anyone age 50 and over. Benefits include travel discounts with a number of tour companies, car rentals and more. ~ 601 E Street NW, Washington, DC 20049; 800-424-3410; www.aarp.org.

Elderhostel offers a number of educational programs in the Philadelphia area and surrounding countryside. Courses address the city's museums, architecture, culture and more. ~ 11 Avenue de Lafayette, Boston, MA 02111; 877-426-8056; www.elderhostel.org.

The **National Park Service** has a Golden Age Passport that grants lifetime access to National Park sites, including parks,

◆◆

THE EDUCATED CITY

With more than 120,000 students in the city and an additional 180,000 in the surrounding areas, Philadelphia is one of the largest college towns in the United States. It's home to the Ivy League's University of Pennsylvania and the universities of Drexel, Temple and LaSalle, as well as 16 other institutions of higher learning. In the suburbs, many nationally recognized colleges and universities are clustered along Philadelphia's Main Line, including Villanova University, Haverford College, Bryn Mawr, Swarthmore College and Ursinis.

monuments, historic sites and recreation areas for a $10 fee to anyone age 62 and older. ~ 888-467-2757; www.nps.gov/fees_passes.htm.

When traveling, take care to monitor your health. Be sure to take along extra prescription medication, if possible, and carry your doctor's name, phone number and address with you.

DISABLED TRAVELERS

Many of Philadelphia's old buildings and uneven walking paths pose challenges to the wheelchair-bound and physically disabled, but the city has taken measures to ensure that most sites are accessible. Often, wheelchair-access doors are tucked at street level along the sides or in the rear of buildings. City sidewalks have been cut at intersections to facilitate wheelchair traffic, but be aware that some streets and sidewalks are uneven. Parking is a challenge in Philadelphia, and not just for the disabled. However, handicapped spots are rare, and those traveling with special needs should allow extra time to find parking if they plan to drive into the city.

Most hotels have special rooms for disabled travelers, but if you plan to stay in a bed and breakfast, be sure to ask if they can accommodate you. Many are in historic residences and cannot be altered for elevators.

For basic information on disabilities and access in Philadelphia, contact the **Mayor's Commission on People with Disabilities**. ~ 1401 JFK Boulevard; 215-686-2798.

For information on public transportation for the disabled, the **South Eastern Pennsylvania Transit Authority** publishes a transit guide. All SEPTA buses are lift-equipped and two subway stations, Market East and University City, are wheelchair accessible. Most other stops are not. ~ 1234 Market Street, 4th floor; 215-580-7145; www.septa.org.

Philadelphia has more public art than any other American city, according to a Smithsonian Institution survey.

Many of the national car-rental companies have hand-controlled cars available with advanced notice. Be sure to inquire when you make a reservation.

The **Moss Rehabilitation Hospital** in Philadelphia runs a travel information site—Accessible Travel—on the web with information for disabled travelers planning their trips. ~ www.moss resourcenet.org.

The **Travelin' Talk Network** also operates a website for disabled travelers and a monthly newsletter. ~ P.O. Box 1796, Wheat Ridge, CO 80034; 303-232-2979; www.travelintalk.net.

Easter Seals Project ACTION maintains a National Accessible Traveler's Database with more information on accessibility. ~ projectaction.easterseals.com.

Another organization that provides online travel resources is the **Society for Accessible Travel and Hospitality**. SATH helps its members find tour groups, travel agents and assistance when planning a trip. ~ 347 5th Avenue, Suite 610, New York, NY 10016; 212-447-7284.

The **National Park Service** has a Golden Access Passport that grants free lifetime access to National Park sites, including parks, monuments, historic sites and recreation areas. ~ 888-467-2757; www.nps.gov/fees_passes.htm.

And the **American Foundation for the Blind** provides information for those traveling with service dogs. ~ 800-232-5463; www.afb.org.

Some services of interest available for the disabled in the city include the Free Library of Philadelphia's **Library for the Blind and Physically Handicapped**, containing talking books, CDs, large-print books and Braille. The library was built especially for the disabled. ~ 919 Walnut Street; 215-683-3213.

The **Associated Services for the Blind**, operating out of the same building as the library, also offers assistance for the visually challenged. ~ 215-627-0600.

FOREIGN TRAVELERS

Philadelphia is expanding in popularity as a destination for foreign visitors, rising in the past decade from 24th on a list of U.S. cities to visit to 12th, according to the U.S. Department of Commerce. New regulations have made travel to the United States trickier in the past five years. Check your nearest U.S. Embassy or Consulate if you are unsure of requirements.

Passports and Visas　Most foreign visitors are required to have a passport and tourist visa to enter the United States, with visitors from all but 27 countries required to schedule an interview with their nearest U.S. Embassy or Consulate for their visa. Visitors from the 27 "visa waiver countries" must have machine-readable passports to enter the United States. Visitors should expect to have their fingerprints scanned during their consular visit or on arrival in the United States. Entry from Canada calls for a valid passport, visa or visitor permit for all foreign visitors. Starting in 2008, Canadian and U.S. citizens will be required to show a passport to travel between their two countries.

Customs Requirements　Foreign travelers are allowed to bring in the following: 200 cigarettes (1 carton), 50 cigars (not from Cuba) or 2 kilograms (4.4 pounds) of smoking tobacco; one liter of alcohol for personal use (you must be 21 years or older to bring in alcohol) and US$100 worth of duty-free gifts that can include an additional quantity of 100 cigars (again, not Cuban). You may bring in any amount of currency (more than US$10,000 requires a form). Carry any prescription drugs in clearly marked containers—you may have to provide a doctor's statement or written prescription to clear customs. Meat or meat products, seeds, plants, fruits and narcotics may not be brought into the U.S. Also, merchandise from certain countries, including Cuba, Liberia, Sudan and others, is prohibited. Check with the U.S. Embassy or Consulate before leaving if you plan to carry questionable items. Contact the **U.S. Customs and Border Protection** for further information. ~ 1300 Pennsylvania Avenue NW, Washingotn, DC 20229; 202-354-1000, 877-227-5511; www.cbp.gov.

Driving   If you plan to rent a car, an international driver's license should be obtained before arriving. Some rental car companies require both a foreign license and an international driver's license along with a major credit card, and they require that the driver/lessee be at least 25 years of age. Seat belts are required for drivers and front passengers, and they are required for passengers ages 8 to 18 regardless of where they sit in a vehicle. Children under four years of age are required to use a car seat and children four to eight years old must be securely fastened, in an appropriate booster seat or with a seat belt. Most rental car companies have child safety seats available. Pennsylvania does not require motorcyclists to wear helmets. Be aware that U.S. traffic signs differ from international signs; for more information, speak with your car rental agency.

Currency   The U.S. currency is the dollar. Bills in the United States come in seven dominations: $1, $2, $10, $20, $50 and $100 ($2 bills are rare, however, and you likely won't encounter any during your trip). Dollars are divided into 100 cents. Coins are the penny (1 cent), nickel (5 cents), dime (10 cents) and quarter (25 cents); half-dollar and dollar coins are used infrequently, but they do exist. You may not purchase goods or services in the United States with anything but U.S. dollars. When purchasing traveler's checks, buy them in dollar amounts. You can also use credit cards affiliated with U.S. companies such as Interbank, Barclay Card, Diners Club, VISA and American Express. Depending on your bank's affiliations or networking system, your automated teller machine (ATM) card will dispense U.S. dollars from your home account.

Electricity and Electronics   Electric outlets use currents of 110 volts, 60 cycles. To operate appliances made for other systems, you'll need a transformer and plug adapter. Travelers who use laptop computers for telecommunications should know that modem configurations in the U.S. may differ from their European or Asian counterparts. Similarly, when making any electronics purchases or accessories for electronics, ask about compatibility before buying.

Weights and Measurements   The United States uses the English system of weights and measures. American units and their metric equivalents are as follows: 1 inch = 2.5 centimeters; 1 foot = .3 meter; 1 yard = .9 meter; 1 mile = 1.6 kilometers; 1 ounce = 28 grams; 1 pound = .45 kilograms; 1 quart (liquid) = .9 liter. (To compare gas prices, 1 gallon = 3.8 liters.)

Philadelphia lies along the prime transportation corridor linking the southeastern United States with the
Northeast and the large cities of New York and Boston.

Transportation

Route 95 is the primary roadway for most of the Eastern
Seaboard; it runs from Maine to Florida and is most congested
between Boston and Washington, DC. Although Route 95's con-
tinuity becomes fragmented in the Philadelphia area, the interstate proper enters Philadelphia at its northeast from Bucks
County, and exits south below the airport through Delaware
County heading for Delaware.

CAR

Another major corridor linking the city with other parts of
the country is the **Pennsylvania Turnpike** (called Route 276, 76
and 476 in different parts), which stretches westward toward the
state capital of Harrisburg, Pittsburgh and Ohio, and northward
toward Wilkes-Barre and the state of New York. **Route 76** runs
through the western part of the city, including University City
and Fairmount Park, before becoming part of the turnpike.
Broad Street essentially runs north–south the entire stretch of the
city (becoming the Avenue of the Arts south of Center City). City
streets are in a grid pattern with four quadrants centered on City
Hall—a design proposed by William Penn and his surveyor
Thomas Holmes.

Major corridors in surrounding counties includes **Route 476**,
through Delaware County, which runs from the Delaware River
northward to the "Main Line," including Chanticleer Garden and
the university towns of Villanova, Bryn Mawr and Haverford.
Route 1 also crosses Delaware County, leading to the Brandywine Valley region, Longwood Gardens and Chadds Ford.
Smaller, local roads lead through most of Bucks County, including **State Route 611** (the same State Route 611 as Broad Street
in Center City), which leads to Doylestown, and **Route 202**,
which forms a wide arc to the west of Center City, linking places
like Valley Forge in Chester County, Gwynedd in Montgomery
County and Lahaska and New Hope in Bucks County.

Philadelphia International Airport is seven miles from Center
City and is served by most domestic airlines, including AirTran

AIR

PHLASHING THROUGH PHILLY

The **Phlash** trolley is one of the least expensive ways to get to city attractions besides walking. For $1 every time you board, or a $4 day pass, you
can ride the Phlash to 18 sites in a downtown loop. Phlash runs daily
from March 1 to November 30, with service every 12 minutes. ~
www.gophila.com/phlash.

Airways, America West, American Airlines, Continental Airlines, Delta Air Lines, Frontier Airlines, Midwest Airlines, Northwest Airlines, Southwest Airlines, United Airlines, US Airways, several affiliates of the larger carriers and smaller charter airlines. International carriers include Air Jamaica, Air Canada, Air France, British Airways and Lufthansa. The airport has a number of shops, restaurants and bars for passenger comfort. ~ 215-683-9840; www.phl.org.

The area transit authority, SEPTA, runs a high-speed train from the airport to Center City, as well as a number of bus routes. ~ 215-580-7800; www.septa.org. Taxis and van pools are available at the airport for a flat-rate fee to the downtown area as well.

BUS

To travel to Philadelphia by bus, the city is served by **Greyhound Bus Lines** (800-231-2222; www.greyhound.com) and **Peter Pan Bus Lines** (800-237-8747; www.peterpanbus.com); both share a downtown terminal. ~ Filbert and 10th streets.

TRAIN

Amtrak operates primary rail service in and out of the Philadelphia area along its busy Northeast Corridor, with links to New York, Boston and Canada to the north, Chicago to the west and Baltimore, Washington, DC, and other stops to the south. Train service varies from express-style trains between Boston and Washington, DC, to local trains that stop at smaller U.S. cities along the rail lines. Service leaves from 30th Street Station, a few blocks from the Pennsylvania Convention Center and Center City. ~ Market Street between 29th and 30th streets; 215-349-2270, 800-872-7245; www.amtrak.com.

SEPTA runs an extensive commuter rail service between the city and the suburbs. This clean, well-timed transportation mode is popular among locals for traveling into the city for both work and pleasure. Tickets are available at stations or, if the station is closed, on the trains for a small fee. Day and weekly passes can be purchased as well. If riding the commuter trains into the city, be aware that parking fills early at local station lots. Major train hub stations downtown include 30th Street Station, Market East and Suburban Station. ~ 215-580-7800; www.septa.org.

The **Port Authority Transit Corporation** runs high-speed trains across the Delaware River, linking Philadelphia with southern New Jersey, including Camden and beyond. ~ 215-922-4600; www.drpa.org.

CAR RENTALS

Most major car rental agencies have offices at the Philadelphia International Airport, including **Alamo Rent A Car** (800-327-9633), **Avis Rent A Car** (800-331-1212), **Budget Rent A Car** (800-527-0700), **Dollar Rent A Car** (800-800-4000), **Enterprise**

Rent A Car (800-736-8227), **Hertz Rent A Car** (800-654-3131)
and **National Car Rental** (800-227-7368).

SEPTA operates bus service throughout the city, running buses, articulated buses and trolleys in many neighborhoods. Senior citizens and persons with disabilities receive special fares and discounts, including free ridership for the elderly during off-peak hours. SEPTA offers a day pass good for unlimited transportation on all city transit vehicles; passes can be purchased at the Independence Visitor Center or the SEPTA information station. ~ 6th and Market streets; 215-580-7800; www.septa.org.

PUBLIC TRANSIT

The Delaware River Port Authority runs its **RiverLink Ferry** from April 1 to November 15 between Penn's Landing and Camden, NJ. Primarily used by visitors to carry them from downtown Philadelphia to the New Jersey attractions of the Adventure Aquarium, the battleship USS *New Jersey* and Camden sports and entertainment venues, RiverLink is a lovely way to see Philadelphia from the water. Tickets can be purchased at Penn's Landing or in Camden near the aquarium. ~ 121 North Columbus Boulevard; 215-925-5465; riverlinkferry.org.

FERRY

Area taxi companies such as **City Cab** (215-492-6600) and **Quaker City Cab** (215-728-8000) can ferry you throughout the city, and have a set rate to the airport.

TAXIS

Philadelphia travel and tourism companies offers a number of unique ways to traverse and view the city, including horse-and-carriage, double-decker bus, trolley, amphibious landing vehicles (also known as ducks), walking tours and Segway rides. Many of these tours begin near Independence Hall. Information is available at both the Independence Visitor Center and area ticket kiosks.

TOURS

The **Big Bus Company** runs double-decker bus tours to key stops. Guides are informative, friendly and funny, and your ticket is valid for 24 hours, meaning you can hop on and off at any of their 20 drop-off points. Fee. ~ 111 South Independence Mall East, Suite 740; 215-923-5008, 866-324-4287; www.bigbus.co.uk.

For a wacky tour of Philadelphia with some of the city's most quacky tour guides, try **Ride The Ducks.** It offers an 80-minute trip past the city's historic sites and on the Delaware River in a World War II–era amphibious truck—the type that carried supplies to Omaha Beach on D-Day. On a duck tour, you'll be handed a duck-bill shaped "quacker" and egged on by your tour guide to "honk" at pedestrians. Kids will love the animated guides and the chance to make as much noise as they please. Closed December to mid-March. Fee. ~ 6th and Chestnut streets; 215-227-3285; www.phillyducks.com.

Ghost tours have popped up in U.S. cities both large and small, but of the ones I've taken, the Philadelphia versions offer a fine blend of folklore and historical fact that pleases both believers and skeptics. The opportunity to walk through the streets of Philadelphia by candlelight is reason enough to try one of these adventures because the historic area is quite beautiful in the dark (although to fully appreciate the impact, you'll want to take your tour September through November, when it's dark at 7:30). **Philadelphia Ghost Tour** organizers claim that the city is the nation's "most haunted." You can decide after listening to their stories of Ben Franklin, Benedict Arnold and deceased Revolutionaries. Purchase tickets at the Independence Visitor Center or CremaLita Ice Cream Shop (401A Chestnut Street). Closed December through March. Fee. ~ 5th and Chestnut streets; 215-413-1997; www.ghosttour.com.

TWO

History & the Outdoors

Although William Penn gets much of the credit for founding the area now known as Philadelphia, the region was settled long before Penn arrived—up to 10,000 years before. There is much debate over when exactly the first humans arrived, but there is no doubt that the earliest settlers were drawn to the land's wealth, its fertile soil and abundant animal life. Since prehistoric times, Pennsylvania has been covered in dense forests—first rich, lush jungles that fossilized into the state's plentiful oil and coal reserves and, later, the pine and deciduous forests that continue to cover most of the state today. Prehistoric Pennsylvania was home to mastodons, moose, elk and deer—a hunter's paradise that eventually drew the native settlers. The first humans, Eastern Woodland American Indians, established semipermanent agricultural villages along the region's rivers. This subset of American Indians included the Algonquian, Delaware (also called the Lenape) and Shawnee tribes, among others. At their population peak, in the early 1600s, there were more than 20,000 American Indians inhabiting the area near the banks of the Schuylkill and Delaware rivers.

In 1604, the first Europeans arrived, Dutch and Swedish explorers who scouted potential settlements. Nineteen years later, the Dutch established the first trading post in the area, near the Schuylkill. By the mid-1600s, more Swedes and Dutch arrived, joined by Finnish and British settlers. These colonists established a strong fur and tobacco trade, and drafted treaties with the Indians, setting the stage for Penn's later successes in negotiating with the natives.

Penn wasn't to arrive in the colonies until 1682. Born in England in 1644, Penn was the son of wealthy Anglicans, his father a British Navy admiral. Penn studied and became a soldier, but after spending time in the military and witnessing bloodshed in his country, he turned to the Society of Friends, or Quakers, drawn to their beliefs of pacifism and personal freedom, including freedom of religion, assembly and trial by jury. Because of his religious convictions and activism, Penn ran afoul of the law and spent time in prison. But when King Charles II decided to make good on a debt he had with Penn's father after the elder's death, he did so by granting the younger Penn land in the colonies, a large area west of New Jersey. Charles called the land "Pennsylvania"—Latin for "Penn's Woods"—to honor the older Penn.

Penn set sail for the colonies on September 1, 1682, to embark on his "Holy Experiment," a dream to found a place where members of all religions could worship in peace without fear of persecution. Penn landed at New Castle, Delaware, on October 27, 1682. He later moved upriver to a settlement that is now Chester, Pennsylvania, and on to the site of his future "green country towne." Penn named his new city Philadelphia, the "City of Brotherly Love," a place he hoped would be a city on a grand scale like London or Paris, but better. Penn hoped to plan a city with a country feel—one that also embraced the ideals of the Quakers, supporting the rights of people, in the words of Quaker and theorist John Locke, to pursue "life, liberty and estate."

Penn's idealized vision is considered one of the first efforts toward urban planning in the Americas. Working with surveyor Thomas Holme, Penn mapped a city of wide streets and broad city blocks arranged in a grid pattern, 22 squares by 8 squares. Each quadrant featured its own public square; at the center of the grid lay a main city square. Penn wanted the city's houses to be built on large lots, creating a feeling of gentility, even at its urban core. The city would be surrounded by countryside, and landowners in the city could also receive a country lot. This greenway would provide a place for city dwellers to escape should disease or fire ravage the city—disasters that befell London during Penn's childhood that he sought to avoid. The plan called for a great port, encouraging commerce, and it allowed room for expansion.

Unfortunately for Penn, he spent little time in the city to monitor its growth. Penn traveled much throughout his stay in the colonies, attending to political matters in New York and elsewhere. He drafted treaties with the Indians, insisting that his colony would only expand legally under treatise with the American Indians. He also battled Maryland's governor, Lord

A SHORT TENURE

William Penn, to whom the city of Philadelphia and the United States owe so much for his early attempts to secure individual rights, spent less than four years in the Americas. He traveled the colonies from 1682 until 1684, and lived in Philadelphia and his Pennsylvania country home from 1699 until 1701. He died in 1718 and is buried in a Quaker meeting house in Bucks, England.

Baltimore, over a dispute regarding their respective colonies' boundaries. Business forced Penn to return to England in 1684, and he didn't see Philadelphia again for 15 years.

By the time Penn returned to Pennsylvania in 1699, Philadelphia had a population of 7000. It had prospered, its economy thriving as a result of Pennsylvania's natural bounty, including lumber, fur, hemp, tobacco, iron and copper. The waterfront along the Delaware had become the center of town, with homes, warehouses and businesses springing up along the wharves and rises over the river. Some of these original houses still exist in Elfreth's Alley, Queen Village and Society Hill. Although he was delighted with the growth of his new city, Penn spent much of his second trip to the colonies at his country home 24 miles north of Philadelphia—Pennsbury Manor. Penn left Pennsylvania for England again in 1701, with Philadelphia well on its way to becoming the colonies' finest city. Certainly, it was one of the most sophisticated, boasting the colonies' first hospital, its first library, its first volunteer fire department and first fire insurance company.

The 1700s marked Philadelphia's finest century, a time of growth, prosperity, ideals and independence. In 1723, a young apprentice named Benjamin Franklin arrived in Philadelphia, having run away from his post as a printer for his brother in Boston. Like Penn, this youngster—who eventually became America's most indefatigable Founding Father—would leave a mark on the city that still resonates 300 years later.

REVOLUTIONARY TIMES In Franklin's Philadelphia, city residents enjoyed life in a sophisticated city. Many were loyal subjects to the Crown, and William Penn's descendants still governed the land. As the 1700s wore on, however, relationships between the colonists and the Crown soured. The Stamp Act of 1765 was met with irritation, while later taxes and policies threatened the colonies' ability to thrive economically and independently. After Britain passed the Intolerable Acts, 12 colonies (Georgia abstained) decided to send representatives to Philadelphia for the First Continental Congress in 1774. Delegates debated their future and agreed to meet again in 1775 if relations had not improved. By the time they met again in Philadelphia seven months later, the situation had worsened. The Battles of Lexington and Concord had already taken place, and while the delegates initially had wanted to reach an accord with England, they soon voted, on June 14, 1775, to raise an army. Three days later, American patriots fought against the British near Boston at the Battle of Bunker Hill.

This second meeting, the Second Continental Congress, remained in session for more than a year. In April 1776, the mem-

Text continued on page 34.

Philadelphia's Favorite Adopted Son

Most Americans know at least one "Franklinism," even if they don't know who originated the adage. "A penny saved is a penny earned" and "Early to bed, early to rise, makes a man healthy, wealthy and wise" are so ingrained in American catechism that it's easy to forget that Philadelphia's favorite founding father Benjamin Franklin was responsible for them and so many American "firsts." Franklin helped steer the course of history with genius and brilliance. As a scientist, inventor, statesman, philosopher, musician and economist, you could call him the archetypical American overachiever.

Franklin was born on January 17, 1706, in Boston, Massachusetts, the tenth son of a soap and candle maker. Although he only attended formal schooling for two years, he showed promise as a writer and reader and was apprenticed to an older brother, a printer, to learn a craft. Frustrated by the pace of his studies—and abused by his brother—he ran away to Philadelphia to strike out on his own. In this new city, 17-year-old Franklin began doing print work and soon moved to London to finish his studies.

On his return to the City of Brotherly Love in 1726, he threw himself into numerous projects, starting with the purchase of the *Pennsylvania Gazette* in 1729. At the *Gazette*, he penned numerous articles, but made his mark drawing the first political cartoon. Less than five years later, he started publishing *Poor Richard's Almanack*, a calendar that stood apart for its style and witticisms. In the 1730s, he emerged as a civic activist, launching the first subscription library, a fire insurance company and the nation's first hospital. By the 1740s, he had sold off his printing business and absorbed himself in science and politics, conducting his famous lightning experiments and inventing the Franklin stove, an iron fireplace insert designed to heat homes more efficiently. By the 1750s, he was immersed in politics, and with the passage of the Stamp Act, began contemplating an independent America. His notable political acts include signing both the Declaration of Independence and the Constitution (he was one of six that did so) and negotiating the Treaty of Paris ending the Revolutionary War.

Franklin's private life was as complex and rich as his public one, a life filled with love, loss and passion. Franklin fathered a child out of wedlock, a son named William who later served as royal governor of New Jersey and split with his father over politics, remaining loyal to the crown as his dad became a patriot. Franklin married Deborah Read, a woman he met on his first day in Philadelphia, and had two children. His son died at age four while his daughter outlived them both. His wife pre-deceased him as well. Although he suffered from gout and far-sightedness and near-sightedness—afflictions that led him to invent bifocals—as he aged, he maintained his joie de vivre and passions for learning, humor and women, celebrated from the court of Louis XVI to the parlors of the fledgling nation.

Franklin's life is showcased at museums and homes throughout the city. For an in-depth look at his accomplishments and life, check out the Independence Hall National Historical Park area, the Benjamin Franklin National Memorial in the rotunda of the Franklin Institute, and the Franklin Institute.

bers decided to draft a declaration of independence, crafting words that would mean all-out war to the Crown. Virginia delegate Thomas Jefferson was named to lead the small committee charged with writing the document. With some assistance from James Madison and the guidance of Benjamin Franklin, the committee's document was considered by Congress on July 2, 1776. It was formally approved on July 4, and on July 8th, was read to a crowd of 8000 people in Independence Square. The Founding Fathers could have been tried for treason, a crime punishable by death. Certainly they were well aware of the risks. At the signing of the Declaration of Independence, Benjamin Franklin uttered the immortal words, "We must all hang together, or assuredly we shall all hang separately."

Six men signed both the Declaration of Independence and the Constitution: George Clymer, Benjamin Franklin, Robert Morris and James Wilson, all of Pennsylvania; Roger Sherman of Connecticut; and George Read of Delaware.

The Revolutionary War years were tumultuous for the city. Washington led his troops to victory on Christmas 1776, crossing the Delaware roughly 34 miles north of Philadelphia. Less than a year later, the British invaded the city after defeating George Washington's army at the Battle of Brandywine. British and Hessian soldiers took up residence in many area homes and institutions, by and large enjoying their stay as they were hosted by several wealthy Philadelphians who remained loyal to the Crown. Washington attempted to break through British lines at Germantown in October 1777, but suffering another defeat, retreated with his men to Valley Forge. There, his armies endured a bitter winter with limited supplies and dwindling resources. By summer 1778, however, France had thrown its strength behind the American forces and Washington's troops returned to the fight. The British left Philadelphia in June 1778. The Revolutionary War ended with the stroke of a fountain pen in Paris in 1783. The Crown acknowledged the existence of the colonies as sovereign entities.

The states had been operating under the Articles of Confederation, drafted in Philadelphia by John Dickinson in 1776, amended by the Second Continental Congress and ratified by all 13 colonies by 1781. This document left most of the power of government in states' hands, binding them loosely as a "league of friendship." But it was soon evident that the states needed a more binding relationship than was presented in the Articles, and in 1787, delegates met again in Philadelphia for the Constitutional Convention. George Washington was appointed president of the convention, a group of delegates that included an elderly Benjamin Franklin, Alexander Hamilton and James Madison. For four months, delegates debated various versions of a plan. Keeping the windows and doors shut in the summer heat to avoid being overheard, the men entertained plans that included one calling for a powerful federal government, another granting much sovereignty to state governments and, in one case, a plan with a powerful executive akin to a monarchy. After much wrangling and discussion, they settled on a compromise, submitting it for signing on September 17, 1787. As the document was ratified by the states, Philadelphia became the new nation.

The federal government operated out of the city from 1790 to 1800, with the U.S. Supreme Court, the House of Representatives and the Senate and the Executive Branch housed in buildings adjacent to Independence Hall. When the government moved to Washington, DC, Philadelphia continued to prosper as a center for banking and shipping. As the importance of railroads grew in the expanding nation, Philadelphia maintained its hold as a hub for commerce; the city's iron and locomotive works contributed significantly to economic growth and Western expansion.

Before the Civil War, Philadelphia became a hotbed for abolitionism. The city and its suburbs remained strongly influenced by the Quakers, who actively pursued freedom for slaves and promoted anti-slavery organizations. The abolitionists took the Pennsylvania State House Bell as their symbol, calling it the "Liberty Bell" for its inscription of Leviticus, Chapter 25, Verse 10, which contains the phrase "Proclaim Liberty throughout all the Land unto all the Inhabitants thereof." During the Civil War, several of Philadelphia's homes were used to house runaway slaves and many buildings were used to house wounded soldiers. The war also brought prosperity to many Philadelphia industries, which manufactured goods including uniforms and woolens, ammunition and weapons.

Following the Civil War, Philadelphia expanded, with port activity on the upswing, development of the commuter railroad and the construction of new buildings, institutions and cultural attractions. In 1876, Philadelphia hosted the first world's fair held in the United States, the Centennial Exposition. New buildings were completed in Fairmount Park to house more than 30,000 displays, inventions and natural wonders. At Machinery Hall, Edison unveiled his telegraph and Alexander Graham Bell, the telephone. The Exposition was the United States' opportunity to show the world how technologically and culturally far it had come, and to that end, it was a success. Nearly 10 million people attended.

THE 20TH CENTURY At the turn of the century, Philadelphia underwent a building boom. Its new City Hall, the nation's largest, neared completion and Center City became a major center for finance and commerce. Evidence of the Gilded Age was everywhere in the city, with new rowhouses constructed for workers and manor homes built or renovated to celebrate wealth and prosperity. Yet the good times weren't to last. By World War I, farm prices entered into decline, affecting the entire state, and during the Great Depression, it was estimated that a quarter of Philadelphia's work force was unemployed. By 1933, more than 70,000 Philadelphians suffered from malnutrition. Only America's support and entry into World War II could help stabilize the economy of Philadelphia, and even that prosperity wouldn't last.

Philadelphia's population peaked at 2.1 million in 1950, and as manufacturing jobs were lost and public schools and institutions fell into decay, much of the city's white population fled to the suburbs. The city struggled—and continues to do so—with the issues of employment, education, health care and services for its residents, many of whom continue to live below the poverty line. In 1976, the city celebrated the Bicentennial with much fanfare, opening newly refurbished and reconstructed buildings. Still, Philadelphia remained plagued by issues that affect many large urban centers, including crime, drugs and homelessness. The city had lost much of its manufacturing base—down from 50 percent of its jobs to 9 percent—and struggled to replace these lost businesses.

In the late 1980s and 1990s, Philadelphia's government began to act, launching a massive campaign to improve the city's image. New stadiums and the $522 million Pennsylvania Convention Center were built. Money was directed toward cleaning up the parts of the city that attract visitors, and the city created a marketing corporation for the city.

While critics have noted that the amount of money being spent on improvements should go toward helping the residents themselves, especially in the areas of education, health care and employment services, Philadelphia is seeing results of its efforts. Businesses and commercial enterprises have returned to Center City. Many buildings within Penn's original city plan are experiencing rebirth through reuse. Former parochial schools, warehouses and stores are now upscale condominiums; neighborhoods like Fishtown near Kensington that were once avoided now attract families, artists and new businesses to live, work and play. In 1996, Philadelphia completed a $26 million streetscape project, installing 400 trees and walking-tour signage. The airport completed a $1 billion capital improvement plan. New attractions, including a tourist shuttle to Camden and a renovated cruise ship terminal, have made Philadelphia more attractive to development. New facilities, such as the National Constitution Center and the Kimmel Center for the Performing Arts, draw people to the city for day trips as well as overnight stays.

INTO THE MILLENNIUM   Philadelphia's population continues to decline, yet it appears the city is on the edge of rebirth. Improvements made to tourist attractions are drawing in new dollars. New business headquarters, including pharmaceutical company SmithKline Beecham, hospitality giant Aramark, CIGNA Insurance and Comcast, have created jobs. Even projects in the city's neighborhoods, such as the mural arts program that has placed more than 2000 works of art on buildings and in lots throughout the city—many in some of Philadelphia's worst neighborhoods—are improving previously overlooked or ignored areas.

The oldest rocks in the area have been found in Chestnut Hill. Called Bryn Mawr Gravel, these rocks date to the Paleozoic Era, back 400 million years.

Sure, Philadelphia's city government continues to struggle with problems, including poverty, crime, education and welfare. But in the past five years, there's been much to celebrate. In 2000, the city was selected to host the Republican National Convention. In 2005, it was chosen as the only U.S. city to participate in the global Live 8 concert. And in October 2005, *National Geographic Traveler* magazine featured Philadelphia on its cover, with the headline "Next Great City: Philly, Really."

The cheers went up at City Hall. "For many years, we were overlooked," said Cara Schneider with the Greater Philadelphia Tourism Marketing Corporation. "But there's been a resurgence of interest in patriotic destinations, and certainly, Philadelphia is one of the nation's most historic cities."

The Land

GEOLOGY

Geographically, Philadelphia rides a line—literally—between two regions: the Piedmont Plateau, characterized by a substrate of metamorphic rock, hills and temperate deciduous forest; and the Atlantic Coastal Plain, a flat region of sand and gravel earth, level terrain, wetlands and woody copses. The line that separates the two is called the Fall Line, a low ridge that runs from New Jersey to the Carolinas, paralleling the Atlantic Coast. Not only does the Fall Line separate the Paleozoic-era rock of the Piedmont from the Mesozoic and Tertiary sedimentary rock of the Plain, it is the geologic cause for waterfalls along rivers such as the Schuylkill, the Potomac and the James—cascades that hosted industries based on water power, giving rise to the cities of Philadelphia, Baltimore, Washington, DC, and Richmond.

Characteristics of the Piedmont Plateau are evident in the northwest sections of Philadelphia and Fairmount Park, where metamorphic rocks of schist, gneiss, serpentine and quartzite jut from the soil, forming crags, cliffs and outcroppings.

A trip through Fairmount Park is your best bet for viewing the geology that characterizes the Piedmont. Cruise in the eastern part of the park along Kelly Drive and you'll encounter jutting crags. Near the Girard Avenue Bridge is Promontory Rock, a giant mass of Wissahickon Schist that thrusts from the soil. Park engineers bore through the rock in 1871, making way for the roadway. Another beautiful outcropping is located near the East Park Canoe House, a mass that has been eroded over time to look like it rose in the opposite direction of other outcroppings in the park.

The geology of the Atlantic Coastal Plain is largely sedimentary, made up of sands and brick clay. The abundance and beauty of these native rocks can be seen not only along the sandy shores of the Delaware, but in the Colonial houses of Philadelphia, most of which were constructed of locally made bricks. The redness of the bricks draws its color from the high iron content in the base material. An 1880 geologic survey determined that the bricks also hold a significant amount of disseminated gold—enough to "pay off the national debt" at the time. The survey concluded, however, that since it would cost $10 to extract just one dollar's worth of gold out of Philadelphia area rocks and bricks, it wasn't worth the effort.

FLORA   The pockets of woodland and marshes that make up much of the green space around Philadelphia feature a wide selection of native plant and tree species. Some of the city's most striking scenery, found in the Wissahickon gorge section of Fairmount Park, is beautiful for its majestic trees, including maple, pawpaw, oak, hemlock and sycamore. Aspens are native to the region, and can be found seen in the Houston Meadow, behind the Houston Playground at Wissahickon Avenue and Grakyn Lane, near Forbidden Drive. In the spring, beneath the canopy of the temperate deciduous forest, native redbud and dogwood trees bloom, a show enhanced by the presence of azaleas and rhododendron growing in area gardens and parks. Other native plants and shrubs that can be spotted in the woodlands include bay-

A DEVASTATING PLAGUE

In August 1793, Philadelphia suffered a devastating yellow fever epidemic brought from the Caribbean by infected slaves. At the time, no one realized the fever was transmitted by the mosquito population, which, during that year, was particularly bad as a result of a drought that had reduced wells and cisterns to fetid pools. Nearly half the city's population of 55,000 fled the area, including George Washington. Researchers believe at least 4000 died.

berry, wild hydrangea, blueberries and burning bush. Lucky hikers may come across a number of rare, beautiful wildflowers, including native orchids, jack-in-the-pulpit and columbine. Other flowers that attract butterflies and birds can be found at the forest's edge, including swamp milkweed, asters and wild sweet william. Parks and meadows play host to wildflowers from mid-March to mid-October. Common in these sunny spaces are cone flowers, goldenrod and wild carrots.

In the marshes and lowlands, especially near the airport and the John Heinz National Wildlife Refuge, coastal vegetation provides a habitat for a host of water-loving animals and birds, including grasses, shrubs and ubiquitous cattails.

A great amount of wildlife has learned to coexist with humans in Philadelphia, and the city features vast stretches of habitat for animals, birds and water creatures. Fairmount Park alone is home to 50 species of birds, 20 of mammals, 9 of reptile, 6 of amphibians and 50 of fishes. Hundreds of shorebirds can be found at the John Heinz National Wildlife Refuge along with migratory species in the spring and fall.

FAUNA

The Piedmont region's abundance of small mammals played a significant role in southeastern Pennsylvania's development; early settlers arrived in droves to trap beaver, fox, raccoon, otter, deer and bear. Creatures that lived in Penn's Woods at the time of Penn's arrival included wild pigeons, panthers, black bears and lynxes. No longer will you find bears or medium-sized cats here, but you're likely to encounter a host of mammals both large and small while hiking, including raccoons, squirrels, rabbits, skunks, chipmunks, woodchucks and deer. Birds that you might see in remote spots, wooded areas or meadows include pheasant, quail and turkeys. The Schuylkill River is home to 37 species of fish, and while industrialization in the late 1800s destroyed much of this river habitat, pollution abatement appears to be succeeding. In March 2005, environmentalists rejoiced when a three-foot river otter was spotted at the fish ladder near the Fairmount Water Works. A month later, a wayward beluga whale had found its way upriver to Philadelphia as well.

The wetlands and marshes of the Atlantic Coastal Plain serve as home to numerous shorebirds, amphibians and reptiles. In the John Heinz National Wildlife Refuge and parks along the Delaware, great blue herons, horned owls, cormorants, snowy egrets, geese, mallards and pintail ducks thrive. Woodpeckers share airspace with gulls, doves, cuckoos and barn owls. The refuge also is home to muskrats and two species on the Pennsylvania state endangered list, including the red-bellied turtle and the southern leopard frog. You'll also be surprised to learn that porcupines are a native species to Pennsylvania, and although they tend to live in the mountains or in rocky areas, there is an exhibit at the wildlife center about them.

The waters around Philadelphia are home to a wide range of fish, including trout, smallmouth and largemouth bass, muskie, carp, shad and catfish.

Outdoor Adventures

CAMPING

There are no places to pitch a tent in city limits, but there are at least sixty commercial campgrounds and one state campground within 60 miles of Philadelphia, most of which are open from April through October. Prices vary for the commercial campgrounds, depending on the amenities provided. At state parks, campers can set up their sites at designated camp sites only. Fees vary depending on type of campsite, primitive or with electricity, and whether you are camping during the week or on weekends. See the "Parks" sections of Chapters Seven through Nine for more camping information.

WATER SPORTS

The Philadelphia region is a prime area for boating. The Delaware, Schuylkill and Brandywine rivers offer an array of opportunities for kayaking, canoeing, sailing and rowing. From spring through fall, boaters search out hidden reaches in the city and surrounding counties, finding ample sites for whitewater kayaking, crew and canoeing. The wide waters of the Delaware are popular for both motorboats and sailing, although portions of the Delaware are major ship channels and should be used by only experienced boaters. During the winter, when rivers begin to ice over, you'll see few out on the water, except for hardy individuals—usually members of high-school or collegiate rowing teams—near Boathouse Row in Fairmount Park.

In the state of Pennsylvania, motor boats must be registered with the **Pennsylvania Fish & Boat Commission**. To launch a non-power boat from a commission-maintained launch ramp, a permit is required. For information on boating in Pennsylvania, contact the Pennsylvania Fish & Boat Commission. The agency publishes a boating handbook on rules and regulations. ~ 1601 Elmerton Avenue, Harrisburg; 888-723-4741.

FISHING

Regulations vary, but licenses are required for fishing throughout the state. They can be purchased at a number of venues, including bait-and-tackle shops, sporting good stores, some retail discount stores like Wal-Mart and Kmart, at fishing lodges, in charter shops and at county treasurers' offices. Special permits are required for trout fishing, and those can be purchased where licenses are available.

Philly Phanatics—
The Good, the Bad, the Ugly

Philadelphia is, with no exceptions, a sports town. In fact, the first professional football game was played here in 1936 (the Eagles won, beating Cincinnati 64-0). In the most southern portion of the city lies a cluster of stadiums that house the city's venerated sports teams. This city's sports scene rocks—literally—with frenzied fanatics and flamboyant players. Philadelphia is home to the Eagles football team, the Phillies baseball team, the 76ers basketball team, the Flyers hockey team and the Philadelphia Soul Arena League football team. The city even has a professional lacrosse team, the Philadelphia Barrage.

When Philadelphia's teams win, the entire city rejoices. When they lose, it wails equally as loud. This is a place where the football stadium had a holding cell for ruffians, and fans booed Santa Claus for delay of game. A Philadelphia team hasn't won a major championship since 1983, and some fans say it's because the city government, which once restricted building heights to the height of William Penn's statue atop City Hall, allowed a skyscraper to be built in 1987 that towers over Penn by 397 feet. Called the "Curse of Billy Penn," this mystery has been cited for Philadelphia team losses in the finals for the Stanley Cup, the World Series, the NBA Championship and the Super Bowl. But despite their inability to snag a championship, Philadelphia teams are among the nation's top-rated, and professional sports fans would do well to catch a game while in town.

In addition to pro sports, Philadelphia boasts a wide-ranging collegiate sports scene. Nearly every week of the year, with the exception of a few weeks in summer, Philadelphia area colleges are playing in a game, tournament, playoff or match. With more than 30 colleges and universities in the region, nearly every sport played in America is represented, and some of the more uncommon activities, including fencing and water polo, are among the most fun to watch.

Around Philadelphia, anglers gravitate toward the Schuylkill, the Brandywine and Valley Forge (see Chapter Nine) for fishing. There also are numerous ponds and lakes in the region that welcome fishermen. You can drop a line behind the Philadelphia Museum of Art at the Water Works and perhaps score a bass or catfish; you're likely to find a number of fellow anglers along with you. A top spot for stocked trout within city limits is **Wissahickon Creek** near the Forbidden Drive section of Fairmount Park.

For information on fishing in southeastern Pennsylvania, contact the **Pennsylvania Fish & Boat Commission**. The Commission publishes a book of rules and regulations, and its expansive website serves as a tremendous resource for information on catches, rules, tips and insider hints. ~ 1601 Elmerton Avenue, Harrisburg; 717-785-7800.

BOATING, KAYAKING & CANOEING One of the greatest spectator sports in Philadelphia is watching the graceful strokes of the rowers on the Schuylkill in Fairmount Park. Unless you're a member of the U.S. Rowing Association, however, it's unlikely you'll be able to take to this dangerous and often swift section of the river. There are a number of outfitters outside Philadelphia that can help set you up on the water, either in a canoe or kayak. In Haverford, **Eastern Mountain Sports** rents kayaks. ~ 525 West Lancaster Avenue, Haverford; 610-520-8000; www.ems.com.

For information on canoeing in the area, contact the **Philadelphia Canoe Club**. ~ 4900 Ridge Avenue; 215-487-9674; www.philacanoe.org.

Several commercial companies offer river cruises and sails on the water—little or no physical fitness involved. If you'd like to simply take a tour on the Philadelphia waterfront, you can hop the **RiverLink Ferry** and take a 20-minute trip to Camden, New Jersey, or a longer 90-minute tour. Fee. ~ 121 North Columbus Boulevard; 215-925-5465; www.riverlinkferry.org.

The **Spirit of Philadelphia** offers cruises, dinner sails and entertainment on the Delaware, sailing several time a day on the Delaware. The ship leaves Penn's Landing and heads south to the Navy Yard before turning around and passing beneath the Walt Whitman and Benjamin Franklin bridges. ~ 215-923-4354, 866-211-3808; www.spiritcitycruises.com. The **Riverboat Queen Fleet** offers similar tours aboard a steamboat. For family fun much closer to the water, however, rent a **paddle boat** next to the *Riverboat Queen* in good weather. ~ Columbus Boulevard and Market Street; 215-923-2628; www.riverboatqueenfleet.com.

SWIMMING The city has 86 municipal swimming pools, and it's likely that your hotel, if you're staying in a chain, will have one as well.

Locals tend to favor the YMCA swimming pools since they are clean and well maintained. For information on the location of city pools and times for lap swim, contact the **Philadelphia Department of Recreation Aquatics Department.** ~ 1515 Arch Street; 215-683-3663.

If you are a YMCA member elsewhere and want to find out more about the city's YMCA pools, call the **West Philadelphia YMCA.** ~ 5120 Chestnut Street; 215-476-2700.

JOGGING

Fairmount Park has miles of trails, including a popular 8.5-mile loop that begins at the Museum of Art, runs north up the east bank of the Schuylkill, crosses the river at Falls Bridge and wends its way back to the museum. The western section of the park also has a number of running trails, and the **Forbidden Drive** section is ever-popular with hikers, runners and bikers for its beautiful scenery. For interesting sites and a familiarization tour of the city, you can't beat a run through the historic area and Old City, running past Independence Hall, heading east toward the river and north to the Benjamin Franklin Bridge. Run across the bridge and back and you've added 3.5 miles to your trip. The Fairmount Running Club has information and maps on its website. ~ www.runfairmount.org.

GOLF

The city of Philadelphia has five public 18-hole courses. Several rank as local favorites, with **Cobbs Creek Golf Club** topping the list. Cobbs Creek offers a challenging par-71 course with a lengthy back nine, but is easily the most well-maintained course in the city system. ~ 7200 Lansdowne Avenue; 215-877-8707.

Another local favorite is the **John F. Byrne Golf Club**, with scenic Torresdale Creek and a number of water traps. ~ 9500 Leon Street; 215-632-8666.

Juniata Golf Course offers an urban golfing experience, with twelve par-4 and six par-3 holes. A creek winds through the course, yet this course lies in the heart of the city—placement that creates its own unique challenges. ~ 1391 Cayuga Street; 215-743-4060.

Also within city limits is the **Franklin D. Roosevelt Golf Club**, which features a number of water hazards, wetlands and tall grasses to challenge the most experienced players. ~ 20th and Pattison Avenue; 215-462-8997.

TENNIS

Fairmount Park boasts 150 courts for public use. For information and hours, call the Fairmount Park Commission. ~ 1515 Arch Street, 10th floor; 215-683-0200; www.fairmountpark.com.

WINTER SPORTS

Philadelphia's winters are clearly defined: creeks freeze over and trails often are covered with snow. For outdoor fun, consider hitting the trails of **Fairmount Park** with cross-country skis or snowshoes, or lace up some skates and head onto the ice.

A number of outfitters outside Philadelphia rent snowshoes and cross-country skis. In Haverford, **Eastern Mountain Sports** rents snowshoes. ~ 525 West Lancaster Avenue, Haverford; 610-520-8000; www.ems.com.

Buckman's Ski and Snowboard Shops rent cross-country skis and snowboards during the season. Buckman's has five stores in the Philadelphia suburbs. The closest to Center City is in Ardmore, on the Main Line. ~ 26 Lancaster Avenue, Ardmore; 610-658-0470; www.skibuckmans.com.

In winter, visitors can ice skate outdoors at the **Blue Cross RiverRink** at Penn's Landing, from late November until March. Skate rentals and lessons are available. ~ Columbus Boulevard and Market Street; 215-925-7465.

BIKING

There are miles of bike trails in and around Philadelphia. Near Forbidden Drive in Wissahickon lies dirt and gravel trails for mountain biking. Along Kelly Drive and throughout Fairmount Park are miles of paved trails for street bikes and roller blades; from April through October, West River Drive along the river is closed to vehicular traffic during the day. At Lloyd Hall, the closest boathouse to the Philadelphia Museum of Art is a kiosk for renting wheels, **Bell's Bike Shop**. It rents bicycles, in-line skates, baby joggers, helmets and pads. ~ 1 Boathouse Row; 215-232-7900.

You can also rent bicycles at the **Bike Line** in Manayunk, with the aim of riding to Valley Forge on the Schuylkill River Trail. ~ 4159 Main Street; 215-487-7433; www.bikelin.com.

The **Bicycle Club of Philadelphia** can assist with maps and information on trails in the city and local neighborhoods. ~ 215-735-2453; www.phillybikeclub.org.

HIKING

Fairmount Park has miles of quiet trails and remote regions. In the **Wissahickon** area, hikers hardly believe they are less than ten miles from Center City; Wissahickon has the added advantage of being restricted to vehicular traffic. The **John Heinz National Wildlife Refuge at Tinicum** also is a great place to explore, with wetland trails, birding opportunities and the smell of salty marshes. (The proximity to the airport tends to be a distraction, but it doesn't seem to bother the birds.)

THREE

Historic Philadelphia

More than 16 million people visit Philadelphia each year, attracted to the city for a variety of reasons, including business, conferences, dining and sports events. But most come to experience its rich history, and Philadelphia's Independence Hall area is the main draw. Nicknamed the "nation's most historic square mile," this part of the city housed our nation's founding fathers from October 1774, when the First Continental Congress met, through 1800, when lawmakers moved the U.S capital to Washington, DC.

Much of historic Philadelphia has changed radically since 1776, but significant portions haven't—or at least, they've been rebuilt to look like they haven't. Along Chestnut Street, visitors stroll where Franklin, Jefferson and Washington trod. At City Tavern and Christ Church, they can dally where these famous men spoke, dined and worshipped. And throughout the quarter, visitors will enter numerous sites that offer a sense of life in the turbulent 1770s. Transformation can often be a setback for historic areas, but improvements made to Independence National Historical Park in the last decade have only enhanced its appeal: two new facilities, the Liberty Bell Center and National Constitution Center, aim to promote a better understanding of Philadelphia's history and the country's ideals as a whole, and other improvements, including updates to signs and exhibits and costumed actors, have made the park more user-friendly and edifying.

Old City lies northeast of the park, and was so named to distinguish it from the historic district. Historic in its own right, Old City boasts the nation's oldest residential street—Elfreth's Alley—and contains the remnants of the city's Industrial Age factories and homes. Today, it's a thriving community known for its art galleries, restaurants and nightlife.

Along the waterfront, from the Benjamin Franklin Bridge to South Street, lies Penn's Landing, a focal point of Philadelphia fun, boasting restaurants, museums, watering holes and concert venues. In 1682, William Penn arrived at his new North American home via the Delaware River, landing at the spot now aptly named after him. He was greeted by the settlers that had preceded him, including

Swedish and Dutch pioneers and American Indians. The area became the heart of Philadelphia trade and maritime business, and while shipping continues to be an important part of southeastern Pennsylvania's economy, much of the marine activity has moved north and south of the city, leaving Penn's Landing as a riverfront promenade for recreational activities.

Penn's Landing serves as the city's main music stage during such events as the Memorial Day Jam on the River and 4th of July concert and fireworks extravaganzas. Other festivals are held throughout the year as well. From Penn's Landing, you can catch a ferry to Camden, NJ, home to an aquarium and the battleship USS *New Jersey*.

South of the national park and west of Penn's Landing lies Society Hill, a neighborhood that earned its name from the Society of Free Traders, an organization that built offices along Front Street in the late 1600s. Homes sprang up in the vicinity, with many members of state and federal government choosing this neighborhood to live. Markets, such as the one founded at the Shambles and Headhouse Square, provided goods for this expanding population, and taverns and churches arose amid the homes of the wealthy.

Given the area's charm, with its cobblestone streets, brick rowhouses and hidden parks, it's hard to believe that Society Hill had deteriorated significantly by the mid-20th century, its homes turning into slums, its green spaces buried in rubbish and waste. The decline of Society Hill began years before, during the 19th century, when the growth of wharves, warehouses and markets sent wealthy residents packing for nicer neighborhoods. Left behind were those without the means to care for the district's historic structures. But in the early 1950s, the city—and a group of intrepid residents—embarked on a substantial renewal project in Society Hill. The results are evident today in the neighborhood's homes, businesses, schools and parks, and in the real estate assessments as well.

The park, Old City, Society Hill and Penn's Landing are in close proximity with one another, seen easily by foot. The Independence Visitor Center offers maps, brochures and self-guided tours for these areas. There also are numerous options for exploring the district by professional tour, and many of these activities feature unique transportation modes, including double-decker bus, trolley car, amphibious landing vehicle or Segway. You'll find information on commercial tours at the Independence Visitor Center or at their origination points, mainly along 6th Street between Market and Chestnut streets.

▼▼▼▼▼▼▼▼▼▼▼▼▼▼
Independence National Historical Park Area

From Arch to Walnut streets, between 3rd and 6th streets, lie two of America's most historic icons, the Liberty Bell and Independence Hall. But Independence National Historical Park, which spans 45 acres, also contains the buildings in which Congress first met, an army was raised, and momentous, treasonous decisions were made. Within the boundaries of this park, nearly every significant document framing the United States government was penned or introduced, including the Declaration of Independence, the Articles of Confederation, the Constitution, and the Bill of Rights. This part of the city

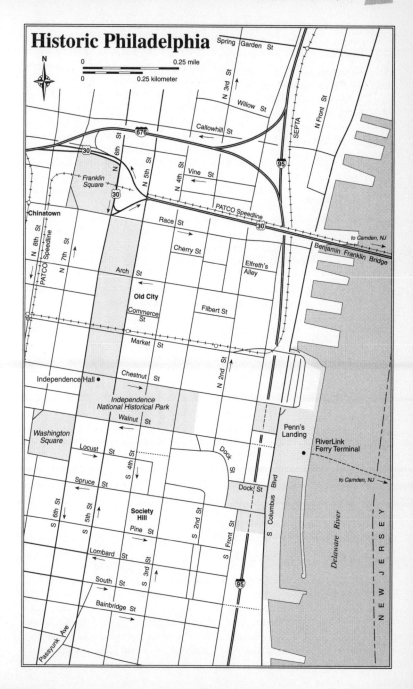

Historic Philadelphia

N

0   0.25 mile

0   0.25 kilometer

Spring Garden St

N 3rd St

Willow St

Callowhill St

676

30

N 6th St

N 5th St

N 4th St

Vine   St

Franklin Square

30

SEPTA

N Front St

95

PATCO Speedline

30

Chinatown

N 8th St

PATCO Speedline

N 7th St

Race   St

Cherry St

Elfreth's Alley

to Camden, NJ

Benjamin Franklin Bridge

Arch   St

Old City

Commerce St

Filbert St

Market   St

N 2nd St

Chestnut   St

Independence Hall •

Independence National Historical Park

Walnut   St

Penn's Landing

RiverLink Ferry Terminal

Washington Square

Locust   St

S 4th St

Dock St

Spruce   St

Dock St

S Columbus Blvd

to Camden, NJ

S 6th St

S 5th St

Society Hill

S 2nd St

S Front St

Pine   St

Delaware River

Lombard   St

S 3rd St

South   St

95

Bainbridge St

Passyunk Ave

N E W   J E R S E Y

hosted the country's most influential men in the 1700s; later, it housed the nation's capital, with Washington living in residence and the Congress and Supreme Court meeting in buildings adjacent to Independence Hall.

The new Liberty Bell Center was built nearly on top of the site of George Washington's home in Philadelphia. Ironically, the Virginian kept slaves while living in Philadelphia, despite laws against the practice.

Today, the National Park Service oversees Independence Hall and the Liberty Bell, but also manages several restored Colonial homes, a portrait gallery, an archaeology laboratory, Benjamin Franklin's home site, parks and gardens. Admittance to most of the attractions is free, although the National Park Service willingly takes donations. Some attractions require tickets; those are denoted in their individual sections.

While many visitors cram their visits to the Independence Hall area into one morning, it's impossible to fully appreciate this area in less than a day. Independence Hall National Historical Park has more than 20 buildings of its own to see, and the surrounding neighborhoods hold their own treasures. Allow at least a day or more to fully experience the history, attractions, restaurants, nightlife and ambiance of this preserved locale.

SIGHTS

First-time travelers should start their tour at the **Independence Visitor Center**, a sparkling new addition to the Independence Hall area that provides visitors with information on the entire city, not just the historic district. The visitors center issues guides to National Park Service–run sites, movies, exhibits and tickets for area attractions, but most importantly, it is where you pick up timed tickets for entry to Independence Hall. While admission to the historic building is free, tickets are required. They can be ordered online before your visit (consult the National Park Service's website: reservations.nps.gov) or picked up at the center. Same-day, walk-up tickets are available for Independence Hall; arrive between 8:30 a.m. to 10:30 a.m. to get your choice of tour time. During peak summer season, tickets often are gone by 1 p.m. Tickets to other Colonial homes run by the park service are available here as well.

The visitors center opens a half-hour before the historic sites, allowing you to get in early and plan your day. Park rangers and travel assistants can help plan your stay and print itineraries, and the center also features several self-service computer kiosks for planning purposes. The visitors center shows a 30-minute film introduction to the area and airs documentaries throughout the day in its three theaters; there's a gift shop and coffee bar as well. Parking is available under the center for a fee. ~ 6th and Market streets; 215-965-7676, 800-537-7676; www.independencevisitor center.com.

Most visitors want to start off in Philadelphia seeing the Liberty Bell and Independence Hall, but if you can restrain yourself, begin your trip at the **National Constitution Center**, a museum dedicated to the U.S. Constitution and the history of U.S. government that opened in 2003. With this museum as a starting point, you'll better appreciate the trials facing the Founding Fathers and enjoy a richer experience as you tour the historic sites later. While you may wonder how a museum devoted to the lofty ideals of the Constitution can be worth the time or admis-

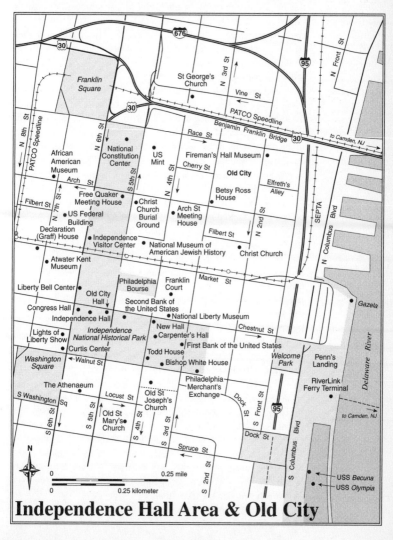

Independence Hall Area & Old City

sion, the center's 17-minute multimedia presentation, "Freedom Rising," will dispel any questions. It provides an excellent overview of the historic events that occurred in Philadelphia between the years 1775 and 1789, and is so well-scripted that the U.S. State Department sends foreign visitors to see it for perspective on the United States' democratic principles. The museum's interactive exhibits pay tribute to the three branches of federal government; children and grownups alike will enjoy participating in such activities as taking the presidential oath of office on a stage mock-up of the U.S. Capitol steps and deciding a Supreme Court case. In Signer's Hall, visitors walk among life-size sculptures of the framers and decide whether to add their names to the 39 who signed the Constitution or stand with the 3 who refused. Admission. ~ 525 Arch Street; 215-923-0004; www.constitutioncenter.org.

The **Liberty Bell**, once housed in the foyer in Independence Hall, has moved several times and was relocated most recently in 2003 to its new home catty-corner to Independence Hall. The newly constructed **Liberty Bell Center** allows the famous ringer to be seen around the clock from the outside and against the backdrop of Independence Hall from inside. The center features interpretive signs, exhibits and information about the bell, ordered in 1751 from Whitechapel Foundry, London, for the Pennsylvania State House (now Independence Hall). The 2080-pound bell cracked on its first strike in Philadelphia and was recast in 1753 by two local artisans, John Pass and John Stow. On July 8, 1776, it was rung to call Philadelphians to the first reading of the Declaration of Independence. Later, during the Revolutionary War, the bell was smuggled to Allentown, 60 miles north, by wagon to keep it from falling into the hands of the British, who captured the city. Just when the recast bell cracked remains a mystery. Both the fixed fissure and the long hairline fracture visible alongside the repair occurred between 1830 and 1846. Some say the bell broke in 1832 or 1835 when it was rung to mark George Washington's birthday, but others say it happened during the funeral of Chief Justice John Marshall in 1835. The National Park Service maintains that it was last rung—and cracked—during Washington's birthday celebration in 1846. ~ 6th and Chestnut streets; 215-965-2305; www.nps.gov/inde/liberty-bell.html.

The Liberty Bell's former home, the Liberty Bell Pavilion, now houses Independence Hall's security screening checkpoint. Studies are underway to raze it or relocate it, a move that would make the area between Independence Hall and the National Constitution Center a true "mall."

An iconic symbol of the United States' birth, **Independence Hall** is where the Declaration of Independence was adopted, the

Articles of Confederation were written and the Constitution of the United States was discussed, drafted and signed. It was selected as the site of the Second Continental Congress, which convened on May 10, 1775. From that day until September 17, 1787, the hall sheltered men whose works and ideas directed the course of American history. By the time Congress convened in 1775, the battles of Lexington and Concord had taken place, and the delegates, elected by their Colonial assemblies, met to coordinate a response to George III's demands on the colonies. The delegates, whose ranks included Virginian Thomas Jefferson, Pennyslvanian Benjamin Franklin, New Yorker Alexander Hamilton and Massachusetts' John Adams, met with a hopes to avoid war, but by June, that optimism had disappeared. Congress organized an army, appointing George Washington commander-in-chief, and less than a year later, on July 2, 1776, delegates voted for independence in the hall's Assembly Room. Two days later, they approved Jefferson's eloquently worded Declaration of Independence. More than a decade after that historic event, Independence Hall hosted the Constitutional Convention, a meeting attended by 55 delegates, including Washington and Franklin. On September 17, 1787, the U.S. Constitution—the document that formed one nation out of a disparate 13 states and created a three-branch federal government—was signed.

The term "Liberty Bell" didn't come about until 1839, when abolitionists adopted the bell as an anti-slavery symbol. It is tapped 13 times each year on Independence Day by descendents of the Founding Fathers, and rings in the note of E flat.

Independence Hall can only be seen by guided tour. The National Park Service issues timed tickets at the Independence Visitor Center. The rooms of Independence Hall are preserved as they are thought to have been furnished in the late 1700s. Assembly Hall's most notable treasure is Washington's speaker's chair, with its engraved sun. Across the hall from the Assembly is the former chamber of the Pennsylvania Supreme Court, which contains an elaborate coat of arms of the Commonwealth of Pennsylvania, as well as a prisoner's dock, where suspects stood throughout their legal proceedings, giving rise to the phrase "standing trial." Upstairs in the hall are the governor's council chambers and the Long Gallery, once the largest public room in Philadelphia, used for receptions, balls and dinners. The "Great Essentials" exhibit, found in the west wing, displays artifacts including the final draft of the Constitution, a copy of the Articles of Confederation, the first printing of the Declaration of Independence and a silver inkstand, designed by silversmith and Franklin political ally Philip Syng, that was used during the signing of the Declaration of Independence and the Constitution. ~ Between 5th and 6th streets and Chestnut and Walnut streets; 215-965-2305; www.nps.gov/inde.

Facing Independence Hall in Independence Square, **Congress Hall** is on the left, a building that housed the U.S. Congress from 1790 until 1800. President George Washington took the oath of office for his second term on the hall's second floor in the Senate chambers; John Adams' inauguration was held in 1797 in the House of Representatives on the first floor. In the ten years Congress met in this building, it passed the Bill of Rights, authorized the collection of customs revenues and established a national bank and mint. ~ Between 5th and 6th streets and Chestnut and Walnut streets; 215-965-2305; www.nps.gov/inde.

To the right of Independence Hall are two buildings, **Old City Hall** and **Philosophical Hall**. Old City Hall, completed in 1791, served as the city's municipal offices from 1791 to 1834 and housed the U.S. Supreme Court from 1791 to 1800. Philosophical Hall is the privately owned headquarters of the American Philosophical Society, an organization founded by Ben Franklin to "promote knowledge." The hall contains a free, small museum containing rotating exhibits and displays about the sciences, arts and humanities. Closed Monday through Wednesday from February 18 through Labor Day, and Monday through Thursday from Labor Day to December 11, with evening hours on Wednesday during the summer. ~ 104 South 5th Street; 215-440-3427.

Across the street from Philosophical Hall is **Library Hall**, a reproduction of a 1789 building that houses the country's oldest subscription library, founded by Benjamin Franklin. It holds several research collections, including books belonging to the American Philosophical Society. Among them is a first edition of Darwin's *Origin of Species* and Newton's *Principia*. ~ 105 South 5th Street; 215-440-3400.

A block east from Independence Hall is the **Second Bank of the United States**, an imposing stone Greek Revival structure constructed between 1818 and 1824. The bank's design, by renowned architect William Strickland, became a standard for many U.S. bank buildings. The Second Bank was chartered in

AUTHOR FAVORITE

sights

No trip to Philadelphia would be complete without a visit to **Independence Hall**, the veritable birthplace of the United States. Built between 1732 and 1756, this magnificent red-brick Georgian building was designed by Philadelphia lawyer Andrew Hamilton and master carpenter Edmund Wooley for use as the Pennsylvania State House. Here you can envision significant moments of American history, from the adoption of the Declaration of Independence to the signing of the U.S. Constitution. For more information, see page 50.

1816 by James Madison but closed in 1832 after a dispute arose between President Andrew Jackson and powerful bank president Nicholas Biddle. Today, the bank building houses an outstanding **Portrait Gallery** of 18th-century American heroes, including Jefferson, Alexander Hamilton, Robert Morris and Patrick Henry. Eight-five of the 185 portraits were painted by noted artist Charles Willson Peale. Be sure to see Gilbert Stuart's image of Jefferson, the only known likeness depicting the third President with red hair. George Washington's death mask is also found here. ~ 420 Chestnut Street; 215-965-2305.

Across the street from the Second Bank is the **National Liberty Museum**, an eclectic collection of memorabilia and exhibits dedicated to the ideals of freedom and diversity. Galleries include memorials to America's Nobel Peace Prize recipients and international Philadelphia Liberty Medal winners; tributes to religious tolerance and freedom and photographs of the hundreds of firefighters, police officers and military personnel who died on September 11, 2001. The museum's art collection includes a 20-foot glass "Flame of Liberty" by Dale Chihuly, and "Jellybean People" by Sandy Skoglund, a whimsical sculpture of life-sized children made of jelly beans. While the museum bills itself as appropriate for all ages, young children may be disturbed by images and statistics on youth violence and other subject matters. Closed Monday from Labor Day to Memorial Day. Admission. ~ 321 Chestnut Street; 215-925-2800; www.libertymuseum.org, e-mail liberty@libertymuseum.org.

The First Continental Congress met in 1774 at **Carpenter's Hall**, a red-brick Georgian building constructed in Flemish bond of glazed and plain bricks, a technique that gives the façade a checkerboard appearance. The facility was the original home of the Carpenter's Company, a guild of builders, architects and carpenters. It has been preserved to look as it did during the first Congress, when 12 colonies (Georgia abstained), under Congressional president Peyton Randolph, met to ease tension between the British Crown and the colonies. Displayed artifacts include original Windsor chairs, carpenter's tools and sconces. The privately owned building still serves as guild headquarters. Closed Monday and Tuesday in January and February, and Monday from March through December. ~ 320 Chestnut Street; 215-925-0167; www.carpentershall.org, e-mail carphall@carpenters hall.com.

Next to Carpenter's Hall is **New Hall**, a reconstructed 1790 building that served as the offices of the Secretary of War. New Hall houses a small collection of Revolutionary War items, including some weapons and uniforms. The first floor is dedicated to the Continental Marines while the second floor addresses the formation of the Continental Army and Navy. In this building, the U.S. Navy and U.S. Marine Corps were established in 1798, although veterans will note that the continental Navy and Marines were founded in 1775 by congressional acts. ~ 320 Chestnut Street; 215-965-2305.

Heading east toward the waterfront and south on 3rd Street, you'll find the **First Bank of the United States**, the oldest bank building in the country. This Federal-style edifice was designed by Samuel Blodget, Jr., a trader, insurance executive and amateur architect. Constructed between 1795 and 1797, it is considered to have the oldest classical façade in the United States. Notable architectural details include the ornate Corinthian columns and the portico above, which depicts an eagle, shield and globe, carved from mahogany. The interior is closed to the public. ~ 120 South 3rd Street.

HIDDEN ►   Across the street from the First Bank is the **Independence Living History Center**, an urban archaeology laboratory where National Park Service scientists publicly catalogue, photograph and piece together findings from area construction sites, including soil taken from beneath the National Constitution Center. Among the samples archaeologists plan to study over the next few years is detritus from a trash pit belonging to James Oronoko Dexter, a coachman and early leader of blacks in Philadelphia. Dexter, whose home was located on North 5th Street, is thought to be a founder of the Free African Society and the city's first black church. Visitors to the history center can view a small cache of Dexter House artifacts already on display and speak with archaeologists as they work. ~ 3rd and Chestnut streets; 215-965-2305.

The most famous resident of the **Todd House** isn't known by the name of Todd. Before she married future president James Madison in 1794, Dolley Payne Todd lived in this house at the corner of 4th and Walnut streets with first husband, John Todd. Todd died in 1793 during a yellow fever epidemic; Dolley married James Madison the following year. The house is furnished in Quaker simplicity, a stark contrast to Dolley's later residences such as her orange Virginia plantation home, Montpelier, and the White House. Visits by tour only, tickets available at the Independence Visitor Center. ~ 4th and Walnut streets; 215-965-2305.

Across the street from the Todd House is the **Philadelphia Merchant's Exchange**, a Classical Revival building designed by William Strickland, architect of the Second Bank building. This facility once housed the Philadelphia Stock Exchange. While the building is closed to the public, its architecture should be noted: the semicircular portico that faces the river was shaped to fit the land bordered by a tidal estuary known as Dock Creek. That waterway has been paved over and is now Dock Street, one of the city's few curved roads. ~ 3rd and Walnut streets.

Toward the Delaware River from the Merchant's Exchange is **Welcome Park**, the site of William Penn's Philadelphia home from 1699 to 1701. The park was named for Penn's ship, the *Welcome*. The statue of Penn is a miniature of the one atop City Hall, designed by Alexander Milne Calder, the grandfather of mobile sculptor Alexander Calder. ~ 240 South 2nd Street.

Two blocks west from Welcome Park on Walnut Street is the lavishly decorated **Bishop White House**, representative of an upper-class home during the Federal period. The 1786 residence housed Bishop William White, the rector of Christ Church and St. Peter's Church and the first Episcopal bishop of Pennsylvania. White, who also served as chaplain to the Continental Congress, entertained such luminaries as Washington and Franklin in the house, and many furnishings are original. Viewed by tour only, in conjunction with Todd House tours; tickets are available at the Independence Visitor Center. ~ 309 Walnut Street; 215-965-2305.

Across Walnut Street from the Bishop White House is **Old St. Joseph's Church**, the oldest Catholic parish in Philadelphia. The current church building was erected in 1838 and is the third building at this site. The interior features several works of religious art, including an 1850 stained-glass window above the altar, mosaics and the painting, *The Exaltation of Saint Joseph into Heaven*, by Filippo Costaggini, whose frescos also adorn the U.S. Capitol. The entry to Old St. Joseph's is located in an alley. Stop at the rectory to request entry. ~ 321 Willings Alley; 215-923-1733, fax 215-574-8529; www.oldstjoseph.org, e-mail germane@oldstjoseph.org.

On 4th Street, near Old St. Joseph's, is **Old St. Mary's Church**, the second-oldest Catholic congregation in Philadelphia (and the oldest Catholic church building). This building dates to 1763, although a Gothic-style façade was added in 1880 and the interior was renovated in 1979. Highlights include brass chandeliers that hung in the Founders Room at Independence Hall. Several notable Americans buried here include the great-great grandfather

INDEPENDENCE AND MORE

In addition to setting the scene for the birth of the United States, Independence Hall has seen much in terms of history. The British used it as a hospital during the Revolution; the body of Abraham Lincoln lay in state in its foyer in 1865 and John F. Kennedy addressed the nation from it on July 4, 1962. Each year around Independence Day, the Philadelphia Liberty Medal is presented here to a person whose leadership demonstrates democratic ideals. Recipients include Nelson Mandela, F.W. de Klerk, Lech Walesa and Thurgood Marshall.

of Jacqueline Bouvier Kennedy Onassis, Michel Bouvier, Constitution signer Thomas FitzSimons and Commodore John Barry, the "Father of the U.S. Navy." ~ 252 4th Street; 215-923-7930.

HIDDEN ►

Heading west on Walnut, back toward Independence Square, be sure to drop into the **Curtis Center** to see the city's most spectacular piece of public art. **Dream Garden**, a 15-by-49-feet glass mosaic, was created by artist Maxfield Parrish and executed by Louis Comfort Tiffany studios. Featuring more than 100,000 pieces in 260 shimmering hues, the 1916 Tiffany masterpiece was purchased in 1998 by Las Vegas casino mogul Steve Wynn, who wanted to spirit it off to one of his Las Vegas hotels. But city residents and artists mobilized to thwart Wynn, and thanks to a $3.5 million endowment to the Pennsylvania Academy of Fine Arts from the Pew Charitable Trusts, the work was purchased and remains in Philadelphia. The lobby of the 1890s-era Curtis Center also features other fine examples of stained glass. The Curtis Publishing Company created the *Saturday Evening Post*, the *Ladies' Home Journal* and other publications. Closed Sunday. ~ 601 Walnut Street; 215-238-6450.

LODGING   Philadelphia's historic area isn't replete with hotels, but there are several to satisfy your desire to stay among the city's famed attractions. The 36-room **Independence Park Inn**, located in an 1856 dry-goods store, seems more like a bed and breakfast than a Best Western hotel, which it is. Located two blocks from Independence Hall, this hotel on the National Register of Historic Places features high-ceilinged rooms with traditional 18th-century-style furnishings. Rooms are outfitted with Queen Anne– and Chippendale-style furniture, including poster beds, swag draperies and wing chairs. The Grand Parlor, the main seating area, has French doors and Palladian windows, comfortable wing chairs and a working fireplace. Continental breakfast is served daily in a glass atrium, and tea and snacks are offered every afternoon. ~ 235 Chestnut Street; 215-922-4443, 800-624-2988, fax 215-922-4487; www.independenceparkhotel.com, e-mail information@independenceparkinn.com. ULTRA-DELUXE.

For a hotel as close as possible to the historic district, **The Omni Hotel at Independence Park** is unparalleled. This towering 150-room facility overlooks the park. The stylish rooms are decorated in shades of plum and beige and feature European furnishings; in-room amenities are typical for a luxury hotel, with marble baths, hairdryers, robes, safe deposit boxes, minibars and complimentary WiFi internet access. The hotel also has an indoor lap pool and fitness center, as well as a restaurant, lounge and 24-hour room service. ~ 401 Chestnut Street; 215-925-0000; www.omnihotels.com. ULTRA-DELUXE.

The Georgian-style **Thomas Bond House** sits on Welcome Park, directly across from the City Tavern. Its 12 bedrooms are decorated in 18th-century style, with period furnishings and opulent swag valances, painted wainscoting and oriental carpets; all have private baths. Two rooms have fireplaces; the Delaware River can be seen from the cozy Robert Fulton room on the attic floor. Breakfast is served, as are evening wine and cheese. Thomas Bond is conveniently located to the historic district and also to the bars and nightclubs on 2nd and South streets, which can be a plus or minus, depending on your needs. If you go on a weekend, especially when the weather is fine, expect to hear street traffic. ~ 129 South 2nd Street; 215-923-8523; www.winston-salem-inn.com/philadelphia. MODERATE TO DELUXE.

DINING

In the immediate vicinity of Independence Hall, **The Bourse**, a late-19th-century building that served as a stock and maritime exchange, now houses offices, shops and a food court. The food court's selection is basically what you'd find at your neighborhood shopping mall, including a Sbarro's Italian kiosk, Bain's Deli and Salad Works, but you can't beat the convenient location and budget prices. There's also a coffee bar for a quick pick-me-up. ~ 111 South Independence Mall East; 215-625-0300. BUDGET.

Several restaurants thrive in the western reaches of the historic section, including Stephen Starr's comfort food sanctum **Jones**. The menu is a culinary romp through a 40-something's childhood, laden with choices like macaroni and cheese, fried chicken, meatloaf, and salads made with iceberg lettuce. For dessert, there's Duncan Hines' devil's food cake with a glass of milk and Jello. The interior's shag rugs, naugahyde booths and

AUTHOR FAVORITE

If money is no object, experience **Buddakan**, created by Philadelphia restaurateur Stephen Starr. Starr is to Philadelphia's dining scene what Steve Wynn is to Las Vegas hotels: beget a theme, spare no expense and reel in the beautiful people. Buddakan is Starr's Asian fusion creation set in a refurbished post office. A ten-foot Buddha dominates the dining room and the glass-encased waterfall lends an air of tranquility to an otherwise noisy experience. The food is top-rate, with superb dishes such as cashew chicken and lamb chop with Thai basil pesto. ~ 325 Chestnut Street; 215-574-9440; www.buddakan.com. DELUXE TO ULTRA-DELUXE.

red bucket chairs would scream "rec room" if the place wasn't so stylish—you wish your parents' basement had looked this good. ~ 700 Chestnut Street; 215-223-5663; www.jones-restau rant.com. MODERATE.

Fans of the *Iron Chef* television show and devotees of Japanese fare shouldn't miss the dining experience at **Morimoto**. Set in a dining room designed to evoke the neon flash of Tokyo's Ginza district, Morimoto serves up remarkable sushi, tempura and Japanese fusion fare. Chef Masahura Morimoto was lured to Philadelphia by master restaurateur Stephen Starr, and delivers a menu that includes sushi and sashimi but reaches beyond, offering oyster fois gras, Kobe short ribs with poached lobster, and pan-roasted free-range chicken. ~ 723 Chestnut Street; 215-413-9070; www.morimotorestaurant.com. DELUXE TO ULTRA-DELUXE.

HIDDEN ► **Portofino Restaurant** is not exactly hidden, being right across the street from the historic Walnut Theatre, but it is a favorite among locals for pre-theater dining, especially since theater-goers receive a 20-percent discount on their meals. This storefront restaurant is cozy, decorated in rich cherry and jewel-notes. The menu is classic Italian, featuring a mix of tomato-laden southern Italian fare with lighter selections from the northern regions, including fettuccine portofino, fresh pasta tossed with asparagus, fresh tomatoes and smoked salmon in lemon-pepper sauce. Some nights a violinist serenades you before the show. ~ 1227 Walnut Street; 215-923-8208; www.portofino1227walnut.com. DELUXE.

Closer to the historic area in terms of location and style is the **City Tavern**, reconstructed for those who want to dine in a historic setting and be waited on by costumed staff. Though the building is a reconstruction of the 1773 version frequented by Jefferson, Adams and Washington, it has the atmosphere of the real thing, with plaster walls, paneled doors, wainscoting and wrought-iron light fixtures. Tables are set with period-style china, pewter goblets and hurricane lanterns. The food here is "inspired by the customs and foods of 18th-century Colonial

BOOTH SAVES LINCOLN

Edwin Booth, the pre-eminent actor of his day and the brother of John Wilkes Booth, bought the Walnut Theatre in 1865 and, together with business partner John Sleeper Clarke, modernized it. Ironically, Edwin Booth saved the life of Abraham Lincoln's son, Robert, just a few years before buying the theater—the same year his brother John would take Abe's life. Booth grabbed the young Lincoln after he'd been jostled onto the railroad tracks at a station in New Jersey and pulled him to safety before he was run over.

America," and the menu is a meat-and-potato-lover's feast. The spicy West Indies pepperpot soup mixes beef, pork and greens, while the turkey pot pie, "Martha Washington Style," is stuffed with chunks of turkey, red potatoes, mushrooms and peas. The Tavern is a tourist haunt, but the bar, with an interesting assortment of Colonial recipe ales—is worth a stop. ~ 138 South 2nd Street; 215-413-1443; www.citytavern.com. DELUXE.

Across the street from City Tavern lies another Philadelphia landmark restaurant, the **Old Original Bookbinder's Restaurant**. In its heyday, Bookbinder's was *the* place to be seen in Philadelphia. Patrons included John Wayne, Frank Sinatra, Bob Hope and Joe DiMaggio. The restaurant, an 800-seat behemoth, fell on hard times and closed in 2002. But after a three-year hiatus, Bookbinder's is back and ready for business with new executive chef David Cunningham, formerly of New York's Lespinasse. The restaurant's rich interior, with dark woods, crisp cinnamon accents and butter-yellow walls and linens, is enhanced by hallway galleries exhibiting photos of famous diners. Seafood is still tops here and the lobby boasts one of the world's largest lobster tanks, filled with 350 tasty crustaceans. ~ 125 Walnut Street; 215-925-7027; www.bookbinders.biz. ULTRA-DELUXE.

People go to Independence National Historical Park to sightsee, not shop. Nevertheless, visitors will find souvenirs at a number of museum shops and gift stores, including those at the Independence Visitor Center and the National Constitution Center. **SHOPPING**

The Bourse houses a number of stores, such as **The Best of Philadelphia** (215-629-0333) and **Making History** (215-574-8822). You'll find T-shirts, postcards, throw blankets, snow globes, earring, key chains and nearly anything you want in a Colonial or red, white and blue theme. ~ 111 South Independence Mall East; 215-625-0300.

Farther west of the historic district, along Sansom Street near 8th Street, and on 8th between Chestnut and Walnut streets, lies the nation's oldest and second-largest diamond district, known as Jeweler's Row. More than 350 vendors sell diamonds, gemstones, watches, gold, platinum and silver here. The 700 block of Sansom crowds jewelers into one city block, both above and below ground. At **Sydney Rosen**, customers are directed to three parts of the store, depending on their wants—the "perfect stone" for those searching for impeccably clear diamonds; "the pragmatist" for those who desire quality and a fine cut; and "the rock" for shoppers wanting big diamonds. ~ 712–714 Sansom Street; 215-922-3500.

Harry Sable is known as "king of the wedding bands," and has been selling wedding jewelry for more than 50 years. ~ 8th and Sansom streets; 215-627-4014. ◄ HIDDEN

NIGHTLIFE   The **Lights of Liberty** is a sound-and-light tour through the historic area during warm summer nights. Groups receive headsets and listen to narrators relate the history behind Independence Hall. Kids get their own versions, narrated by Whoopi Goldberg and other actors who are slightly more animated than Walter Cronkite, who performs the adult soundtrack. ~ 600 Chestnut Street; 215-574-0746; www.lightsofliberty.org.

Northwest of the park, as you move toward Center City, you'll find the **Walnut Street Theatre**, the oldest operating theater in the United States. It's the venue for traveling Broadway musicals, drama and comedy. The building dates to 1807 and the first theatrical production here was attended by Thomas Jefferson and the Marquis de Lafayette. A number of award-winning shows have debuted at the Walnut before moving to Broadway, including *A Streetcar Named Desire* with Marlon Brando, *A Raisin in the Sun* with Sidney Poitier, and *Mister Roberts* with Henry Fonda. ~ 825 Walnut Street; 215-574-3550; www.wstonline.org.

▼▼▼▼▼▼▼▼▼▼
Old City Area

Old City, located north of Independence National Historical Park, is the name given to distinguish the original part of the city from the historical park area. This neighborhood was the heart of William Penn's Philadelphia, giving rise to commercial operations that built the city, including wharves, warehouses and taverns. In early days, artisans, craftsmen and builders lived here; Old City's working-man roots paved the way for later development, including the establishment of industry and wholesale distributors. The architecture is mainly late 18th- and early 19th-century, although the country's oldest residential street is here as well. Many of the district's iron-façade buildings are now loft-style apartments whose names relate their original missions, including the Hoopskirt Factory, the Chocolate Works and the Wireworks.

SIGHTS   There is much to see north of Independence National Historical Park, beginning in a wide arc from the Independence Visitor Center at the **Atwater Kent Museum of Philadelphia**. This museum is the city's repository of its own history, containing more than 100,000 objects relating the Philadelphia story. The museum was established in 1938 by radio magnate Atwater Kent, and while it has its share of antique radios, there's much more here, including a wampum belt given to William Penn by the Indians, furniture used by George Washington and one-of-a-kind African-American Quaker dolls. In 1996, the museum received a collection of Norman Rockwell posters once housed at the Curtis Center, home of the *Saturday Evening Post*. Kids will enjoy stomping over the giant floor map of the Delaware Valley region and taking in the collection of more than 2000 toys and dolls. The Greek-revival building was designed by architect John Haviland, whose works include the Eastern State Penitentiary. Open Wednesday through Monday afternoons. Admission. ~ 15 South 7th Street; 215-685-4830; www.philadelphiahistory.org.

The **Graff House**, also referred to as the Declaration House, is a reproduction of the home where Thomas Jefferson retreated to write the Declaration of Independence. Jefferson, head of the congressional committee charged with writing the document, rented two rooms of this home, which had been built just a year before by bricklayer Jacob Graff. The original house was torn down in 1883 but rebuilt in 1975 to celebrate the Bicentennial. Features include an exhibit on the Declaration, complete with Jefferson's own edits and the committee's redaction of passages that would have abolished slavery. Hours vary, call ahead. ~ 7th and Market streets; 215-965-2305.

Two blocks north, at Arch and 7th streets, is the **African American Museum in Philadelphia**. This museum consists mainly of rotating exhibits with three themes: Africa, Philadelphia's black history and contemporary narratives, captured in art, sculpture, photography and artifacts. The museum was founded and funded in 1976 by the city of Philadelphia to celebrate the Bicentennial and is affiliated with the Smithsonian Institution. Given that Philadelphia's history is so closely entwined with that of black America, this museum—if it were adequately funded—could be so much more. Still, for a population long-overlooked in mainstream museums, it's a venue to celebrate the contributions of African Americans to the development

AUTHOR FAVORITE

sights   An edifice taking up an entire city block, the **U.S. Mint** is a favorite stop. On a public self-guided tour, visitors can watch money being made from large windows overlooking the production floor. The mint can produce 30 million coins a day, worth roughly $1 million. This factory also forges the U.S. military's Bronze Star and Purple Heart medals. The current building is the fourth mint site in Philadelphia and was constructed in 1969. Peter, a bald eagle that once lived at the U.S. Mint and whose stuffed body is on display in the lobby, is thought to have been the model for the eagle on the silver dollar and the Flying Eagle pennies, which were minted from 1856 to 1858. Adults should be prepared to show identification at the door. Closed weekends. ~ 151 Independence Mall East (5th and Arch streets); 215-408-0112; www.usmint.gov.

of the United States. Closed Monday. Admission. ~ 701 Arch Street; 215-574-0380; www.aampmuseum.org.

Southeast of the museum lie **Mikveh Israel**, Philadelphia's oldest Jewish congregation, and the **National Museum of American Jewish History**. The congregation dates to 1740 and was founded by Nathan Levy, a merchant whose ship, the *Myrtilla*, brought the Liberty Bell to the United States. The museum, which dates to 1976, shares space with the synagogue. Its small exhibit room features rotating programs on Jewish art and culture in the United States, as well as a preview gallery of the permanent facility to be built on the site. Today, visitors can enjoy the synagogue and small gift shop. At the entrance stands the Entebbe Memorial, a tribute to the men who took part in a daring raid to free the crew and Jewish hostages in Uganda in 1976. Closed Saturday. ~ 55 North 5th Street; 215-923-3811; www.nmajh.org.

While the term "Fighting Quaker" appears to be an oxymoron (the Quaker religion is based on pacifism), a faction of Quakers earned the nickname during the Revolution. This group met at the **Free Quaker Meeting House** for worship and to throw their support behind the Revolutionary War effort. Free Quaker members included flag-maker and patriot Betsy Ross and Constitution signatory Thomas Mifflin. The group disbanded after the war and the 1783 building, designed by Samuel Wetherill, later served as a school and warehouse. Hours vary, call ahead. ~ 500 Arch Street; 215-965-2305.

Facing Arch Street on the same block of Mikveh Israel lies the grave of Philadelphia's most famous statesman, inventor and philosopher, Benjamin Franklin. At **Christ Church Burial Ground**, Franklin shares a plot with his wife Deborah, who predeceased him in 1774, and their son Francis, who died at age four. Also interred in the cemetery are Dr. Benjamin Rush, father of American psychiatry and signer of the Declaration, Commodore William Bainbridge, captain of the USS *Constitution*, and various other Colonial patriots, including three more signers of the Declaration. The cemetery, closed for nearly 25 years for preservation and restoration, is now open year-round, weather permitting. Franklin's grave can always be seen from the sidewalk on Arch Street, even when the cemetery is closed. It lies behind an iron fence built into the cemetery's brick wall. The pennies tossed onto it for good luck are a tribute to Franklin's motto "a penny saved is a penny earned." ~ 5th and Arch streets; 215-922-1695; www.christchurchphila.org.

Heading down Arch Street, you'll pass **Loxley Court**. Iron gates hide several beautiful restored homes. It's believed that the key used by Benjamin Franklin during his famous kite experiment fit 2 Loxley Court, the home of Franklin's friend and builder Ben Loxley. ~ Between 321 and 323 Arch Street.

Serene and beautiful in its simplicity, the **Arch Street Meeting House** is the world's largest Society of Friends meeting house. Built in 1804 for the Philadelphia Quakers' yearly meeting, this facility is still used for that function as well as weekly services. The East Wing houses dioramas depicting William Penn's life, and visitors can view a slide show of his accomplishments. Famous members who worshipped here include abolitionist and suffragette Lucretia Mott. United States Marines also will find the grave of Samuel Nicholas, the Corps' first commandant, here. Open Monday through Saturday, with services held Sunday. ~ 4th and Arch streets; 215-627-2667; www.archstreetfriends.org.

> Nine-year-old Ben Franklin invented swim fins and paddles to swim faster; he's the only founding father inducted into the International Swimming Hall of Fame.

With so many original historical buildings found in Philadelphia, it's hard to believe that the house belonging to the city's most famous resident, Benjamin Franklin, was torn down by his grandchildren to build townhouses. **Franklin Court** is where the house stood, and its structure is outlined in a unique "ghost house" sculpture designed by architect Robert Venturi. The court contains windows showing exposed parts of the home's foundation, including the kitchen area, privy holes and other sections. (The only remaining Franklin home in the world is located near Trafalgar Square in London.) Franklin Court also has an alleyway used by Franklin, as well as a Colonial-era print shop and post office where visitors can receive hand-cancellations for their letters that read "B. Free Franklin" (Franklin was the nation's first postmaster general, a factoid recalled in the U.S. Postal Service museum above the post office). Beneath Franklin Court lies a museum dedicated to this statesman and scientist. It includes artifacts from Franklin's home and a small portrait gallery. Much of this exhibit is vintage 1976. The "Franklin Exchange," a once-popular exhibit where you dial different numbers on its bank of Trimline phones to hear famous people discuss Franklin, is often empty, and a hall of mirrors featuring neon phrases describing Franklin seems corny in a Colonial venue, but the center's 20-minute documentary on Franklin's life is informative and a timeline located outside the theater entertains. ~ 314–322 Market Street; 215-965-2305.

The Revolutionary who's who of worshippers at Philadelphia's historic **Christ Church** includes Ben Franklin, George Washington, Betsy Ross and Declaration signers Robert Morris and Dr. Benjamin Rush. But this building also has its own history; it's considered to be the birthplace of the Protestant Episcopal Church in the United States. Rector William White, who served as chaplain to the Continental Congress and, later, chaplain of the Senate, was one of two Americans consecrated in England to serve as bishop in the United States after the nation split with England and its Anglican Church. When it was completed in 1794, the Georgian-style church was one of the largest buildings in North America. The sanctuary is dominated by towering columns and a Palladian window. It also contains the 600-year-old baptismal font used to baptize William Penn, a donation from All Hallows Church in London. ~ 2nd Street at Market Street; 215-922-1695; www.christchurchphila.org.

On Arch Street, in the heart of Old City, sits the **Betsy Ross House**, which, when combined with Independence Hall and the Liberty Bell, completes the triumvirate of Philadelphia's most popular tourist sites. Ross ran an upholstery shop at this home with her third husband John Claypoole. The exhibits in this tiny Colonial house provide insight into this remarkable woman's life. Ross, raised in a Quaker family of 17 children, was cast out by her family after she married Episcopalian John Ross at the age of 21. John Ross was killed three years later in the war effort, and Betsy, also known as Elizabeth Griscom Ross Ashbourn, was left to fend for herself as a business woman. She would lose two more husbands and two daughters during the remainder of her life, but she also became an American hero. Closed Monday from September through May. Admission. ~ 239 Arch Street; 215-686-1252; www.betsyrosshouse.org.

HIDDEN ► Fans of MTV's **Real World** will recognize the Philadelphia house from the show's 15th season at 249–251 Arch Street.

Elfreth's Alley, with its 33 homes, is considered the nation's oldest residential street. Many of the tiny rowhouses were built by blacksmith Jeremiah Elfreth, who rented them to sea captains and craftsmen such as cabinetmakers and silversmiths. Today, most of the nearly 300-year-old homes are privately owned. HIDDEN ► **Bladen's Court**, located halfway down the street, leads to a charming courtyard, allowing views of more houses, including one

◆◆◆

A FLAG IS BORN

According to a tale handed down by her descendants, Betsy Ross often retold the story of General George Washington's visit to her shop. Washington had asked that she make a flag with six-pointed stars. Ross suggested the use of five-pointed stars because she found them more attractive. When Washington said that five-pointed stars would be too difficult to cut quickly, Ross folded a piece of paper and, with a few snips of her scissors, formed a perfect five-pointed star. The winning design is history.

with a spinner's balcony, a second-floor gallery where women went for fresh air and to knit. The **Elfreth's Alley Museum** spans two restored Colonial homes: No. 124, the home of a Windsor chairmaker, and No. 126, a dressmaker's house. Both contain authentic furnishings. Hours vary. Closed Monday. Admission for museum. ~ Between Front and 2nd streets and Arch and Race streets; 215-574-0560; www.elfrethsalley.org.

Like a typical firehouse, the **Fireman's Hall Museum** overflows with sparkling, clean equipment. The museum focuses on nearly three centuries of firefighting; its collection includes an 1815 hand-pumper, a fireboat and information about the fire marks seen on Philadelphia's Colonial houses. You can see badges, helmets, parade hats, vintage fire trucks, pumping machines and a beautiful stained-glass window that pays homage to the brave men and women of this dangerous profession. Closed Sunday and Monday. Admission. ~ 147 North 2nd Street; 215-923-1438.

Look to your right as you leave the Fireman's Hall to appreciate the **Benjamin Franklin Bridge**, once the world's longest suspension bridge. Built in 1926, this steel and concrete structure, painted in "Benjamin Franklin Blue," connects Philadelphia with Camden, NJ. Pedestrian walkways on both the north and south sides of the bridge are open from dawn until dusk, allowing pedestrians unfettered views of the city, New Jersey and the northern port facilities. ~ 5th and Vine streets; 215-218-3750.

Off the beaten path, in the part of Old City north of the Benjamin Franklin Bridge, is **St. George's Church**, the world's oldest Methodist church in continuous use. This is where Revolutionary War–backer Robert Morris prayed all evening on New Year's Eve 1776 for the means to finance the Continental Army. Originally constructed by a German Reform congregation in 1769, the building houses many artifacts of American Methodism. Tours by appointment. ~ 235 North 4th Street; 215-925-7788.

◄ HIDDEN

In 2006, **Franklin Square**, a long-neglected city park that was designed as part of William Penn's original city plan, will be revitalized under a state-sponsored initiative, coinciding with Franklin's 300th birthday celebrations. Plans for the park include a heritage fair with a carousel, a playground, arts and crafts, performers, storytellers and a mini golf course. ~ Between 6th and 7th streets and Race and Vine streets.

◄ HIDDEN

The **Bank Street Hostel** offers a bargain for travelers on a budget. Located two blocks from Independence National Historical Park, the hostel has 70 beds in a dormitory setting. Genders are separated, except in the summer months when there is sometimes a co-ed third floor. Amenities include a kitchen and dining areas,

LODGING

◄ HIDDEN

nightly movies and a pool table. ~ 32 South Bank Street; 215-922-0222, fax 215-922-4082; www.bankstreethostel.com, e-mail thebankstreethostel@hotmail.com. BUDGET.

DINING

On the Delaware River and along the major thoroughfares of Market, Chestnut and 2nd streets, down to South Street, are some of Philadelphia's trendiest spots and old favorites.

Philadelphia Fish & Co.'s bold menu and crisp, modern dining room make it a popular destination for seafood fans. Decor is retro-mod with touches of metal and cherry woods. Food is inspired by regional America. There's a yummy Maine lobster roll for starters and a grilled barbecue shrimp entrée served with cheese grits, sausage and collards. If the weather's nice, ask for outdoor seating; the deck is a top spot to people watch. ~ 207 Chestnut Street; 215-625-8605; www.philadelphiafish.com. DELUXE.

One of several trendsetters along 2nd Street between Chestnut and Market, Havana-inspired **Cuba Libre** is fun, although who knows how close the charming courtyard atmosphere resembles pre-Castro Cuba. The guayaberan-wearing waitstaff at this hotspot serves mojitos, regional fare and a large selection from the Caribbean and the Americas under palm fronds and ceiling fans. To avoid crowds, visit during the week. ~ 10 South 2nd Street; 215-627-0666; www.cubalibrerestaurant. com. DELUXE.

Down 2nd Street is **Café Spice**, another geographic-inspired nightspot with a party vibe. The decor is contemporary in shades of curry, cardamom and cinnamon, and the drinks are martinis instead of rum. The fiery vindaloo is eye-watering and pungent. Milder selections include tandoori chicken and *malai* kebab, cubed chicken marinated in yogurt and ground cashews. ~ 35 South 2nd Street; 215-627-6273; www.cafespice.com. DELUXE.

HIDDEN ▶

Reasonably priced **Kabul** features ethnic fare in a charming BYO, without the pick-up-bar vibe of nearby restaurants. In this setting, diners can choose to eat in the dining room, adorned in native rugs and artwork, or call ahead for a genuine Afghan dining experience on the *taqh*, a raised platform with pillows and rugs in the rear of the restaurant. Lamb tops the entrée selections, but vegetarians will appreciate the pumpkin and eggplant dishes. The delicate scallion dumplings are a popular treat. ~ 106 Chestnut Street; 215-922-3676; www.phillyrestaurants.com/kabul. MODERATE.

Tangerine offers Mediterranean fare in a dark, hip, Bedouin-fantasy realm lit by candles and Moravian stars. The entrée list provides a selection from countries surrounding the Med and includes such ingredients as tabbouleh, Greek olives and gorgonzola. ~ 232 Market Street; 215-627-5116; www.tangerinerestau rant.com. DELUXE TO ULTRA-DELUXE.

For a bite to eat on the go, perhaps to enjoy on a bench in Independence National Historical Park, **Campo's Deli** whips up   ◄ HIDDEN
enormous sandwiches at reasonable rates. Sure, they make cheesesteaks here, but the big draw are the fresh and delicious hoagies. Campo's makes salads and grilled chicken breast dishes as well. ~ 214 Market Street; 215-923-1000. BUDGET.

Head south on 2nd Street toward Market Street and you'll continue wending through the collection of fine restaurant choices.

The **Continental Restaurant and Martini Bar**'s outer shell, an old diner glossed up and gleaming, misrepresents what's inside— an uber-cool Asian-fusion eatery with a Rat Pack bent. The orange, black and beige interior, with diner counter and martini olive light fixtures, brings to mind a 1960s airport lounge, while the black-attired waitstaff reminds us that this is the 21st century and we can order a martini made of something other than gin and vermouth. Salads tower on plates and the cheeseburger never disappoints, but you may want to explore the Szechuan french-fried potatoes with wasabi. You'll wonder how it's possible to cut potatoes so thin and pile them so high. Other offerings include teriyaki filet mignon and dim sum. ~ 134 Market Street; 215-923-6069. MODERATE.

To placate a raging sweet tooth, **Petit 4 Pastry Studio** has the   ◄ HIDDEN
goods. It also makes an excellent cup of coffee to accompany its sugary treats. The molasses cookies get rave reviews, as does the bread pudding, but the eclairs, with their light, flaky dough stuffed with thick cream filling topped with rich chocolate, are *incroyable*. ~ 160 North 3rd Street; 215-627-8440. BUDGET.

Locals stop at **Café Ole** for its free wireless internet access   ◄ HIDDEN
and fresh roasted La Colombe coffee. A small soup and sandwich menu satisfies net surfers. ~ 147 North 3rd Street; 215-627-2140. BUDGET.

AUTHOR FAVORITE

FORK is a favorite among both locals and visitors, offering fresh takes on bistro standards, using locally grown ingredients. The menu, which changes daily, is consistently good, with choices including melted mozzarella with radicchio, pan-seared monkfish and house-made herbed gnocchi. The stylish, pleasant dining room, with its open kitchen, draws a young, hip business crowd, and the bar at night is ideal for chatting it up with friends in an elegant yet vivacious and fun atmosphere. The excellent wine list won't drain your wallet. ~ 138 Market Street; 215-625-9425; www.forkrestaurant.com. DELUXE.

SHOPPING　The city's widest selection of African-American books can be found at the **African American Museum of Philadelphia's Gift Shop**. Literature, coffee-table tomes and books on black culture, history and drama are stocked next to home decor items, including sculptures, knickknacks, jewelry, fabric and more. ~ 701 Arch Street; 215-574-0380; www.aampmuseum.org.

Old City is home to many galleries, one-of-a-kind furniture stores and home-decorating shops, many set in former manufacturing buildings and stores. The Old City Arts Association, a collection of more than 50 galleries and museums, celebrates **First Fridays** each month from 5 p.m. to 9 p.m., with exhibits, receptions and open houses.

Among the members of the association is the **Wexler Gallery**, an internationally acclaimed gallery exhibiting both decorative and fine arts. Furniture finds bear such names as Escherek, Stickley and Saarinen. Wexler also has an ever-expanding collection of hand-blown glass. Closed Sunday and Monday. ~ 201 North 3rd Street; 215-923-7030; www.wexlergallery.com.

Flotsam & Jetsam is an inspiration for anyone who has ended up with an eclectic mix of furniture and can't seem to pull it together. Owners R.J. Thornburg and Meltem Birey have thrown an array of furniture styles into their store and artfully matched them with unusual accessories and colorful paint to tie everything together. Somehow, at Flotsam & Jetsam, a wrought-iron side table looks correct next to a Louis XIV chair. They do home design as well. Closed Monday. ~ 149 North 3rd Street; 215-351-9914.

HIDDEN ▶　**Foster's Urban Homeware** seems to have nearly everything you need to dress your house, from flare lamps and unique wall clocks to mix-and-match bedding in the newest chic colors. Foster's has a quirky side as well, selling "Breezy Singers Parakeets," plastic renditions that sing and move but don't need parental guidance, and a Crazy Cat Lady Action Figure, in case you don't have one living next door and feel you're missing out. ~ 124 North 3rd Street; 267-671-0588; www.shopfosters.com.

AUTHOR FAVORITE

Retro, modern and vintage furnishings catch the eye at **Mode Moderne**, an ultra-cool shop full of sleek chairs, desks, lamps, chairs and more. Fans of Lucite, Naugahyde, aluminum and Danish design will enjoy this story; check out the collection of whimsical Vitra clocks, shaped like asterisks, fish and those neat stars that used to top Holiday Inn signs. Closed Monday and Tuesday. ~ 159 North 3rd Street; 215-627-0299; www.modemoderne.com.

For one-of-a-kind fashions, **Vagabond** carries vintage and contemporary clothing by local designers and well-known labels. You might be lucky enough to find a Diane von Furstenberg wrap dress or discover something similar (and less expensive) by local designers, including shopkeepers Mary Clark and Megan Murphy. Other fun items include printed T-shirts, scarves, lace-up jeans and crocheted sweaters. ~ 37 North 3rd Street; 267-671-0737.

NIGHTLIFE

There's an Old City bar for everyone—the trick is finding one that fits. In the historic downtown area, there are bars for fraternity-boy types, yuppies, GenXers, GenYers, students, singles, couples, blue-collar workers and professionals.

Swanky Bubbles tickles the nose and the palate with 11 champagnes by the glass and 27 bottled varieties. The champagne cocktail list is intriguing: a champagne and Red Bull at the start of the night is reputed to allow the drinker to tipple for hours. Decor and food menu are Asian fusion. ~ 10 South Front Street; 215-928-1200.

For soul, jazz and blues served with a side of Southern fare, **Warmdaddy's** is the venue. This could be Memphis off-Beale, with the blues played cool and the catfish served hot. Junior Wells and Koko Taylor are among the musicians who have played here. ~ 4–6 South Front Street; 215-627-8400.

◀ *HIDDEN*

A number of Philadelphia taverns focus on Belgian brews. **Eulogy Belgian Tavern**, located in the original 1832 home of Bailey, Banks and Biddle, features 185 bottled beers and 15 on tap. Food is Belgian as well, with mussels being the most popular menu item. Decor is unusual, to say the least; a table on the second floor is made from a coffin. ~ 136 Chestnut Street; 215-413-1918; www.eulogybar.com.

◀ *HIDDEN*

Raucous, noisy and just plain fun, **Buffalo Billiards**, part of a chain, is a relaxed place for grabbing a bite to eat, watching games, listening to the jukebox and, of course, playing pool. The waitstaff is among the friendliest you'll find in Philadelphia and the ten pool tables draw players of all levels. ~ 118 Chestnut Street; 215-574-7665; www.buffalobilliards.com.

Sugar Mom's is a throwback to your best friend's basement, where you molded Play-doh as a child and later snuck in beers as a teen. This dark club with low ceilings and *That '70s Show* decor even has toys scattered throughout the catacombs, as well as pinball machines and a foosball table. The beer selection changes seasonally and the menu is typical bar fare. Go on, re-live your adolescence. ~ 225 Church Street; 215-925-8219.

◀ *HIDDEN*

A large danceclub in Philadelphia's warehouse area, north of Old City, **Shampoo** has an outsized dancefloor and throbbing techno that attract a young crowd. On Wednesday, Shampoo goes goth/industrial, an evening dubbed "Nocturne." Thursday offers parties for the teenage set in the early evening and dancing for those 18 and older later on. Friday ("Shaft" night) is one huge gay dance party, among the largest in the city. ~ 417 North 8th Street; 215-922-7500; www.shampooonline.com.

Originally a spot for swing dancing, the **Five Spot** has added other genres and live bands to its evening schedule. Two levels allow for a deejay to play downstairs while bands entertain upstairs. Atmosphere is nightclub—plush booths, beads and stainless steel swing lamps. ~ 5 South Bank Street; 215-574-0070; www.thefivespot.com.

For live rock music nearly every night, **The Khyber** is a must. Internationally renown artists as well as local musicians take the stage at this hip Philadelphia institution. The bar—an ornate behemoth carved with gargoyles—dates to 1876. Behind it, servers can pony up more than 100 types of international and domestic beers. ~ 56 South 2nd Street; 215-238-5888; www.the khyber.com.

As for the performing arts, Old City has its share of fine theaters. The **Arden Theatre Company** holds five productions a year and two children's works. Offerings include new plays as well as classic drama, comedy and musicals (which are heavy on the Sondheim since the master of musicals spent his childhood in Bucks County, tutored by Oscar Hammerstein). The Arden's production of *Sweeney Todd* won a local theater award for best musical in 2005. ~ 40 North 2nd Street; 215-922-1122; www.arden theatre.org

It's hard to classify **The Painted Bride Art Center**, a multidisciplinary arts center that celebrates dance, music, the visual arts, performance and poetry. Founded in 1969, the arts center provides a venue for emerging performers and artists, and prides itself on embracing artists pushing for social change. The center features daytime and nighttime events, including concerts and performances at its 250-seat theater, and shows in its two galleries. Past performances include jazz concerts, hip-hop and modern dance and one-man plays. ~ 230 Vine Street; 215-925-9914; www.paintedbride.org.

Penn's Landing and Society Hill

Penn's Landing is Philadelphia's answer to a riverwalk, a wide, tree-lined promenade with a museum, restaurants, a hotel and great views of the Delaware River. Society Hill, spanning between Walnut and Lombard streets and Front and 8th streets, is Philadelphia's residential showcase, a collection of 18th-century homes that have been painstakingly restored in period detail. This picturesque neighborhood of Federal, Colonial and Georgian rowhouses set along cobblestone streets and alleyways houses some of the city's most affluent residents, much as it did when founded in the 1700s.

SIGHTS

Events abound at Penn's Landing throughout the year, from concerts in the spring and summer to ice skating in the winter. For year-round fun, check out the **Independence Seaport Museum**, which pays tribute to the area's maritime heritage. Its collection of artwork, nautical artifacts, interactive exhibits and models relate the importance of the shipping industry to both Philadelphia and U.S. history. Children and boat enthusiasts will enjoy displays that allow you to blow a ship's whistle, learn about buoyancy and unload a model cargo ship using a crane. The museum also manages two of Penn's Landing's most noted attractions, the USS *Olympia*, the flagship of Commodore George Dewey, and the USS *Becuna*, a World War II–era submarine. Admission. ~ 211 South Columbus Boulevard; 215-925-5439; www.phillyseaport.org.

The cruiser **USS Olympia** is best known as the only U.S. vessel remaining from the Spanish American War. From this ship, built in 1892, Admiral Dewey issued the command "You may fire when ready, Gridley," launching the Battle of Manila during that war on May 1, 1898. The *Olympia*'s final major sail, in 1921, was to France to retrieve the unknown remains of a World War I soldier for internment at Arlington National Cemetery. The ship has been restored to its grandeur as a flagship and most areas are accessible by tour, including the bridge, the galley, the engine rooms, batteries and state rooms. ~ Penn's Landing at Spruce Street.

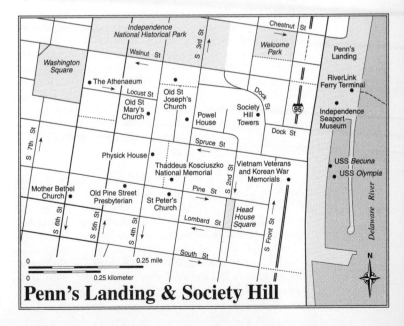

Penn's Landing & Society Hill

Lodged between the pier at Penn's Landing and the USS *Olympia* is the **USS Becuna**, a Balao-class submarine built in 1944. The *Becuna* took part in several South Pacific patrols toward the end of World War II and was responsible for sinking several vessels, including a 7500-ton freighter and an oiler. Later, it was renovated to become a swift Guppy-class vessel and served in the Atlantic and Mediterranean Sea during the Korean and Vietnam wars. A tour of the Becuna provides interesting insight into the life of a submariner. Claustrophobes and those with sensitive noses should note that quarters are close and the boat is odiferous, with the lingering smell of diesel and lubricants.

Virginians Edmund Randolph and George Mason and Massachusetts delegate Elbridge Gerry refused to sign the Constitution because they wanted it to have a bill of rights. The Bill of Rights was ratified in 1791.

The two other large vessels seen along Penn's Landing are the **Gazela** and the *Moshulu*, now a restaurant. The *Gazela* is an 1883 barkentine vessel, the last of a fleet of sailing cod-fishing ships. It is the oldest and largest wooden square-rigger still underway and is used extensively during the summer for ceremonial events and goodwill trips along the Eastern Seaboard. When *Gazela* is in port, she welcomes visitors on the weekends. Usually docked near the *Gazela* is the 1902 tugboat *Jupiter* and the barge *Poplar*. All three are maintained by the Philadelphia Ship Preservation Guild. ~ 801 South Columbus Boulevard; 215-238-0280; www.gazela.org.

Society Hill has numerous historic sites, yet much of its charm is enjoyed by simply walking its streets, appreciating the architecture, gardens and houses, including such decorative touches as fire marks, boot scrapers, door knockers and working shutters. Begin your tour by heading south from Welcome Park on 2nd Street. You will encounter three enormous apartment buildings as you approach Society Hill. The concrete-and-glass **Society Hill Towers** were designed by architect I. M. Pei, and the complex, which includes townhouses and sculpture, received top honors in 1965 from the American Institute of Architects for its efforts to establish aesthetically pleasing high-density residential development in a historic area.

Near the towers is the **Philadelphia Vietnam Veterans Memorial**, a monument to the 600 Philadelphians who died in the war and the 80,000 who served in the military during that period. Adjacent to it, on 38th Parallel Place, is the **Korean War Memorial**. ~ Located on Front Street between Spruce and Delancey streets.

While in the vicinity, check out the **Man Full of Trouble Tavern**. This 1759 Colonial bar is the real deal, unlike City Tavern, which has been reconstructed. It's likely that the tavern won't be open when you walk by, but it's fun to imagine what it was like when sailors bunked here, the maids slept in the cellar, and it was called "Man with a Load of Mischief." ~ 125–127 Spruce Street.

Delancey Street and **American Street** are among Society Hill's most charming residential lanes, harkening to an era three centuries past. At Delancey and 4th streets is the **Physick House**, a sumptuously decorated Federal mansion owned by Dr. Philip Syng Physick, the "Father of American Surgery." The home, built in 1786, is a rare freestanding period home in Society Hill (most were rowhouses). The home was built by Henry Hill, importer and executor of Benjamin Franklin's estate. Notable items in this finely furnished abode include an inkwell bearing Franklin's fingerprints. Closed Monday through Wednesday. Admission. ~ 321 South 4th Street; 215-925-7866; www.philalandmarks.org.

At 2nd and South streets stands the **Shambles**, a historic marketplace that's stood here since 1745, and the **Head House**, a building that oversaw market operations and doubled as a fire-engine house. The area comes alive on summer weekends as an open-air market for crafts and art. ~ 2nd Street between Pine and South streets; 215-790-0782.

The **Powel House**, an elegant 1765 brick Georgian owned by Samuel Powel, the last mayor of Philadelphia before the Revolution and the first mayor after, is reputed to have been the finest home in Philadelphia at the time and still ranks among the prettiest. Samuel Powel and his wife, Elizabeth Willing, threw lavish parties for Colonial leaders, including George Washington and wife Martha, John Adams and the Marquis de Lafayette. The mansion was slated for demolition in 1930 after having been used as a warehouse, and most furnishings were sold off to the Philadelphia Museum of Art and the Metropolitan Museum in New York. Today, however, it has been restored and is filled with 18th-century Philadelphia-made furniture. Closed Sunday through Wednesday. Admission. ~ 244 South 3rd Street; 215-627-0364.

The **Philadelphia Contributionship for the Insurance of Houses from Loss by Fire** is one of the nation's earliest fire insurance companies, founded in 1752. Its building dates to 1836 and contains a small museum on the history of fire insurance. Homes in Philadelphia that were insured by the Contributionship boast firemarks featuring four interlocking hands. The Greek-revival building was designed by architect Thomas U. Walter, who created the U.S. Capitol dome, and is still used for offices by the Contributionship Companies. Closed weekends. ~ 212 South 4th Street; 215-627-1752.

In 1794, Reverend Richard Allen, a former slave, founded the first African Methodist Episcopal Church in the world. **Mother Bethel Church** welcomed black Methodists who wanted to worship in a non-segregated church, and was used as a stop on the Underground Railroad. The current building, the fourth on this site, is a Romanesque revival dating to 1889. The museum contains such artifacts as antique church ballot boxes, muskets dating to the War of 1812 and a pew from when services were held in the original blacksmith's shop on site. Closed Monday. ~ 419 South 6th Street; 215-925-0616.

The sunny yellow classical façade of **Old Pine Street Presbyterian** belie the horrors that occurred here during the Revolutionary War. The current structure was built in 1857, but the Revolutionary War–era structure, also of classical design, was occupied by British troops, who used it as a hospital and, later, a stable. The pews and pulpit were torn out for firewood and horses destroyed the flooring and walls. The British soldiers desecrated the cemetery and, when they left, buried the bodies of 100 Hessian soldiers on the grounds. Those graves still lie beneath the churchyard's east walk. ~ 401 Lombard Street; 215-627-2493; www.oldpine.org.

When George Washington worshipped in Philadelphia, and didn't attend Christ Church, he sat in pew 41 at **St. Peter's Episcopal Church**. This church has been in continuous use since it was built as an Anglican church in 1761. Designed by Robert Smith, architect of Carpenter's Hall and the steeple at Christ Church, the interior features a large Palladian window, high box pews and an altar and pulpit on opposite ends of the nave. Buried in the cemetery here are Commodore Stephen Decatur, artist Charles Willson Peale, Second Bank of the United States president Nicholas Biddle and eight American Indian chiefs who contracted smallpox in 1793 while visiting George Washington. ~ 313 Pine Street; 215-925-5968; www.stpetersphila.org.

Who was Thaddeus Kosciuszko and why does he have his own monument? Without Thaddeus Kosciuszko, the American

OF MASONS AND MARINES

Tun Tavern is considered the birthplace of the Marine Corps because tavern owner Robert Mullan began recruiting customers for the service once Congress ordered two battalions of Marines on November 10, 1775. The tavern is also considered to be the birthplace of the Masonic brotherhood in the United States. Tun Tavern was located on Water Street at what is now the base of the Benjamin Franklin Bridge. Efforts are underway to reconstruct it near Pier 11 at Penn's Landing.

Revolution may not have succeeded. This Polish military engineer and general helped revolutionaries build fortifications to protect themselves against the British, namely at Saratoga and West Point, New York. Inspired by his experience, he returned to Poland and led an unsuccessful revolt against the Russian Czar. After he was wounded in battle, he returned to the United States and stayed in Philadelphia at the boarding house that is now the **Thaddeus Kosciuszko National Memorial**, now run by the National Park Service. The home features a small museum dedicated to the Polish general and his rooms have been preserved. Hours vary, call ahead. ~ 301 Pine Street; 215-965-2305.

◄ HIDDEN

When William Penn designed his city, he envisioned a city of commercial and residential streets divided into quadrants, each quadrant having its own park square. **Washington Square** is one of the four, a tidy greenspace among neat houses and straight streets. (Penn's fifth open space, at the center, is where City Hall now stands.) Washington Square is reminiscent of a London city park. While Washington Square today is a fine spot to play, rest and picnic, it holds tragic secrets. It is the final resting spot for 2600 British and American Revolutionary War soldiers and an unknown number of victims of the city's 1793 yellow fever epidemic. The Tomb of the Unknown Solder of the American Revolution is found here. ~ Walnut and Locust streets between 6th and 7th streets.

The **Athenaeum**, a research library on the eastern side of Washington Square, stands out among this neighborhood's buildings by its construction—this 1845 Italian revival structure is one of Philadelphia's oldest brownstone buildings. In addition to housing rare architectural drawings, books and collections, the Athenaeum's reading rooms contain numerous fine and decorative arts dating between 1800 and 1850. Open for tours by appointment. ~ 219 South 6th Street; 215-925-2688; www.phila athenaeum.org.

When you've topped your cerebellum with all the history it can handle, **South Street** is the place to unwind. This avenue of funky shops, restaurants, bars and stores is a walk on the wild side with few chain establishments (although some, including the Gap, Starbucks and McDonald's, have managed to slip in). For more about South Street, check out the shopping and dining sections later in this chapter.

The **Comfort Inn Downtown/Historic Area** is one of the most moderately priced hotels in the area. But its location, at the base of the Benjamin Franklin Bridge, has its drawbacks. Still it boasts a good view of the river and rooms have been soundproofed to shield guests from noise coming from the bridge. The mauve

LODGING

Text continued on page 78.

Camden, New Jersey

Camden, New Jersey, is one of the state's largest cities. It's also one of its poorest, battling a host of urban challenges such as crime and decay. Yet this city of nearly 80,000 has embarked on a $175 million redevelopment effort, counting on its waterfront's appeal to erase its reputation as the nation's most dangerous urban center. Today, numerous attractions draw Philadelphia visitors across the Delaware River to this historic place, which recently celebrated its sesquicentennial. Camden is accessible by the Benjamin Franklin Bridge and the quick and scenic **RiverLink Ferry**. The ferry runs daily from April through November, but is also open before and after special events in Camden, including concerts at the Tweeter Center and Riversharks baseball games. ~ 215-925-5465; www.riverlinkferry.org.

The **Adventure Aquarium** opened in 2005 with more than 5000 marine creatures, including sharks, rays, eels, octopus and fish, as well as penguins, hippos and seals. The "Ocean Realm," a 760,000-gallon habitat for sea creatures, is breathtaking; here, visitors can watch sharks, stingrays, sea turtles and tuna pass by. The Jules Vern gallery shows off the ocean's darkest reaches while touch tanks satisfy the curiosity of children and grownups alike. Admission. ~ 1 Riverside Drive; 800-616-5297; www.adventureaquarium.com.

The **USS New Jersey** was one of the last great battleships of the U.S. Navy. Decommissioned in 1991, her career ranged from operations in the South Pacific, including naval battles in the Marshall Islands and Okinawa during World War II to providing fire support for U.S. Marines in Beirut, Lebanon, in 1983. This massive vessel underwent a $22 million overhaul to become a museum, opening in 2001. Visitors can take self-guided or two-hour docent-led tours to see most of the ship, including her guns, teak deck, bridge, officers' quarters, chiefs' mess and more. There's also a weapons-systems specialty tour called the Firepower Tour, and personal behind-the-scenes tours are available to veterans who served on board. Limited hours in January and February. Admission. ~ Beckett Street at the Delaware River; 856-966-1652; www.battleship newjersey.org.

The four-acre **Camden Children's Garden** provides outdoor and indoor fun for youngsters. The garden hosts a carousel, a train ride, a maze, a tree house and storybook gardens based on the Three Little Pigs, Jack and the Bean Stalk, the Frog Prince and Alice in Wonderland. Indoors, there's the ever-popular butterfly house and a tropical conservatory. Hours vary, call ahead. Admission. ~ 3 Riverside Drive; 856-365-8733; www.camdenchildrensgarden.org.

Camden's **Tweeter Center** amphitheater—an open-air venue in the summer and enclosed stadium in the winter—hosts big-name concerts and stage productions. ~ 1 Harbour Boulevard; 856-365-1300; www. tweetercenter.com.

Campbell's Field is home to the Camden Riversharks minor-league baseball team. ~ Located at the base of the Benjamin Franklin Bridge; 866-742-7579; www.riversharks.com.

rooms are functional with queen beds, desks and nightstands. The hotel has a cocktail lounge, and continental breakfast is included with the room rate. Other amenities include an exercise room and a free shuttle to historic attractions. ~ 100 North Christopher Columbus Boulevard; 215-627-7900; www.comfort inn.com. MODERATE.

For rooms with a view, the **Hyatt Regency**, located on the waterfront, offers choices. Built in 2001, it's the only high-rise on the Delaware at Penn's Landing, and guests staying in exterior rooms can see the river, Camden and the New Jersey pine barrens or look out over Philadelphia's historic district and majestic skyline. The rooms feature contemporary decor in shades of beige, brown, gold and aqua, and offer amenities like hairdryers, high-speed internet, ironing boards, clock radios and large televisions. The hotel itself offers WiFi, a glass-wrapped indoor pool, a health club with stunning views and a restaurant with outdoor seating on Penn's Landing. If you have a view in mind, request it when making reservations. ~ 201 South Columbus Boulevard; 215-928-1234; www.pennslandinghyatt.com. ULTRA-DELUXE.

If you'd like to stay in a historic urban setting, Philadelphia has a number of small hotels and bed and breakfasts in the historic district and Society Hill to suit your taste. The **Penn's View Hotel** is a sweet boutique inn with 51 rooms located near the waterfront at Front and Market streets. Run by a family who also owns several upscale restaurants, including Ristorante Panorama and La Famiglia, this European-style hotel is set in a refurbished 19th-century commercial building. Some rooms have exposed brick walls and Delaware River views while premium rooms offer fireplaces and whirlpool tubs; all are decorated with lovely European-style furnishings. The location is convenient, although some guests may be put off by this hotel's proximity to Route 95 and the subsequent noise. Ask for a room in the rear when making reservations if you would like a quieter room. Be sure to make dinner reservations for the hotel's restaurant, Panorama, when you reserve your room if you want to eat there during your stay. ~ Front and Market streets; 215-922-7600; www.penns viewhotel.com. DELUXE.

HIDDEN ▶ For those who can't afford the dream of living in an elegant home in one of the country's finest neighborhoods, the **Gaskill House** fulfills that fantasy for a night or weekend. Located in Society Hill near South Street, this three-bedroom bed and breakfast is a double townhouse built in 1828 and run by a man with an eye for interior design. Gaskill House is draped in fine art, fabrics and Turkish carpets. The well-appointed rooms feature original art, antiques, fireplaces and private baths; two have jacuzzi tubs. The opulent Girard Room is a favorite, with lovely wallcoverings and a unique blue-and-white Delft tile fireplace.

Those with allergies should be aware that Zephyr, a friendly whippet, lives in the home. Breakfast is served fresh; proprietor Guy Davis has a knack for making omelets. ~ 312 Gaskill Street; 215-413-0669; www.gaskillhouse.com. DELUXE.

Also located in Society Hill is the 15-room **Morris House   ◄ HIDDEN Hotel,** a 1787 brick Federal-style residence that was once home to the Morris family, whose members include Anthony Morris, one of Philadelphia's early mayors. The Morris' wealth is illustrated by the large windows and Palladian transom over the door. Rooms are decorated with 18th-century period-style pieces but have televisions, clock radios and telephone service. A typical room features beautiful moldings, a poster bed, wing chairs and opulent bedding and draperies. The house's elegant garden is a well-kept secret. After a day of sightseeing, afternoon tea can be enjoyed alongside its manicured lawn and gazebo. The hotel is located within walking distance to Society Hill sites and Independence National Historical Park. There is no elevator in this historic residence and rooms are on the second and third floors. ~ 225 South 8th Street; 215-922-2446; www.morris househotel. DELUXE TO ULTRA-DELUXE.

The **Sheraton Society Hill** is a Neoclassical low-rise hotel roughly four blocks from Independence National Historical Park. This hotel has all the amenities business and family travelers could want, including minibars, internet access, a health club, restaurants, a bar, an indoor pool and those dreamy Starwood beds. Rooms are decorated in 18th-century style, mostly in florals, paisleys and plaids. The best views from the hotel are from the fourth floor facing the Delaware River. Several rooms open onto the decently sized indoor pool, but guests who don't like noise or the faint odor of chlorine would do well to request other rooms when making reservations. The hotel's main lobby area is a beautiful atrium design whose seating gives a sense of being outdoors. Pets are allowed, with restrictions. ~ 1 Dock Street; 215-238-6000; www.sheraton.com/societyhill. DELUXE TO ULTRA-DELUXE.

◆◆

SOULFUL SUNDAY SERVICE

Visitors lucky enough to be in Philadelphia on the third Sunday of the month should go to church—at least to experience the **Jazz Vespers** at Old Pine Street Presbyterian. Geared toward those who "seek non-traditional worship," the vespers feature music from Philadelphia's historic jazz community. Musicians who have appeared at this interdenominational service include Grover Washington, Jr., Shirley Scott and Tex Wyndham. ~ 401 Lombard Street; 215-627-2493.

DINING   Front Street hosts a triad of Italian restaurants. At **La Famiglia**, you'll find ornate, Old World–style dining, jacket required. The spaces are finished in marble and dark woods, with gilded accents, candelabras and ceiling frescos. La Famiglia prides itself on impeccable service and flawless presentation. The veal dishes are a specialty; the *vitello al tartufo*, veal served with black truffle and porcini sauce, is sublime. La Famiglia's menu is arranged traditionally, with an antipasti course, a pasta course, entrées and dessert. Closed Monday. ~ 8 South Front Street; 215-922-2803; www.lafamiglia.com. ULTRA-DELUXE.

The atmosphere of **Ristorante Panorama** is more relaxed than La Famiglia, its sibling—more Tuscan villa dining room than Roman rococo. The rich yellow walls, fresh flowers and substantial wine-by-the-glass list (up to 120!) invite lingerers. The handmade pastas can be delicate, as in the agnolotti, served with a light spinach sauce, or substantial, demonstrated by spaghetti *alla chitarra con agnello*, braised lamb in red wine sauce. ~ Penn's View Hotel, Front and Market streets; 215-922-7600; www.pennsviewhotel.com. DELUXE.

For Italian fare at reasonable prices, **Spasso Italian Grill** serves authentic dishes in a casual atmosphere. Exposed brick walls, friendly service and delicious food draw large lunch and dinner crowds, many who come for the fresh seafood and homemade pasta. The grilled calamari is a popular appetizer. The lounge area has become a place for local business types to relax; no stuffed-shirts or too-cool-for-you GenYers here. ~ 34 South Front Street; 215-592-7661; www.spassoitaliangrill.com. MODERATE.

The birthplace of BYOB restaurants in Philadelphia, South Street hosts a number of restaurants, including those where you can order a drink. The restaurant that spawned the BYO spurt is **Django**, a European eatery set behind a storefront. The casual at-

AUTHOR FAVORITE

Given its ubiquitous advertising, prime location and unusual venue—a four-masted sailing ship parked at Penn's Landing—the **Moshulu Restaurant** could easily be marked a tourist trap. But management has carefully avoided the pitfalls that often plague theme restaurants, instead offering delicious New American fare complemented by the superb views. For starters, the ceviche is nicely accented with a touch of mango, while the spice-encrusted ahi entrée, with a touch of cilantro and avocado, takes off with Southwestern panache. The 600-seat ship has a casual dining area and a comfortable bar that are subtly South Pacific, making your outing here feel like a mini-break. ~ 401 South Columbus Boulevard; 215-923-2500; www.moshulu.com. ULTRA-DELUXE.

mosphere of golden walls and unmatched furniture sets the stage for a complex, seasonal menu of European and French fare, which could include fresh corn and fruits, venison or bison. Django ranks as one of Philadelphia's top BYOs; this 38-seat restaurant fills quickly and reservations are usually made up to 30 days in advance. ~ 526 South 4th Street; 215-922-7151. DELUXE.

It may not look like much, but **Alyan's** delivers when it comes to inexpensive Middle Eastern fare. Locals come here to stock up on hummus and babaganoush, and the falafel is toasty, with a crispy exterior and a delicious, soft inside. The spicy french fries, with peppers and onions, are great, too. ~ 603 South 4th Street; 215-922-3553. BUDGET.

◄ HIDDEN

Many Philadelphians consider **Jim's Steaks** to be *the* place to get cheesesteaks, huge sandwiches overloaded with meat, onions and dripping cheese. Be prepared to order fast and correctly—the line at this mainly takeout place is usually down the sidewalk—and the cooks can be snarly. There are some tables and chairs upstairs. ~ 400 South Street; 215-928-1911. BUDGET.

Native Philadelphians highly recommend **Hosteria Da Elio** both for its unassuming decor and food that's on par with Tuscan trattorias. This reasonably priced BYO offers numerous daily specials, mostly centered around fresh, delightful hand-made pastas. The gorgonzola-filled white gnocchi melts in your mouth while the marinara dazzles. ~ 615 South 3rd Street; 215-925-0930. MODERATE.

◄ HIDDEN

The **Jamaican Jerk Hut**'s backyard hangout earned a starring role in the 2005 movie *In Her Shoes*; we hope Hollywood fame—and a subsequent increase in patrons—doesn't spoil the Hut's casual island air and festive menu of Johnny cake, jerk pork and jerk chicken. For summer fun, the Hut's garden is the place to be; you can listen to a steel-drum band while eating Caribbean fare by tiki torch. ~ 1436 South Street; 215-545-8644. MODERATE.

Although many "Main Street" shopping districts have popped up in and around the Philadelphia area, few have the unique boutiques, eateries, cafés and people-watching of South Street. A byway of more than 300 stores (95 percent independently owned), South Street has "something for everyone," whether you're a stoner looking for incense, a fan of vintage wear searching for a Nehru jacket or a tourist browsing for antiques.

SHOPPING

A store that has gotten much attention—and giggles—for years is **Condom Kingdom**. ~ 437 South Street; 215-829-1668.

Zipperheads is the place for punk rockers to get their tongue studs, leather jackets and dog collars. ~ 407 South Street; 215-928-1123.

Fun urban duds can be found at a variety of clothing shops on South Street. **Guacamole** is the place to go for whatever's in style, right now. The price is right for shoes, including pretty good imitations of Doc Martens and Steve Maddens, and the selection of teensy T-shirts will make under-25 females swoon. ~ 422 South Street; 215-923-6174.

HIDDEN ▶   The art students hanging around the double doors at **Pearl Art Supply & Crafts, Inc.** indicate the popularity of this store among professionals, but hobbyists enjoy shopping here as well. Strolling down the aisles of canvases, colors and brushes at this three-story store may inspire you to explore your creative side. ~ 417 South Street; 215-238-1900.

In addition, South Street has "denim bars" that can fit you in the right pair of jeans and stores that sell everything from games and holistic gems, to used books and CDs, new music and more.

Dr. Denim is a Philadelphia original, a place to purchase men's urban wear, including oversized T-shirts and casual jeans from Ralph Lauren, Tommy Hilfiger and DKNY. The shop has jackets, button-down shirts, shorts, belts and accessories for all occasions. To top off your ensemble, check out the array of embroidered ball caps and knit hats. ~ 331 South Street; 215-922-7199.

For the latest trends in gal and guy fashions, head to **Europe Moda,** a great place to get hand-painted T-shirts, snug jeans, cute halter dresses and leather jackets. The store also has one of the widest selection of hoodies and casual wear for women in Philadelphia. Beware, however—the prices are as upscale as the swanky merchandise. ~ 524 South Street; 215-629-5525.

NIGHTLIFE   **Il Bar**, inside the Ristorante Panorama at the Penn's View Hotel, has the largest wine preservation system in the world, allowing it to have a weekly-changing "wine-by-the-glass" menu that tops 120 selections. To enjoy it to its fullest, the proprietors have a special tasting offer with samples of up to five wines. ~ Front and Market streets; 215-922-7600; www.pennsviewhotel.com.

HIDDEN ▶   Fans of quirky art films and independents will love the **Ritz Theatres** near Society Hill, at the Bourse and on 2nd Street. ~ Locations at 125 South 2nd Street, 214 Walnut Street and 400 Ranstead Street; 215-925-7900; www.ritzfilmbill.com.

HIDDEN ▶   The **Laff House,** Philadelphia's original comedy club, aims to please and comics are on more than they are off. Small tables, a decent snack menu, a no-drink minimum and edgy humor keep people coming back. ~ 221 South Street; 215-444-4242; www.laff house.com.

The **Theatre of the Living Arts** is a concert venue for roughly 1000 patrons on South Street. Past performers include Wilco and Sixpence None The Richer. ~ 334 South Street; 215-922-1011.

Since the 1960s, **Society Hill Playhouse** has been Philadelphia's "off-Broadway" venue, staging new comedies and East Coast premiers. Past shows include *Menopause the Musical* and improv troupe N Crowd Live. ~ 507 South 8th Street; 215-923-0210; www.societyhillplayhouse.com.

FOUR

Center City

The heart of Philadelphia is Center City, where you'll find City Hall as well as new office towers that gleam like jeweled minarets against the evening sky. From Washington Square west to the Schuylkill River, and from Arch Street to South Street, Center City houses city government agencies and the components of working Philadelphia, including municipal offices, courts, corporate headquarters and financial institutions. But Center City also accommodates Philadelphia's culture houses, including spacious new performing arts venues and top-rated museums, hundreds of public art installations, upscale retail stores, chic boutiques, fine restaurants and opulent homes.

Before 1987, Center City was a cluster of low-rise buildings, none taller than 548 feet, thanks to a gentleman's agreement that limited height to the level of William Penn's hat atop City Hall. But in 1984, developers proposed breaking that rule, and although a dispute erupted over whether Philadelphia should retain its small-city feel or move architecturally into the 20th century, the city granted permission for a skyscraper, One Liberty Place, to be built. Today, Center City has at least six buildings that tower over William Penn, creating an urban skyline that has come to symbolize the city's rebirth.

Like the Independence National Historic Park area, Center City has much to see, packed into an area easily traveled by foot. We've divided Center City in half; City Hall, the country's largest municipal building, is seated on the dividing line—Broad Street—between the eastern and western portions. You could tour the eastern portion one day and the western the next, or visit the important sites on one side in the morning, eat lunch, and tour the other side in the afternoon, depending on time. Shoppers will want to permit extra time for the western part around Rittenhouse Square; the city's finest stores are located here, as are numerous nationally rated restaurants.

▼▼▼▼▼▼▼▼▼▼▼▼
Center City East

Between the historic area and City Hall lie residential neighborhoods, unique storefronts, department stores and historic sights that date anywhere from the city's founding to its industrial expansion. Along Broad Street and John F. Kennedy Boulevard, Philadelphia's courts and administrative offices bustle during the week. The large Pennsylvania Convention Center, which opened in 1993, usually is filled during the workweek as well, hosting special events and meetings. Reading Terminal Market, one of the country's finest indoor bazaars, is in constant whirl; Philadelphians shop and dine here morning, noon and night. In eastern Center City, you'll find Philadelphia's famed Antique Row and Pennsylvania Hospital, the nation's oldest medical center, founded by Ben Franklin and Dr. Thomas Bond, as well as other places of historic significance.

Like a wedding cake festooned in lacy filagree, Philadelphia's **City Hall** is a grand contrivance of French Second Empire architecture and uncommon engineering. Built between 1871 and 1900, the hall is the world's tallest masonry building, having no internal steel structure. To bear the weight of its seven stories and 700 rooms, the first floor is made of solid granite, 22 feet wide in some places. Much of the remainder is brick with marble or steel cladding. City Hall was designed by architect John McArthur, Jr., and at the time of its grand opening, the $23 million office complex was the tallest usable building in the world. (The Eiffel Tower and the Washington Monument are taller, yet these structures aren't considered true buildings.) Take time to wander around the building and through the arches that lead to the courtyard; the ornate façade is decorated with hundreds of statues by Alexander Milne Calder, who also created the 37-foot bronze statue of William Penn on top of the City Hall tower. City Hall sits on Penn Square, the center park in Penn's original design for Philadelphia. Tours of this vast structure are offered weekdays at 12:30. ~ Broad and Market streets; 215-686-2840.

SIGHTS

Across John F. Kennedy Boulevard from City Hall is the **Masonic Temple**, a Norman structure that contains some of Philadelphia's most exquisitely decorated interiors. The temple serves as a meeting place for 28 Philadelphia-based Masonic organizations and is the Grand Lodge of the Free and Accepted Masons of Pennsylvania. The Masons is one of the oldest and largest fraternal organizations in the world. Members swear allegiance to a brotherhood of man and a belief in one God. They have built grand monuments throughout the United States, and Philadelphia's temple is among their most opulent. Oriental Hall is of Moorish design, decorated in colors and fabrics matching the Alhambra castle in Granada, Spain; Egyptian Hall is awash in turquoise and gold, featuring brightly painted columns, hieroglyphs and statues; the grand Norman Hall pays tribute to the Knights Templar, the monastic order of Crusaders who, among other things, were instrumental in developing the banking industry and special elite military forces. ~ 1 North Broad Street; 215-988-1917; www.pagrandlodge.org.

HIDDEN ▶

Farther up Broad Street at Cherry Street is the **Fabric Museum and Workshop**. Fans of Marimekko prints and the artist Christo will love this gallery and studio dedicated to textiles and unique uses of these materials in art and performance. Contemporary art aficionados will enjoy exhibits that explore the uses of woven media in art and daily living, and the museum's collection of more than 3500 artifacts. A working print studio allows visitors to watch artists at work. ~ 1315 Cherry Street; 215-568-1111; www.fabricworkshop.org.

When you're ready for lunch or a snack, head to **Reading Terminal Market**, a bustling bazaar that has been the site of an operating farmer's market since 1653. Crowded below the train shed of the Reading Railroad, the market brings together locals and tourists with more than 80 stalls of produce, meats, cheeses, baked goods, ready-to-eat meals, crafts, books and jewelry. At Termini Bros. bakery, you'll find the best cannoli in Philadelphia. Delilah's booth features Oprah Winfrey's favorite macaroni and cheese. The northwestern corner of the market is run by Amish and Mennonite families who bring in farm-fresh items and baked goods from Lancaster County Wednesdays through Saturdays, including handmade sausages, scrapple and shoofly pie. Closed Sunday. ~ 12th and Arch streets; 215-922-2317; www.readingterminalmarket.org.

The Masonic Temple museum has one of four glass paintings of Washington in existence.

Upstairs from the market is the grand **Reading Railroad Train Shed**, a terminus for the Reading Railroad from 1893 to the early 1970s. The cavernous building is the nation's only surviving single-span, arched train shed. Remnants of the shed's earlier purpose can be seen in the floor, which features 13 pairs of embedded stainless steel tracks. The shed is now the entryway to the **Pennsylvania Convention Center**, a 1.3-million-square-foot meeting facility that plays host to the famed Philadelphia Flower Show in March as well as other special events throughout the year. ~ 1101 Arch Street; 215-418-4700; www.paconvention.com.

Northeast of the convention center, **Chinatown** whirls with shoppers, diners and residents of this six-block area, home to more than 3500 Chinese and Asian residents. Chinatown dates to the 1870s, when settlers opened the first Chinese laundry at 913 Race Street. Marking the neighborhood's entryway over 10th Street is the 40-foot-high Friendship Gate, the largest Chinese gate outside China. The gate was built in 1983 by artisans from Tianjin, Philadelphia's sister city in China. All materials used to build the structure were donated by Tianjin residents. Chinatown has more than 50 restaurants and shops carrying Oriental furniture, Hello Kitty paraphernalia, souvenirs and fortune cookies. Many of the restaurants in this neighborhood serve traditional ten-course banquets on the Chinese New Year; the

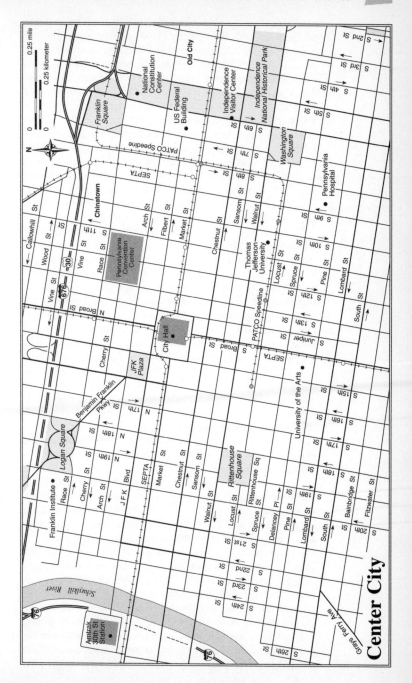

Center City

cash-only **Chinese Cultural Center**'s meal is among the most popular. ~ 125 North 10th Street; 215-923-6767.

Philadelphia has its mainstream museums and its oddities as well. At North 8th and Race streets, by appointment only, is the

HIDDEN ► quirky **Shoe Museum at Temple University's School of Podiatric Medicine.** Dr. Augustus Wilson, a Philadelphia podiatrist who lived from 1853 to 1919, collected shoes from all over the world, and much of his 900-plus collection can be viewed here. The museum's exhibits include sandals dating to biblical Egypt, shoes belonging to several First Ladies and sneakers worn by basketball legend Dr. J. There are modern examples, such as Sally Struthers' funky, fabulous blue satin platform shoes from the set of *All in the Family*, and ancient footwear, including "lily shoes"—bindings used by the Chinese to keep women's feet smaller than four inches long. ~ North 8th and Race streets; 215-625–5243.

From Reading Terminal Market, head south to the tall building bearing the letters "PSFS." Though this office complex looks small compared to the city's new skyscrapers, it was the first international modernist skyscraper built in the United States, and its well-preserved interiors are worth a look. Until the 1990s, the

HIDDEN ► **Philadelphia Saving Fund Society Building** (PSFS), designed by architects George Howe and William Lescaze, housed the nation's first savings bank. The gleaming structure is now the luxurious Loews Philadelphia Hotel, but its hallways, ballrooms and main offices, finished in black granite, limestone and stainless steel, have been carefully preserved. Period details in this the circa 1932 building include Cartier clocks at the elevator banks, exotic wood paneling in the meeting rooms, and enormous casement windows in the ballrooms and guest rooms. The staff at Loews takes pride in their building's heritage and don't mind if you wander around. Be sure to take the elevator to the 33rd floor, where there are several preserved executive dining rooms and conference centers. ~ 1200 Market Street; 215-627-1200.

Down the street from the PSFS Building is a Philadelphia shopping landmark, a **Lord and Taylor** department store that always will be known to Philadelphians as **Wanamaker's.** This city block–wide store was one of the nation's first department stores, and it continues to be one of its most glamorous, an urban retailer that rivals those found on Fifth Avenue in New York City. John Wanamaker was a retail pioneer, opening his store in 1876 in a former railroad station. Wanamaker changed the face of American retail, instituting such practices as return policies, setting customer service standards and establishing themed sales, including the first White Sale in 1879. The store itself has borne a series of firsts: the first department store to have elevators; the first to have electric lights; the first to have a telephone. A 2500-pound bronze American Eagle statue, a purchase from the 1904

St. Louis World's Fair, stands in the emporium's huge center court. "Meet Me at the Eagle" remains a common phrase today for Philadelphians shopping downtown with family and friends. The Wanamaker Organ, also purchased at the 1904 World's Fair, is played daily. Don't miss the holiday light show and concerts held during the Christmas shopping season. ~ 1300 Market Street; 215-241-9000; www.lordandtaylor.com.

Genealogists and history buffs shouldn't skip the **Historical Society of Pennsylvania,** one of the country's largest repositories of family histories and immigrant and ethnic documentation.

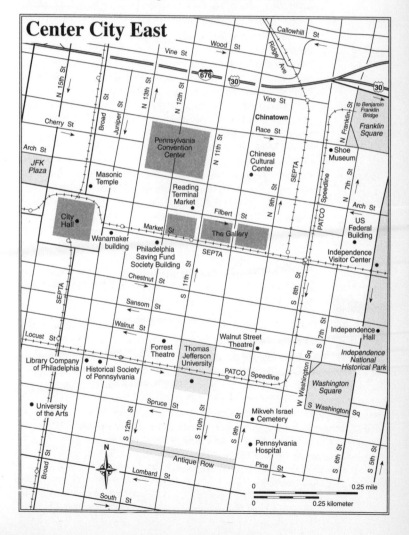

Center City East

The museum's collection includes a first draft of the U.S. Constitution as well as a rare printed copy of the Declaration of Independence. Hours vary, so call ahead. ~ 1300 Locust Street; 215-732-6200; www.hsp.org.

Stroll east on Locust and you'll encounter townhouses and gardens that often are ignored by passersby. Tucked behind the main streets, between 11th and 12th and Spruce and Locust, are

HIDDEN ►

the city's **"littlest streets,"** including Quince, Irving, Cypress and Panama streets, which contain the former homes of servants who ran the city's 19th-century mansions. These tiny alleyways are so small, one can barely fit a car through. For years, this neighborhood has housed Philadelphia artists, artisans and creative arts clubs.

The **Mask and Wig Club** is a clubhouse for the University of Pennsylvania's all-male comedy troupe. Founded in 1889 as a place to showcase student-written satires and comedy productions, the club continues to stage shows annually. The odd Swiss-Alpine building once served as a stable; architect Wilson Eyre converted it into a theater, and its open-beam interior features a number of wall murals painted by artist Maxfield Parrish. ~ 310 South Quince Street; 215-923-4229.

Art history buffs should consider ducking into Alumni Hall of Thomas Jefferson University to see the master work of Ameri-

HIDDEN ►

can artist Thomas Eakins, *The Gross Clinic*. Painted in 1875, the masterpiece portrays surgeon Samuel Gross instructing spectators in a surgical amphitheater mid-operation. With *Gross Clinic*, Eakins, an American Realist known for pushing the boundaries of portraiture and for painting everyday life, explored a subject that had not been touched by American or European painters. ~ 1020 Locust Street.

Farther down Locust toward Broad is the **Library Company of Philadelphia**, a library founded by 50 men, including Benjamin Franklin. Each member paid 40 shillings to join the library, and

sights

AUTHOR FAVORITE

On a clear day, you can enjoy a 30-mile view of Philly from the **City Hall observation deck**—just take the tour that zips you up the tower until you're right below the statue of William Penn. You can pick up timed tickets for your ascent in Room 121 on the first floor of City Hall, and take the elevators to the seventh floor, where you wait for another carriage to the top. The tiny five-person (six if some are small) elevator, with glass doors, allows a unique view of the tower's interior, including a glimpse at the back of one of the 26-foot clock faces that adorn the tower. At the top, the panorama awaits. ~ Broad and Market streets; 215-686-2840.

10 shillings for dues. The company continues to operate as a nonprofit research facility, and its collection includes a half million volumes, including rare manuscripts and artifacts. Permanent and rotating exhibits offer glimpses into this vast historic collection. Closed weekends. ~ 1314 Locust Street; 215-546-3181; www.librarycompany.org.

Off the beaten path, on Spruce Street, you'll find **Pennsylvania Hospital**, the nation's first hospital and the site of its first surgical amphitheater. Founded in 1751 by Benjamin Franklin and Dr. Thomas Bond, Pennsylvania Hospital was designed as a public facility to house the "sick-poor and insane." Its patients, who wandered around their fenced yard for fresh air on Sundays, were considered such curiosities that the hospital eventually began charging a fee to those who stood outside the gate and watched. Self-guided tours of this well-preserved facility begin at the hospital's main treasure, Benjamin West's magnificent 1817 oil *Christ Healing the Sick in the Temple*. This painting is West's second rendition of the subject; the first painting, commissioned originally for the hospital, was sold to Britain's National Gallery under pressure from the British government.

Found in the original hospital building are a beautifully restored library, a portrait gallery, an apothecary and the amphitheater, the nation's first for teaching surgery. The amphitheater seated nearly 180 spectators, and surgeries were conducted between 11 a.m. and 2 p.m. on sunny days to maximize the light shining through the ceiling's oculus. Self-guided tour brochures are available at the information desk near the Spruce Street entrance. Guided tours also are available if you call ahead. ~ 800 Spruce Street; 215-829-3270; www.pennhealth.com/pahosp.

Across the street from Pennsylvania Hospital is the **Mikveh Israel Cemetery**: a burial ground that predates the Mikveh Israel Congregation, located near Independence Hall, by 42 years. The cemetery was founded by Jewish merchant Nathan Levy, who purchased the land from then-Governor Thomas Penn to bury an infant son. Several well-known Philadelphians are interred here, including Levy, a merchant whose ship, the Myrtilla, brought the Liberty Bell to the city. Revolution financier Haym Salomon and socialite Rebecca Gratz, whose personality inspired the character "Rebecca" in Sir Walter Raleigh's *Ivanhoe*, are also buried here. Tours by appointment. ~ Spruce Street between 8th and 9th streets; 215-923-3811.

LODGING

Most of the lodgings found in Center City East are chain hotels and independent lodgings geared toward business travelers, but there are luxury resorts and lesser-priced business hotels here, too, as well as several boutique-style facilities.

Adjacent to the Pennsylvania Convention Center, the 1332-room **Philadelphia Downtown Marriott** caters to the convention crowd, with two restaurants, a lobby lounge and martini bar, a sushi bar, a sports bar and a Starbucks. Rooms are functional, featuring two queens or a king-sized bed, a full-sized desk and chairs. Amenities include an indoor pool, 24-hour fitness center and wireless internet access in the common areas. Visitors will appreciate the hotel's proximity to Reading Terminal Market, City Hall, the Wanamaker Building and other downtown sites. ~ 1201 Market Street; 215-625-2900; www.marriott.com. DELUXE.

The nation's first modernist skyscraper makes a particularly elegant hotel, with Cartier clocks at the elevators, granite walls and limestone flooring. **Loews Philadelphia Hotel** spent $18 million renovating the PSFS building, a National Historic Landmark, into a hotel. The rooms, furnished in contemporary style, feature comfortable beds, desks and chaises longues. Bedspreads, carpeting and draperies are copper or eggplant colored, with accents of beige, blue and taupe. All 583 rooms have faxes, printers and three telephones, including one cordless. Each room features a beautiful city view through large steel casement windows. Amenities throughout the hotel include a spa and fitness facility, an indoor pool and a restaurant. ~ 1200 Market Street; 215-627-1200; www.loewshotels.com. ULTRA-DELUXE.

Business travelers like the location of the **Residence Inn Philadelphia Center City**, directly across from City Hall and a few blocks from the convention center. This Marriott hotel is another example of urban re-use; it is built in a 1920 former art deco–style bank. The rooms, which are decorated in jewel tones and beiges, are adequately furnished with desks, sofas and chairs. All have kitchenettes, perfect for long stays or families. A hot buffet breakfast that features real oatmeal and freshly made waffles is included. Management also hosts evening happy hours with light food and beverages. ~ 1 East Penn Square; 215-557-0005; www.marriott.com. ULTRA-DELUXE.

HIDDEN ▶

Clean, sleek, art deco decor, reasonable rates and an excellent location keep clients coming back to the **Alexander Inn**, a bed-and-breakfast boutique hotel located a few blocks from theaters,

PENN'S EFFIGY

The bronze statue of William Penn on the top of City Hall is 36 feet high and weighs 27 tons. It is the work of Alexander Milne Calder, the grandfather of mobile artist Alexander Calder. The statue faces northeast toward Penn Treaty Park, the site where the legendary treaty between Penn and the Lenni Lenape Indians was signed.

Antique Row and City Hall. The rooms, ranging in size from small to not-so-small, are individually decorated in modern furnishings, with contemporary art hanging on the walls, plants and deco lamps brightening the interiors. A continental breakfast is served daily, featuring breads, yogurts, juices, coffee and pastries, and the facility offers a complimentary snack bar loaded with fruits and pastries. There's also a fitness room for those who don't spend all day walking around the city. ~ Spruce and South 12th streets; 877-253-9466. MODERATE TO DELUXE

Conveniently located across the street from the Kimmel Center for the Performing Arts, and within walking distance to all Center City sites, the **Doubletree** is a solid choice for business travelers and families. The architecture of the building is sawtoothed, affording each room a 180-degree city view (with the top rooms having the most spectacular vistas). Rooms are basic, with creamy wallpaper, jewel-tone bedding and poster beds. The beige, nondescript bathrooms are equipped with hairdryers and irons. Kids will enjoy the chocolate chip cookies on check-in and the indoor pool, set in an atrium. Other amenities include a jogging track, a fitness center, a sundeck, a café and a restaurant. ~ 237 South Broad Street; 215-893-1600, 800-222-8733; www.doubletree.com. DELUXE TO ULTRA-DELUXE.

DINING

Reading Terminal Market has more than 60 kiosks, making it *the* lunch destination for nearly anyone within a ten-block radius. You can choose from gooey cheesesteaks, Greek fare such as gyros and souvlaki, Chinese, comfort food, hoagies, soups and stews. Closed Sunday. ~ 12th and Arch streets; 215-922-2317; www.readingterminalmarket.org.

The best cannoli in town is found at **Termini Bros**. A cannoli, for the uninitiated, is an Italian pastry shell stuffed with a sweet mixture of ricotta cheese and flavorings, such as citrus or chocolate. At Termini Bros., the cannoli shells are crisp and perfect, and the filling is creamy and balanced. The chocolate chip cannoli is a personal favorite. Closed Sunday; also closed Monday and Tuesday from July through Labor Day week. ~ The southernmost aisle in Reading Terminal Market, 12th and Filbert streets; 215-629-1790; www.termini.com. BUDGET.

Also in Reading Terminal Market, the **12 Street Cantina** is a hotspot for takeout Mexican fare, offering a few surprises, such as chicken *mole*, that most takeouts don't. The guacamole is fresh and delicious, served with crispy blue chips, and nearly anything with the restaurant's trademark chipotle maple barbecue sauce is yummy. Try the *tortas*, flour tortillas stuffed with cheese and other toppings, including peppers, sweet potatoes or meats. ~ 1136 Arch Street; 215-625-0321. BUDGET.

Four blocks south of the convention center is **Sal's on 12th,** an Old World Italian bistro. You'll find wonderfully hearty dishes such as lobster ravioli and oversized shrimp stuffed with horseradish and wrapped in bacon. The pasta dishes are outstanding, but if you're not into carbs, Sal's also cooks a wonderful steak and simply prepared seafood. ~ 200 South 12th Street; 215-731-9930. MODERATE TO DELUXE.

HIDDEN ►

Of all the restaurants in Chinatown, **Lee How Fook Tea House** continues to please with its Cantonese menu. A family-owned BYOB, Lee How Fook has a dedicated following of locals, including chefs from other restaurants who drop by after hours. The pulled-pork steamed dumplings are delicious, as is the gingered beef with scallions. The salt-baked shrimp and squid are perennial favorites. Many regulars order huge terrines of sweet-and-sour soup or luscious stews. ~ 219 North 11th Street; 215-925-7266. BUDGET.

Pho Xe Lua, a Vietnamese and Thai restaurant in Chinatown, is well known for its reasonably priced pad thai and *pho.* This place is popular with starving students and artists—the portions are huge and served up quick. The *pho ga,* a filling beef noodle soup, features thin slices of beef simmered gently in a rich broth. Save room—just a little—for the refreshing rainbow ice dessert. ~ 907 Race Street; 215-627-8883. BUDGET.

Philadelphia has its share of high-end chain steakhouses, including the Palm, Ruth's Chris, Smith and Wollensky and Morton's. Of the major steakhouses, the **Capital Grille,** with its selection of aged steaks served in a clubby atmosphere, never disappoints. The calamari appetizer, fried up with peppers and onions, is unbeatable. The large steaks, prepared simply, will satisfy a ravenous carnivore. If you order lobster, go broiled—the nutty flavor is delicious. Be sure to listen to the specials; sometimes they have a few slices of specially prepared filet mignon or other surprises tucked into their dry-aging room. ~ 1338 Chestnut Street; 215-545-9588; www.thecapitalgrille.com. DELUXE.

◆◆

A PHILLY FREEBIE

The Wanamaker Organ, in Lord and Taylor's center courtyard, is a few pipes shy of being the world's largest. (That distinction goes to an organ in Atlantic City, but portions of that instrument are inoperable.) The organ was displayed at the 1904 St. Louis World's Fair and was purchased by Wanamaker. Concerts are held daily at noon, Monday through Saturday, and also at 5 p.m. Monday, Tuesday and Thursday through Saturday. On Wednesday, there is a 7 p.m. show as well.

Center City East has a number of stores, from bargain outlets to upscale apparel shops, fine arts and antique galleries, and museum gift stores. Philadelphia, once known for its fine 18th-century furniture, continues to excel in the antiques and arts trades. Stores offer a complete range of American-made furnishings as well as Asian, English and French antiques.

SHOPPING

Considered one of the finest farmer's markets in the country, **Reading Terminal Market** is a shopper's delight, with booths selling everything from groceries and kitchenware to housewares, books, jewelry and fresh-cut flowers. The market has room for 80 vendors, and on its busiest days (Wednesday through Saturday, when the Amish farmers tote their goods from Lancaster County), Reading Terminal hops. Many Philadelphians shop here for the fine selection of meats, produce and prepared foods, but you'll find loads of other goodies here as well. For gifts and kitchenware, **Foster's Gourmet Cookware** stall (215-925-0950) has a great selection of baskets, servingware, glassware, bakeware and gourmet gift items. For take-home Pennsylvania gifts, stop by **Kauffman's Lancaster County Produce** (215-592-1898) for Amish-made jams, jellies, crafts and home-grown produce. Closed Sunday. ~ 12th and Arch streets; 215-922-2317; www.readingterminalmarket.org.

Lord and Taylor, in the Wanamaker Building, is an elegant urban department store with three levels of designer-label women's, men's and children's wear, accessories, housewares and cosmetics. This store is as close as you'll get to shopping on Fifth Avenue without being in New York. ~ 1300 Market Street; 215-241-9000.

You'll find nearly every store you've got at home at **The Gallery at Market East**, an urban shopping mall with 170 stores, including Strawbridge's Department Store, Burlington Coat Factory, Modell's Sporting Goods, the Gap, Express, Old Navy and others. The Gallery runs four city blocks and is four stories high. The food court has more than 25 vendors and the lowest level serves as a hub for SEPTA's commuter trains. ~ 9th and Market streets; 215-625-4962; www.galleryatmarketeast.com.

I. Goldberg is Philadelphia's Army-Navy store, carrying military surplus items as well as work clothes, footwear, camping equipment and accessories. This is a great place to pick up woolens for your next mountain hike or an inexpensive backpack for a camping trip. ~ 1300 Chestnut Street; 215-925-9393; www.igoco.com.

J.E. Caldwell is a Philadelphia institution, where moneyed Philadelphia has bought its jewelry and silver spoons since 1839. The opulent store is worth a pass-through—if not for the merchandise, then for a peek at the Baccarat crystal chandeliers that hang inside the store. ~ 1339 Chestnut Street; 215-864-7800.

Text continued on page 98.

Off the
Beaten Path

With a bevy of neighborhoods throughout the city, you could write a book about Philadelphia's off-the-beaten-path neighborhoods alone. Here we've assembled a sampling of the neighborhoods north of the Center City area that will give you a feel for the city that you wouldn't get by sticking to the regular routes. However, we've been selective as well, to protect your safety. Along the main thoroughfares, you're not likely to get into trouble in Philadelphia, but avoid straying farther into some of the neighborhoods unless you are with someone who knows the city intimately.

The African-American neighborhoods along Broad Street north of Center City have much to offer in terms of cultural sights. The towering **Divine Lorraine Hotel**, a magnificent historic building that is languishing in disrepair, was Philadelphia's first fully integrated first-class hotel. The French Renaissance–revival building was constructed in the early 1890s as luxury apartments, and in 1949, the property was purchased by a Philadelphia minister, Reverend Major Jealous Divine, for use as apartments and hotel space. The property sold three times to developers between 2000 and 2005; the city hopes it will be renovated and returned to its former glory. ~ 699 North Broad Street.

Just a few blocks north of the Divine Lorraine is the **Legendary Blue Horizon**. A mystical place for boxing fans, it's one of the few boxing venues left in the United States. The "Blue" actually is housed in three mansions that were built in 1865 and converted into one facility for use as a Moose fraternal lodge. In 1961, boxing came to the Blue; the 1200-seat venue has seen a number of big fights and 30 World Champions in its canvas ring. Today, boxing continues to be the headline event with Friday-night fights, and many Philadelphians consider it a great first-date destination. ~ 1314–16 North Broad Street; 215-763-0500; www.legendarybluehorizon.com.

As you move up Broad, you'll enter **Temple University** territory. Temple is the 28th largest university in the country, with more than 34,000 graduate and undergraduate students. Famous alumni of this school, founded in 1888, include entertainer Bill Cosby, musician Daryl

Hall, Philadelphia Mayor John Street and four U.S. congressmen. The Tyler School of Art students show their work at a variety of venues around town. Temple's Liacouras Center is home to Temple's basketball team and also hosts concerts on occasion. ~ 1801 North Broad Street; 215-204-7000; www.temple.edu.

In the neighborhoods and throughout the city, you'll find mom-and-pop stores, local restaurants and watering holes. Cars line up outside **Taconelli's Pizza** as patrons pop in to pick up their pies—pizzas that many consider Philadelphia's best. At Taconelli's, customers must call ahead the day before to reserve their pizza dough. Whether or not this is a gimmick is a favorite discussion topic among Philadelphians, but some swear by the brick oven–baked crust and fresh ingredients. If you like thin-crust pie with a delicate balance of cheese, spices and meats, this might be your place. ~ 2604 East Somerset Street; 215-425-4983. MODERATE.

Near the Mayfair section of town, between U.S. 1 and the Delaware north of the Tacony-Palmyra Bridge, you'll find two bakeries that vie to produce the city's best butter cake. Butter cake should not be confused with pound cake—this German recipe is actually not very cakey (in fact, it's easier to eat with a spoon). Butter cake has a yeast-based bottom layer, topped with a mixture that includes a half-pound of butter and two cups of sugar. You can find butter cake and other regional specialties, including beautiful Italian rum tortes, at **Mayfair Bakery**. Closed Monday. ~ 6447 Frankford Avenue; 215-624-7878; www.mayfairbakery.com. BUDGET.

Competing with Mayfair Bakery for the city's best butter cake is **Haegele's Bakery**, off Frankford Avenue. Haegele's specializes in cookies but offers breads, tortes and cakes as well. Locals swear it's one of the best German-style bakeries in the area. At Christmas, they hand-produce 50 pounds of cookies a day for six weeks, including gingerbread, Viennese walnut cookies and *pfeffernusse*. Closed Sunday and Monday. ~ 4164 Barnett Street; 215-624-0117. BUDGET.

For more of Philadelphia's colorful neighborhoods, see Chapter Six.

Antique Row, on Pine Street from 9th to 12th streets, features more than 25 stores in one small area. **G.B. Schaffer** offers a selection of period 18th- and 19th-century furniture and art, as well as less expensive Centennial pieces. You'll also find a selection of prints, paintings, silver, glass, Federal furniture and decorative arts, from 18th-century Chippendale highboys to convex bulls-eye mirrors. ~ 1014 Pine Street; 215-923-2263.

HIDDEN ▶ SOTA—**Spirit of the Artist** is a gallery gift shop of handcrafted merchandise by American artists. Owner Frank Burkhauser has amassed a collection of gifts for any budget, including handblown glass wind chimes, inlaid wooden boxes, burnished art deco–style switchplates, garden statues, toys, museum-quality glass bowls and more. Burkhauser is especially proud of his large collection of Raku Goddess sculptures. ~ 1022 Pine Street; 215-627-8801; www.sotagifts.com.

HIDDEN ▶ **Robert Anthony Interiors,** also on Antique Row, carries a delightful selection of luxury home decorating items, including prints, art, throw pillows and linens. Merchandise fights for space in this shop, and with so much to see, you'll want to save time to browse. ~ 1106 Pine Street; 215-925-0750.

Unusual jewelry, including necklaces, earrings, rings, pins, bracelets and watches, can be found at the hard-to-find and totally HIDDEN ▶ hip **Halloween,** a store identifiable only by the orange business card propped in the window. This shop sells traditional jewelry and one-of-a-kind pieces, including traditional diamond solitaires and earrings, dragon pins, amber and semi-precious creations. ~ 1329 Pine Street; 215-732-7711.

NIGHTLIFE Bars are spread throughout Center City, with each catering to a specific crowd. East of Center City, in what is usually referred to as Washington Square West, you'll find a number of gay danceclubs and bars. Also, Irish taverns and European bars are popular in this part of town.

Fergie's Pub is Irish through and through, serving eight domestic and international beers on tap and carrying more than 50 bottled brews. Live music plays nightly, and on Tuesdays and Thursdays, Fergie's draws large crowds for Quizo, a team trivia game. There are no TVs in Fergie's; proprietor Fergus Carey loathes them. But you'll find a jukebox with Philly and Irish favorites and a friendly clientele. ~ 1214 Sansom Street; 215-928-8118; www.fergies.com.

Established in 1860, **McGillin's** is the oldest continuously operating tavern in Philadelphia. The bar even has its original license hanging on the wall. McGillin's serves a selection of brews, including two house brands made by Stoudts, a local brewer. McGillin's also carries Pennsylvania-brewed Yuengling on tap. The menu consists mainly of bar fare, but McGillin's also carries some comfort foods, including warm soups, seafood stew and chops. ~ 1310 Drury Lane; 215-735-5562; www.mcgillins.com.

Woody's is a Philadelphia institution, a bar that has served as a gay hotspot since the 1970s. Two levels of partying spaces include a coffee bar, lounges and dancefloors, free computer kiosks for surfing the internet, and outdoor seating in good weather. Something fun is always on the calendar: Fridays and Saturdays attract a young crowd of urbane men cruising the dancefloor to techno. Other nights, Woody's is not as crowded and the clientele tends to be more diverse, in terms of age and gender. Monday nights are for karaoke; two-step lessons are offered on Sunday; and country music is played Tuesday. ~ 212 South 13th Street; 215-545-1893.

> Completed in 1987 and designed by architect Helmut Jahn, One Liberty Place is the first building that broke the "no higher than Penn's hat" rule.

While most of the theater arts are celebrated across Broad Street in Center City West, one former theater—**the Trocadero**—still draws crowds in Center City East. The "Troc" is a former vaudeville theater that now serves as a concert venue, hosting all-ages shows, generally featuring rock and punk bands. The historic building, constructed in 1872 as an opera house, was Philadelphia's longest-running burlesque theater, showing cabaret and vaudeville acts, including Abbot and Costello, and burlesque shows until it closed in 1978. Today, groups such as Sonic Youth and the Reverend Horton Heat regularly take the stage here. ~ 1003 Arch Street; 215-922-5483; www.thetroc.com.

The **Forrest Theatre** is a roadhouse of sorts, a theater that houses the traveling troupes of big-name Broadway musicals. Past shows at the Forrest include *Mamma Mia!*, *Aida* and *Beauty and the Beast*. ~ 1114 Walnut Street; 215-923-1515; www.forrest-the atre.com.

Center City West

Philadelphia's new distinctive skyline is owed to the office buildings in western Center City, the heart of the city's commercial district. The hub for the city's banking, insurance and financial industries, Center City West is home to One and Two Liberty Place, the city's tallest buildings, and the site of the future Comcast Center, soon to be the city's tallest building (and the tallest between New York and Chicago). Center City West is home to Philadelphia's ritziest neighborhood and high-end shopping district near Rittenhouse Square. This is also the center for Philadelphia's performing arts; South Broad Street, between City Hall and Pine Street, is known as the Avenue of the Arts, boasting such well-known institutions as the Academy of Music, the University of the Arts and the new Kimmel Center for the Performing Arts.

SIGHTS   The most visible landmarks in Center City West are One and
Two Liberty Place, the tallest buildings in Philadelphia. **One
Liberty Place** stands 63 stories, at 945 feet high. The art deco–
style building, faintly reminiscent of the Chrysler Building in
New York, seems to have set a precedent for conical-topped
buildings in Philadelphia, although the new Comcast Center will
have a square top. Its sister building, **Two Liberty Place**, opened
in 1991 and houses a hotel, shops and offices. ~ 1650 Chestnut
Street and 1601 Chestnut Street.

The nation's first art museum and school, **The Pennsylvania
Academy of the Fine Arts** houses a trove of American and inter-
national art in a fanciful Gothic Victorian building. The Aca-
demy was founded in 1805; its exquisite facility was designed by
Philadelphia architects Frank Furness and George Hewitt and
built in 1876. The collections include the works of several great
American artists, including portrait artist and Academy founder
Charles Willson Peale, Thomas Eakins, Winslow Homer and
Andrew Wyeth. The contemporary works of artists such as Roy
Lichtenstein and Georgia O'Keeffe can also be found here. ~
118–128 North Broad Street; 215-972-7600; www.pafa.org.

Many locals refer to **John F. Kennedy Plaza**, northwest of
City Hall, as LOVE Park, for the nationally recognized sculpture
that dominates the plaza's southeastern end. The LOVE sculpture,
by pop artist Robert Indiana, is based on the artist's 1960s paintings of the same word. It became a cultural symbol of the '60s
and lives on today in part because the U.S. Postal Service continues to use the logo for stamps. Once considered a Mecca for
Philadelphia's skater crowd, LOVE Park is no longer the skate-rat
hangout it used to be; the city cracked down on skateboard use
in the park in 2002. Today the park is a concert venue in the
summer months and is one of Philadelphia's public WiFi hot-
spots. ~ 15th Street and John F. Kennedy Boulevard.

Another example of public art in western Center City is a 45-
foot **Clothespin** by Swedish-born artist Claes Oldenburg, who
spent a career transforming ordinary objects into pop art. The ten-
ton *Clothespin* was designed to demonstrate the beauty of an
everyday object; for Philadelphians, it's become an identifiable
place for meetings and smoking breaks. ~ 15th and Market streets.

Heading south of City Hall on Broad Street, the Avenue of
the Arts, you'll encounter the magnificent **Bellevue-Stratford
Hotel**, a facility that now houses the Park Hyatt Philadelphia at
the Bellevue, upscale retail shops and offices. This 1710-room
structure complements City Hall with its French Renaissance–
style architecture and white marble façade. Completed in 1904,
the *Philadelphia Inquirer* lauded Bellevue-Stratford as the "most
magnificent hotel in the world" when it opened. It had more than
1000 rooms, and its opulent common spaces, including a grand

staircase and ballroom with moveable stage, hosted lavish parties, debutante balls and cotillions. Like many historic hotels, the Bellevue-Stratford fell into a period of decline by mid-century. In 1976, disaster struck the hotel when conventioneers contracted a mysterious illness—an infection the world now knows as Legionnaires' Disease. Twenty-nine American Legion members died of bacterial pneumonia while staying in the hotel for a Bicentennial convention, having been exposed to a germ found in the hotel's air-conditioning system. The hotel then shut down for three years and reopened as the Fairmont Hotel, operating under that name from 1979 to 1986. Eventually, the building became the multi-use commercial facility it is today, with luxury shops on the first two levels, offices in the middle and the 170-room Park Hyatt on the top floors. ~ 200 South Broad Street.

Next door to the Bellevue-Stratford is the **Union League**, an ornate French Renaissance–style building with double staircase and mansard roof. It's home to a private social club for affluent

Center City West

members of the Republican party. Founded in 1865 by supporters of Abraham Lincoln and the Civil War effort, the Union League houses a small hotel for Union League and affiliate club members. It is closed to the public. ~ 140 South Broad Street; 215-563-6500.

South of the Union League on Broad is the **Academy of Music**, an opera house whose simple stone façade belies the splendor that lies within. This 1857 theater, the nation's oldest opera house in continuous use, was modeled after the La Scala in Milan. Its opulent interior drips with scarlet hangings and carpets, gilded cornices and a 5000-pound crystal chandelier. The Academy hosted the nomination of President Ulysses Grant for his second term in 1872 and was the site of the world premiere of John Phillip Sousa's "The Stars and Stripes Forever" in 1897. Today, the Academy is home to the Opera Company of Philadelphia and the Pennsylvania Ballet. ~ 1420 Locust Street; 215-893-1999; www.academyofmusic.org.

There's nearly always something happening at the **Kimmel Center for the Performing Arts**, the city's newest concert hall and performance venue. This 450,000-square-foot structure was completed in 2001 as the permanent home of the Philadelphia Orchestra. Other resident companies here include the Philadelphia Chamber Music Society, the Chamber Orchestra of Philadelphia, the Philadelphia Dance Company, the Philly Pops and the American Theater Arts for Youth. Concerts and plays are performed in two separate halls, the cello-shaped 2500-seat Verizon Hall and the smaller 650-seat Perelman Theater, which features a rotating stage. Free concerts are given in the center

AUTHOR FAVORITE

Budding physicians, scientists and fans of all things macabre will love the **Mütter Museum at the College of Physicians of Philadelphia**. Historians who have a strong stomach will appreciate this museum as well, especially the facility's fascinating take on the medical challenges behind the 1804 Lewis and Clark Expedition. The museum has more than 20,000 medical artifacts and anomalies, housed in a grand 19th-century building. Two levels of exhibit space show medical oddities dating back 200 years. Highlights include the liver of Siamese twins Eng and Chang, whose autopsy was performed at the college; a piece of John Wilkes Booth's thorax; a cadaver from the early 1800s whose flesh has turned into soap; and miscarried fetuses displaying a host of tragic birth defects. ~ 19 South 22nd Street; 215-563-3737; www.collphyphil.org.

lobby area during the year. ~ 260 South Broad Street; 215-893-1999; www.kimmelcenter.org.

Contemporary art is showcased at the **Rosenwald-Wolf**   ◄ HIDDEN
Gallery at the University of the Arts. Shows focus on trends in modern art and include various media, including performance art, graphic art, sculpture, paintings and film. ~ 333 South Broad Street; 215-717-6480; www.uarts.edu.

West of the Avenue of the Arts lies Philadelphia's swankiest neighborhood, **Rittenhouse Square**. This park, part of William Penn's original city layout, was named for David Rittenhouse, an astronomer, clockmaker and the first director of the U.S. Mint. Houses in this neighborhood were first constructed around 1840, and many have been converted into upscale lodgings and condominiums. Rittenhouse Square is a favorite lunchtime destination in warm weather. Nearly any time of year, you'll find students playing chess or suited businessmen eating lunch. The square also hosts art shows and other special events throughout the year. Its fanciful stone walls, pool and fountain were designed in 1913 by architect Paul Cret, designer of the Rodin Museum on the Benjamin Franklin Parkway. ~ Between 18th and 20th streets and Walnut, Locust and Spruce streets.

The **Church of the Holy Trinity**, an 1859 Norman-style church across from the northwestern corner of Rittenhouse Square, houses a number of architectural wonders, including five Tiffany Studios stained-glass windows and floors constructed of handcrafted tiles made by artist Henry Mercer in Doylestown. A tryptich behind the church altar honors Reverend Phillip Brooks, the church's pastor from 1862 to 1869, who wrote the words to "O Little Town of Bethlehem." Music for the tune was composed by Lewis Redner, the parish's organist, who once served as organist for Old Pine Presbyterian on Pine Street. ~ 1904 Walnut Street; 215-567-1267; www.htrit.org.

Also near Rittenhouse Square, **Delancey Place** is one of the city's prettiest streets, with ornate town homes built in a variety of architectural styles, including beaux arts and Italianate. Number 1810 Delancey features an unusual collection of caryatid statues. The lavish 1900 Delancey Place, now a business, was designed by architect Frank Furness, who created the Pennsylvania Academy of Art. Note the use of cherubim and seraphim on the façade. Other Victorian-era homes include beautiful leaded and stained-glass windows and elegant front porches.

The exclusive **Curtis Institute of Music** is a tuition-free school for the nation's most exceptional young musicians. Graduates of the institute include conductor Leonard Bernstein, composer Samuel Barber and pianist Ignat Solzhenitsyn. The school, founded in 1924 by Curtis Publishing heir Mary Louise Curtis Bok, is housed in several former residences; the main building once belonging to banker George W. Childs Drexel. Free concerts are given October through May on Monday, Wednesday and Friday evenings; the institute also holds children's concerts on weekends in November and February, and other special events throughout the year. ~ 1726 Locust Street; 215-893-7902; www.curtis.edu.

The collection of Union artifacts at the **Civil War and Underground Railroad Museum of Philadelphia** is extensive and includes weapons, camp gear and more from the conflict as well artifacts from the Lincoln presidency. Included in the collection is an 1861 life mask of Lincoln as well as one made just two months before he was killed. There's a lock of the president's hair and a "wanted" poster seeking Lincoln's killers. The museum also features an exhibit that explains the progression of firearms development from the Revolutionary to Civil wars. ~ 1805 Pine Street; 215-735-8196; www.cwumuseum.org.

Tucked off Rittenhouse Square is the **Rosenbach Museum & Library,** an 1863 townhouse filled with rare books and manuscripts, 18th-century antiques, exceptional Persian rugs and priceless Egyptian statuary. Collectors Dr. A.S.W. Rosenbach, a rare book dealer, and his brother Philip Rosenbach, an antiques dealer, amassed more than 130,000 manuscripts and 30,000 rare books, as well as paintings and furniture, which are now available for public viewing. Highlights include James Joyce's handwritten manuscript for *Ulysses* and the only known first edition of *Poor Richard's Almanack*. There's also a first edition of *Don Quixote* and Lewis Carroll's own copy of *Alice in Wonderland*. The museum shop features a good selection of signed prints and books by Maurice Sendak, the children's author who penned and illustrated *Where the Wild Things Are*. ~ 2010 Delancey Place; 215-732-1600; www.rosenbach.org.

HIDDEN ▶ To experience a special Philadelphia residential neighborhood, walk to **Fitler Square,** a hidden gem southwest of Rittenhouse Square. Tucked among single-family homes, Fitler Square is a cherished neighborhood green space, featuring a dog park and

ONE HEROIC HORSE

Among the oddest displays at the Civil War and Underground Railroad Museum is the well-preserved head of General George Meade's horse, "Old Baldy." This is a steed whose heroism outshone his rider's; Baldy was wounded in battle a whopping 14 times, in places such as Gettysburg, Manassas, Virginia, and Antietam, Maryland. He managed to outlive Meade by ten years and served as the riderless horse during the general's military funeral honors.

beautiful Victorian fountain that flows nearly year-round. The square is a hub of neighborhood activity, providing a venue for events such as a spring fair, easter egg hunt and Christmas tree lighting. The neighborhood has several lovely, small restaurants and stores with friendly service and clientele. ~ Bounded by Panama and Pine streets and 23rd and 24th streets.

If you're on a budget, you'll want to stay somewhere else besides Center City.

LODGING

The **Park Hyatt Philadelphia at the Bellevue** is the city's most historic hotel, called the "grande dame of Broad Street" when it opened as the Bellevue-Stratford Hotel in 1904. An elevator takes guests to the Park Hyatt's 19th-floor lobby. Visitors are greeted with sparkling water or wine served in tall flutes. The rooms, above the lobby level, have high ceilings and are nicely appointed, although as in many historic hotels, they are furnished in a fairly simple style. Furniture is traditional—down comforters or patterned spreads on poster beds, and easy chairs or sofas, depending on the room's size. Nonetheless, they have beautiful city views. All rooms are equipped with robes, ironing boards, minibars and televisions. Room service is available, as is a continental breakfast. One of the top perks available to guests at the Hyatt is free access to the Sporting Club, a Michael Graves–designed private health club that features a half-mile indoor jogging track, a 25-meter pool, cardiovascular machines and racquetball courts. ~ 200 South Broad Street; 215-893-1234, 800-223-1234; parkphiladelphia.hyatt.com. ULTRA-DELUXE.

Philadelphia is a city that has mastered the art of building re-use, and the **Ritz-Carlton** is among its showpieces. Situated in the former Girard-Mellon Bank building and a neighboring tower, this hotel is the building double of Rome's Pantheon. The 1908 dome houses a stunning atrium, restaurants and a ballroom. Guest rooms are decently sized, with none smaller than 320 square feet, and are furnished with inlaid cherry furniture, comfortable overstuffed armchairs and luxurious bedding. Large marble baths feature glass-enclosed showers and tubs, fluffy terry robes and hairdryers. Room service is taken to new heights at the Ritz-Carlton, with a special Bath Menu—a butler can come draw a luxurious, soaking bath for you. The hotel also has a fitness center, spa and three restaurants. ~ 10 Avenue of the Arts; 215-735-7700, 800-241-3333; www.ritzcarlton.com. ULTRA-DELUXE.

Looking for some place special to stay? The **Latham Hotel** is a small European boutique-style hotel with graceful lobbies and uniformed doormen. Begun as a hostel for business travelers, this circa-1907 hotel still draws a business crowd during the week and pleasure travelers on weekends. The 139 rooms are decorated in Victorian style, with poster beds featuring floral ruffled bedskirts and pillow shams in jewel tones, heavy draperies, nightstands and elegant desks. Stunning crystal chandeliers hang in the paneled two-story lobby. The hotel's restaurant, Jolly, is more American than European, a place to swig martinis and eat prime rib sandwiches. ~ 135 South 17th Street; 215-563-8200; www. lathamhotel.com. MODERATE TO DELUXE.

Opened in 2000, the **Hotel Sofitel Philadelphia** has quickly found its niche in the city's market, becoming one of Center City's most popular hotels. The Sofitel, part of a French chain, has a sleek, blue granite and marble lobby. Guest rooms are modern and sophisticated, adorned in shades of ocher, black and beige. Luxurious featherbeds top each bed, and some rooms are equipped with comfortable chaises longues. A Zagat-rated French bistro, Chez Colette, is on-site. The lobby bar, La Bourse, is a nice place to unwind after a long day; the name pays homage to the Philadelphia Stock Exchange that once occupied this site. ~ 122 South 17th Street; 215-569-8300, 800-763-4835; www.sofitel. com. ULTRA-DELUXE.

A luxurious hotel at one of the city's top addresses, the **Rittenhouse Hotel** overlooks Rittenhouse Square, with views of the lovely city park from nearly every room. The Rittenhouse is both a hotel and a condominium complex; the building's design gives the rooms interesting shapes and sizes. Choose from guest rooms or suites; all rooms are larger than 450 square feet. Recently redecorated guest rooms are sumptuous and elegant, with rich blue carpeting and bedding, and beige accents. The rooms have separate seating areas and high-speed internet. The marble bathrooms have large glass showers and separate tubs, and come with robes, mini-televisions and Aveda products. Suites vary in decor, but all have separate living rooms with tables, chairs and an entertainment armoire; large bedrooms; a foyer

AUTHOR FAVORITE

The **Rittenhouse Square Bed and Breakfast** is a darling inn just a few blocks off the square. A renovated 19th-century carriage house, the eight rooms and two suites pamper guests with upscale furnishings, including wrought iron beds or queens with upholstered headboards, upholstered valances and custom draperies, Impressionist art and private marble baths. Rooms come with turn-down service, luxury linens and plush robes. Some have gas fireplaces. Continental breakfast is served daily in the breakfast café, while wine and hors d'oeuvres are offered at night in the elegantly appointed living room. ~ 1715 Rittenhouse Square Street; 215-546-6500, 877-791-6500; www.rittenhousebb.com. ULTRA-DELUXE.

and a bathroom. The Mobil four-star restaurant, Lacroix at the Rittenhouse, is in the building; be sure to secure a reservation when you make your hotel plans if you want to dine there. ~ 210 West Rittenhouse Square; 215-546-9000. ULTRA-DELUXE.

La Reserve is a bed and breakfast set in an 1850s townhouse just off Rittenhouse Square. This lovely inn, with three suites and four guest rooms, is mostly decorated in French Provincial style, although several rooms have a decidedly English or American style, such as the Hunt Room and the Liberty Twin Room. The Marquis Room has recently been decorated in sunny yellows and crisp blues. All rooms have private baths and come with bathrobes, ironing boards, clock radios and WiFi access. Breakfast is substantial; the innkeepers whip up pancakes, waffles or eggs between 8 a.m. and 10 a.m. ~ 1804 Pine Street; 800-354-8401; www.lareservebandb.com. MODERATE.

◀ HIDDEN

Rittenhouse Square and "Restaurant Row" along Walnut Street are home to the city's finest dining establishments, with the Mobil five-star Le Bec-Fin leading the troupe. Center City West also has a number of small establishments that will fit any budget. If you'd like to try some of the pricier restaurants but you're on a budget, consider making lunch reservations; you'll often pay half of what you might for a similar dinner bill.

DINING

Homesick Southerners should check out **Zanzibar Blue**'s New American cooking and Southern favorites. Much of the fare has a Creole or Cajun bent, although you can also get simple but tasty meat dishes and macaroni and cheese. Among the entrées are short ribs, fried catfish and an interesting seafood lasagna jazzed up with asparagus, white wine and chervil. Those who hail from south of the Mason-Dixon line will appreciate the collards and sweet potatoes on the side-dish menu. The music in this restaurant and jazz club is unparalleled, so plan to make it a night. ~ 200 South Broad Street; 215-732-4500; www.zanzibarblue. com. DELUXE.

Chef and proprietor **Susanna Foo** has elevated Asian cuisine to a new level at her self-named restaurant, famous for fusing Chinese and Southeast Asian fare with French flavors. The elegant dining room with honeyed walls features silk lanterns, delicate screens, comfortable banquettes and fragile orchids. In this fine yet comfortable setting, prepare to be surprised. The Manila clams with black beans have the heat of jalapeños; coriander jazzes up the seafood pad thai. No need to "save room" for dessert. Portions at Susanna Foo are manageable; some critics say they're on the smallish side. ~ 1512 Walnut Street; 215-545-2666; www.susannafoo.com. ULTRA-DELUXE.

Thirty-five years after opening in Philadelphia, **Le Bec-Fin** remains the city's preeminent restaurant, one of 14 dining rooms nationwide to earn Mobil's five-star rating. When Chef Georges Perrier opened Le Bec-Fin, he began Philadelphia's restaurant revolution, leading the charge with an opulent French dining room and impeccable service. With the swish of a silver-domed plate at Le Bec-Fin, Philadelphia became a restaurant destination. In 2000, Perrier and Le Bec-Fin stumbled, and the restaurant was swiped of its five-star rating. But rather than accept the fate of his aging restaurant, Perrier regrouped. He revamped his dining room, tearing everything out but the crystal chandeliers and firing himself as executive chef. Three years later, the restaurant won back its fifth star. Today, Le Bec-Fin is a stunning Parisian salon upholstered in gold silk, with glittering lights, gilt mirrors and Louis XIV chairs. Diners enjoy a six-course meal served in a carefully choreographed presentation. The crab cake and Dover sole, perennial favorites, are perfect; the roasted breast of squab adventurous. The wine list features more than 500 labels, and its dessert tray is heady with pastries and rich confections, as well as several lighter tarts. ~ 1523 Walnut Street; 215-567-1000; www.lebecfin.com. ULTRA-DELUXE.

HIDDEN ▶ **Le Bar Lyonnais**, downstairs at Le Bec-Fin, serves delicious French bistro fare from an à la carte menu. Enjoy onion soup, Perrier's famous crab cakes, blinis with caviar and crème brûlée prepared with the same care as upstairs but for fewer *francs*. ~ 1523 Walnut Street; 215-567-1000. DELUXE.

Georges Perrier uses Le Bec-Fin to exhibit his mastery of his native cuisine, but he demonstrates his creative flair at **Brasserie Perrier**, itself a Mobil four-star restaurant. Opened in 1997, the Brasserie Perrier features French food with Asian or Italian touches. The steak *frites* are the best in the city, and the chicken breast comes with gruyere and sun-dried tomato pesto. Atmosphere is convivial, with art deco touches, upholstered banquettes and a silver-leafed ceiling. ~ 1619 Walnut Street; 215-568-3000; www.brasserieperrier.com. ULTRA-DELUXE.

Aristocratic Argentina meets cosmopolitan Cuba at ¡Pasion!, a nouvelle Latin eatery. Chef Guillermo Pernot, the Argentina-born force behind the restaurant, has created a rustic dining room

LOVELY . . . BUT DEADLY

The Bellevue-Stratford Hotel's marble staircase was designed to allow women to show off their dresses as they approached the ballroom. However tempting it may be, don't try to slide down the banister. Philadelphia socialite Louise Schoettle died in 1956; she fell 37 feet to her death while demonstrating to friends how she slid down the banister as a child.

with weathered woods and a canopy ceiling. Backlit plantation
shutters give an illusion that it's always sunny outside. Expect
meals to be oriented around seafood, Argentine beef, and ceviche
of ingredients such as ahi tuna, shrimp, clams, fruit and squid
ink. The beef is as tender as butter; the smoked ribeye is marinated for more than 24 hours in a mix of chilis and spices. The
wine selection relies heavily on South America's vineyards with
a smattering of Spanish and Portuguese wines. Mojito fans will
like ¡Pasion!'s version of the unofficial Cuban national beverage.
~ 211 South 15th Street; 215-875-9895. DELUXE.

The line stacks up at lunch outside **Joe's Pizza**. Some Philadelphians consider it the best pie in the city, while others argue that
its less-than-thick (but not thin) crust lacks authenticity. Still, for
cheap on-the-go food, Joe's offers many toppings and service is
quick. Just be sure to get in line and know what you want; any
delay will earn you scorn from the pizza Nazis as well as the waiting customers. ~ 122 South 16th Street; 215-569-0898. BUDGET.

Chez Colette, a little bistro in the Hotel Sofitel Philadelphia
(as well as several Sofitel hotels in the U.S.) is a bit of modern
Paris in Philly, with a red-and-black dining room motif and
1920s-style poster art on the walls. The menu has French standards such as onion soup and steak *frites*, but also offers some
outstanding, not-so-traditional choices, including a savory crabmeat crêpe topped with lobster sauce. Because it's a hotel restaurant, it serves three meals. Perfect croissants and pots of hot
chocolate highlight the authentic continental breakfast. ~ 122
South 17th Street; 215-569-8300; www.sofitel.com. MODERATE
TO DELUXE.

If you're looking for takeout fare to eat at Rittenhouse Square,
you can stop in at **Così**, the chain coffeehouse/eatery, for panini
or a salad. Così servers are efficient, whipping up fresh or signature salads made to order. Polite and urbane, the Cosi staff is
friendly and will make sure you have napkins and flatware for
your meal-to-go. ~ 201 South 18th Street; 215-735-2004; www.
getcosi.com. BUDGET.

One of the prettiest dining venues in Center City, **Le Jardin**   ◄ HIDDEN
in the Art Alliance Building, features an urban garden for outdoor dining in temperate weather and an intimate indoor space
of warm plaster walls, hardwood flooring and leather seating.
The menu's standard French bistro fare is the best bet, from the
well-prepared escargot and onion soup to the dry-aged beef sirloin. Some menu items, including the pan-roasted duck breast,
served with a mango chutney and "seven spice fig sauce," seem
overly ambitious. The white chocolate mousse is a dulcet cloud.
The wine list, which lists French wines as "domestics" and U.S.
wines under "international" is a little obnoxious. ~ 251 South
18th Street; 215-545-0821. DELUXE.

At **Lacroix at the Rittenhouse**, celeb chef Jean-Marie Lacroix, formerly of the Philadelphia Four Seasons Hotel, has established a menu that allows diners to mix and match. The elegant dining room is boxy yet chic, with dark wood booths, earth-toned upholstery and walls, and palms. The menu is split into four tastings; customers can start with a soup such as the double duck consommé or fresh organic greens, and move on to crispy skate wing, salt cod or walleye pike gnocchi in crayfish bisque. Desserts are on the house; the crème brûlée is perfect, but try one of the unique, fresh-made sorbets to top off your experience. ~ 210 West Rittenhouse Square; 215-790-2533; www.rittenhouse hotel.com. ULTRA-DELUXE.

HIDDEN ▶ Opposite the culinary spectrum from Lacroix at the Rittenhouse is **Little Pete's**—a 24-hour, greasy spoon for the all-night coffee-and-cigarette set. The people-watching is awesome, especially in the middle of the night, and the service is friendly. As for the food, the menu of diner fare is typical—burgers, fries, shakes and 24-hour breakfasts. It's all hot, fast and good, and portions are huge. Don't ask about calorie counts. ~ Locations at 219 South 17th Street, 215-545-5508; and 1904 Chestnut Street, 215-563-2303. BUDGET.

Since the 1970s, **The Astral Plane** has been drawing customers with its eclectic, funky decor and fresh menu. The orange-rose walls are adorned with the pics of stars who've dined there, and visitors eat from mismatched plates under poofy, parachute ceilings and 1930s chandeliers. Selections are complex, like the macadamia nut–encrusted Hawaiian sea bass with coconut-rum reduction, or simply prepared with fresh ingredients, like the salmon quesadilla with mozzarella, mango and jalapeños. ~ 1708 Lombard Street; 215-546-6230. MODERATE.

The **Sansom Street Oyster House** is a Philadelphia staple, a fish restaurant that is classic yet comfortable, with the widest raw bar selection in town. Seafood is straight off the boat. Like

AUTHOR FAVORITE

A tiny BYO with an atmosphere that feels like the home of an old friend, **Porcini** serves homemade pastas and light Italian trattoria–style fare. Decor is simple, with white tablecloths and white walls—nothing to distract you from the tasty *bruschetta* and a salad of fresh tomato and basil. Chicken tops the meat menu choices here; the saltimbocca—large, moist chicken breasts prepared with prosciutto—is particularly tasty. This restaurant is tiny and cramped; try going early or on an off-night to avoid waiting in line. ~ 2048 Sansom Street; 215-751-1175; www.phillyrestaurants.com/porcini. MODERATE.

any traditional seafood house, Sansom Street's strengths lie in traditional favorites like fried oysters and chowders. The raw bar has more than 40 different types of oysters, subject to availability, harvested from Virginia to Canada. Spicy Cajun crawdads and clams fill out the selection. The Oyster House is a local favorite. Check out the restaurant's website before you go; money-saving coupons are often posted. ~ 1516 Sansom Street; 215-567-7683; www.sansomoysters.com. DELUXE TO ULTRA-DELUXE.

If you'd prefer to eat Japanese food while picnicking with the worker bees and suits in Rittenhouse Square, try **Tampopo**, a tiny storefront joint that serves noodles swiftly. There are a few tables, but your best bet is to get in and out, if the weather's nice. Vegetarians will like Tampopo's selection of meatless sushi, while meat-eaters should try the shrimp *gyoza* or beef teriyaki. ~ 104 South 21st Street; 215-557-9593. BUDGET.

◄ **HIDDEN**

The hard-to-find **Bistro St. Tropez** offers impressive views of the Schuylkill River and the art museum, as well as a fine menu of French bistro standards and flavorful entrées. The restaurant is on the fourth floor of the Marketplace Design Center—the building with the large Wyland whale mural on its waterfront face. While enjoying the beautiful views, diners can sup on escargots served with a macadamia nut–shiitake butter sauce or steamed mussels, followed by a traditional cassoulet or hefty bouillabaisse. Arrive early and shop for furniture in the Design Center before heading up to dinner. ~ 2400 Market Street, 4th floor; 215-569-9269. DELUXE.

◄ **HIDDEN**

Center City West boasts many galleries and upscale shopping opportunities. The 60 **Shops at Liberty Place** include Ann Taylor Loft, April Cornell, Jos. A. Banks and other national retailers. ~ 1625 Chestnut Street; 215-851-9055.

SHOPPING

The **Shops at the Bellevue** feature designer labels and custom clothing, jewelry and art, with independent galleries seated next door to such well-known shops as Polo Ralph Lauren, Tiffany & Co., Williams-Sonoma and Nicole Miller. ~ 200 South Broad Street; 215-875-8350; www.bellevuephiladelphia.com.

The oldest independent book store in the city is **Robin's**, run by Larry Robin, the grandson of the founder. At Robin's, you'll find a mix of literature, political science, poetry and arts books. Larry Robin takes pride in stocking books for inquisitive minds; the store also hosts book signings and numerous special events. An annex store, at 1837 Chestnut Street, offers discount magazines and great book buys. ~ 108 South 13th Street; 215-735-9600.

Collectors who seek the extraordinary can find volumes at **Bauman Rare Books**. Bauman's is a destination for discriminating buyers of antiquarian books, offering such works as a first edition of Dickens' *A Christmas Carol* or Descartes' *Principia Philosophiae*. ~ 1608 Walnut Street, 19th floor; 800-992-2862.

Knit Wit is a women's wear boutique carrying everything from jeans to evening gowns and pricey baubles. The service is impeccable, proving to be a great help for those needing advice on style. ~ 1718 Walnut Street; 215-564-4760.

The **American Institute of Architects Bookstore and Design Center** features architecture and design tomes, as well as gardening books, children's books and unique gifts. The downstairs gallery features architectural renderings, paintings and sketches. ~ 117 South 17th Street; 215-569-3188.

Urban Outfitters is a home-grown Philadelphia store that now has locations in 27 states, Ireland and the United Kingdom. This is where the target market of 18- to 30-year-olds go to buy clothes that look like the ones 40-somethings wore 20 years ago. Like its sister store, Anthropologie, Urban Outfitters carries clothes, accessories and "apartment" furnishings—nearly everything in the store, from the sweaters on the shelves to the furniture that holds up the merchandise, is for sale. ~ 1809 Walnut Street; 215-564-2313; www.urbanoutfitters.com.

Philadelphia's home for funky, fashionable and comfortable shoes is **Benjamin Lovell Shoes**. This Rehobeth, Delaware, shoe retailer has expanded with two stores in Philadelphia, offering American- and European-made shoes for those who seek comfort as well as style. In addition to carrying Merrell, Mephisto and Birkenstock, Benjamin Lovell offers Cole Haan and Kenneth Cole for men and Steve Madden and Via Spiga for women. ~ 119 South 18th Street; 215-564-4655.

The swanky shops around Rittenhouse Square offer high-end options. If money is no object, dress your little prince or princess at **Born Yesterday**, a children's clothing store that sells fine French-, Italian- and American-made outfits for the wee set. Born Yesterday also sells its own line, including precious sweaters and adorable dresses, as well as toys and accessories for youngsters. Philadelphia moms know that the store marks down merchandise twice a year and after holidays. ~ 1901 Walnut Street; 215-568-6556.

For handcrafted jewelry and Judaica, **Dahlia's** carries necklaces, earrings, bangles and giftware by Israeli artisans. Many of the pieces contain Jerusalem stone and Swarovski crystals and are a perfect companion for evening wear. Closed Sunday. ~ 2003 Walnut Street; 215-568-6878.

HIDDEN ► If you like designer style and don't mind wearing last year's fashions, **Sophisticated Seconds** consignment store has top names in gently used clothes, shoes, handbags and accessories. You might snag a Kate Spade handbag or Prada shoes if you're lucky. The selection of evening bags and accessories is tops. ~ 2019 Sansom Street; 215-561-6740.

Crammed with thousands of titles, the **Joseph Fox Bookshop** carries a wide selection of literature, political nonfiction, history, art, architecture, picture books, poetry and children's books. Joseph Fox prides itself on personal service; it's considered to be one of Philadelphia's top independent bookstores. ~ 1724 Sansom Street; 215-563-4184.

If you like designers but can't afford them, you might luck out at **Daffy's**, a six-story discount store with levels upon levels of women's and men's clothes, accessories, shoes, leather apparel and home decor. Daffy's has 20 discount stores nationwide, and the Philadelphia store is one of its best, with well-maintained and displayed merchandise and a layout that feels more like a department store than an outlet. ~ 1700 Chestnut Street; 215-963-9996.

The well-heeled gentleman shops at **Boyd's**, a Philadelphia institution for suits and menswear. Boyd's service begins with valet parking and ends after the customer picks up his tailored threads. The conservative can find staples from Burberry and Ralph Lauren here, while others can satisfy their wardrobe needs with clothing from Armani, Hugo Boss and Versace. Women won't be disappointed, either; Boyd's boutique carries Vera Wang, Oscar De La Renta, Michael Kors, St. John and Stella McCartney. Closed Sunday. ~ 1818 Chestnut Street; 215-564-9000.

Mysteries, spy thrillers, detective *noir* and horror novels fill the shelves at **Whodunit**, a used bookstore with a cute, creepy, mysterious façade and shelves containing rare finds, first editions, paperbacks and more. Sci-fi fans will find their genre featured here as well. The store often hosts author events. ~ 1931 Chestnut Street; 215-567-1478.

◀ HIDDEN

AUTHOR FAVORITE

Anthropologie's ultra-feminine selection of clothing, accessories and housewares can be found in 23 states, but you still can't beat the original. Founded in Philadelphia in 1992, this store embraces international design, and its merchandise brings to mind far-off lands, from a few traditional offerings of the United Kingdom to the exotic designs of India, Indonesia and the Far East. The store is in the former beaux arts–style mansion of Sara Drexel Fell and Alexander Van Rensselaer. When climbing the interior staircase, be sure to look up at the stained-glass dome. ~ 1801 Walnut Street; 215-568-2114; www.anthropologie.com.

NIGHTLIFE   Around Rittenhouse Square, you'll find some of the best jazz clubs around, as well as expensive watering holes for politicos and power brokers. In Center City West there are dive bars and Irish pubs.

The city's best jazz can be found at the Park Hyatt Philadelphia at the Bellevue at **Zanzibar Blue**, a nightclub and stage that has hosted the kings and queens of modern jazz, including Nancy Wilson, Shirley Horn, Chuck Mangione, Oleta Adams and Lou Rawls. Jazz is played nightly, and on Sundays during brunch. ~ 200 South Broad Street; 215-732-4500; www.zanzi barblue.com.

The **Merriam Theater** at the University of the Arts dates to 1918, when it opened as the Shubert Theater. Famous actors who have performed on this stage include Helen Hayes, Katharine Hepburn, Laurence Olivier and Ethel Merman. In 2005, Hal Holbrook took the stage as Mark Twain in *Mark Twain Tonight!* This elegant building has been carefully renovated; it is among the city's premier venues for national tours. ~ 250 South Broad Street; 215-732-5446.

The **Kimmel Center for the Performing Arts** is Philadelphia's premier concert venue. For information, see the "Sights" section in this chapter. ~ 260 South Broad Street; 215-893-1999; www. kimmelcenter.org.

The **Wilma Theater** has a long history of avant-garde productions and innovations. Created by artistic directors Blanka and Jiri Zizka, the Wilma has put on plays by European and American playwrights, including dramas by Bertolt Brecht, Tina Howe, Romulus Linney and Donald Drake. The Wilma hosts Danceboom! in January, a three-week series showcasing a bevy of dance troupes. ~ 265 South Broad Street; 215-546-7824; www.wilmatheater.org.

Popular with the after-work crowd and Belgian beer fans, **Monk's Café** has nearly 20 imported beers on tap and a beer "bible" featuring hundreds of bottled ales. Atmosphere is like a European street-front pub—dark, narrow and crowded. Get there after about 7:30 p.m., and it's standing room only. Still, the Belgian beer selection is one of the best on the East Coast, and the food is pretty good as well. Belgian mussels are a popular treat, prepared with, of course, beer, and garlic. The french fries, cut large and served hot, make a nice complement to the tasty libations. ~ 16th and Spruce streets; 215-545-7005; www.monkscafe.com.

The **Black Sheep** is a pricey but authentic Irish pub, serving tap beers and ales alongside the fish and chips and bangers and mash. The setting is in a renovated rowhouse, with a dark, pubby, clubby atmosphere. The beer selection is extensive with more than a dozen imported and domestic beers on tap as well as hundreds of bottles. There's a full complement of Irish whiskeys to enjoy as well. ~ 247 South 17th Street; 215-454-9473.

If you're looking for a neighborhood bar with pints, burgers and friendly patrons, head to **Doobie's**. This after-work hangout is full of regulars who watch television, chat or read while relaxing. They've got Guinness on tap but also serve seasonal beers in bottles. ~ 2201 Lombard Street; 215-546-0316.

◀ HIDDEN

The **Philadelphia Theater Company** stages the works of contemporary American playwrights at the 320-seat Plays & Players Theater. The company is known for its fine performances of American contemporary theater, put on by award-winning actors and directors. By 2007, it will have a new home on the Avenue of the Arts at the Suzanne Roberts Theater. ~ 1714 Delancey Place; 215-735-0630 or 215-985-1400.

The **Roxy** is a movie house for serious filmgoers, featuring thought-provoking, sophisticated films, foreign movies, independents and documentaries. It also shows first run Hollywood films on occasion. ~ 2023 Sansom Street; 215-923-6699.

A venue for concerts, original musicals, cabaret and innovative musical performance artists, the **Prince Music Theater,** in a renovated movie house, aims to nurture innovation in American music by promoting new musicians, musical drama and comedy, and opera. The Prince was formerly known as the American Music Theater Festival. The building also is home to the Sharon Pinkenson Film Project, an organization that shows independent films as well as classics in the Prince's large 450-seat theater as well as in its small "black box" movie lounge. ~ 1412 Chestnut Street; 215-893-1570.

FIVE

Benjamin Franklin Parkway & Fairmount Park

A six-lane boulevard lined with trees and often festooned in flags and lights, the Benjamin Franklin Parkway is Philadelphia's Champs Elysées—a wide thoroughfare that connects the city's museums and galleries to Center City. At one end, seated high on its own Acropolis, is the magnificent Philadelphia Museum of Art, holding one of the world's finest collections of paintings, sculptures and decorative arts. Along the roadway are equally impressive buildings, designed by renowned architects, that house a variety of museum exhibits, as well as breathtaking churches and impressive sculpture gardens. At the other end of the Parkway lie beautiful parks, including the fanciful Logan Circle and John F. Kennedy Plaza.

Initially proposed by architect Paul Cret and others in 1907 as a grand boulevard linking City Hall with the art museum, the parkway was intended to become a center for government, education and the arts. Its design was tweaked in 1917 by architect Jacques Greber to showcase the art museum building and highlight the Swann Fountain and Logan Circle, a roundabout of flowers, trees and sculpture. Today, the parkway rivals Philadelphia's historic district for tourist attractions, with the art museum on one end, and the Franklin Institute, the Rodin Museum and the Natural Academy of Sciences alongside the Free Library of Philadelphia, area gardens and churches.

Changes that are under way or planned for this area include improvements to Logan Circle and the stunning Swann Fountain, designed by Alexander Stirling Calder; expansion of the art museum with renovations to the Perelman Building, a former life insurance building now being remodeled to house the museum's collection of textiles and photography; and relocation of the Barnes Foundation's vast collection of Impressionist art, now housed in Merion, Pennsylvania. (For information on the Barnes Foundation, see Chapter Six.)

The Parkway area has so much to offer that it's important to pace yourself. The Philadelphia Museum of Art alone could swallow a day or two of vacation time. Another site that warrants a long visit is the city's premier science museum, the Franklin Institute, especially if you have children in tow.

Many walking tours of this area of Philadelphia begin at JFK Plaza (covered in Chapter Four), referred to as LOVE Park for its famous sculpture. I prefer to start at the Philadelphia Museum of Art, mainly because parking is ample at the museum and it's free. Plus, the facility is so large, if you get tired while touring it, you can leave and save the rest of the Parkway's sights for another day.

One of the finest museums in the United States, if not the world, the **Philadelphia Museum of Art** was built in 1928. The building, even without its incredible collection of more than 300,000 works, is an objet d'art in itself. A design team led by Julian Francis Abele, the first African American to graduate from the University of Pennsylvania's School of Architecture, produced this neoclassical building, which sits atop "Fair Mount" (as the hill overlooking the Schuylkill River was dubbed in William Penn's time). The Greek-revival structure, with its huge Corinthian columns and blue glazed-tile roof, resembles a colossal temple. As you stand at the top of the steps facing the front (having walked or run up the stairs so immortalized by Sylvester Stallone in the movie *Rocky*), note the ten colorful statues of Greek gods and goddesses on the right. Added in 1933, they mark the first use of multicolored terracotta statues on a building in 2000 years.

The entrance of the museum takes you into a great hall adorned with a magnificent staircase dominated by a statue of Diana, the huntress. The bronze statue, by Augustus Saint-Gaudens, served as a weathervane atop New York's original Madison Square Garden until 1892; it was acquired by the museum in 1932. Along the hallways on the second floor are 17th-century tapestries by Peter Paul Rubens depicting the conversion and life of Constantine. And throughout the museum's 200-plus galleries, you'll find hundreds of famous works, including van Gogh's *Sunflowers* and Poussin's *Birth of Venus*. The museum also houses art from the Renaissance to the 19th century, Asian art, American and European furniture, European armor and weapons, and photographic works. Included in the galleries are entire rooms (a Japanese teahouse and Indian temple) and architectural samples that will transport you to other places and times around the globe. You can pick up a map at the ticket counter and wander at your own pace, or choose to take a guided tour or audio tour. The museum's **Art after Five** program features live ◀ *HIDDEN* jazz or international music and cocktails in a festive setting from 5 p.m. until 8:45 p.m. Friday nights. Sundays are "Pay as You Wish," meaning that from 10 a.m. to 5 p.m., you can set your own admission price. Closed Monday. Admission. ~ 26th Street and the Benjamin Franklin Parkway; 215-763-8100; www.phila museum.org.

In front of the art museum, facing City Hall, is **Eakins Oval**, named for Philadelphia painter Thomas Eakins. At the center of the oval is a fountain monument to George Washington, sculpted by Rudolph Siemering in 1897, a gift from the Society of the Cincinnati of Pennsylvania—descendants of officers who served in the Revolutionary War. The four figures and animals overlooking the pools at the fountain's base represent four great U.S. waterways—the Mississippi, the Potomac, the Delaware and the Hudson.

HIDDEN ►

Strolling toward City Hall from the art museum on the right hand side of the Parkway, you pass a series of **Alexander Calder** sculptures, which will remain on display at this site through 2013. In fact, from this vantage point, you can see the works of three generations of Calders: Alexander Milne Calder's statue of William Penn atop City Hall, his son Alexander Stirling Calder's Swann Fountain, and grandson Alexander Calder's sculptures. The works of the three generations of Calders along the Benjamin Franklin Parkway, including the youngest Calder's "Ghost" mobile inside the art museum, are sometimes irreverently referred to as the "father, son and holy ghost."

The parking lot in front of Eakins Oval could be better maintained, but parking is free and usually abundant.

Step into the Benjamin Franklin Memorial Hall at the **Franklin Institute** and you'll realize how much Philadelphia cherishes its adopted founding father. The great hall, whose architecture was inspired by the Pantheon, features a 20-foot-high marble statue of Franklin that resembles the sculpture of Abraham Lincoln found at the Lincoln Memorial in Washington, DC. Featured in the hall are artifacts belonging to Franklin, as well as biographical information about this ambassador, statesman, inventor and naturalist. Inside the main part of the Institute lies a collection designed for learning and fun. Exhibits explore scientific topics such as electricity, medicine and mechanics. You can pass through a giant heart as if you were a red blood cell, step aboard a steam locomotive, figure out the cause of a train accident, shock a heart patient back to life or watch an operation, or fly a jet trainer in a flight simulator. There's a science studio where you can learn about physics, a space exhibit, sports memorabilia and more. As an added bonus, the Fels Planetarium and the Tuttleman IMAX Theatre within the Institute have shows daily. Admission. ~ 222 North 20th Street; 215-448-1200; sln.fi.edu.

Behind the Franklin Institute is the **Please Touch Museum**, a children's museum geared toward ages one through seven, featuring a host of activities for pre-schoolers. In the Alice's Adventures in Wonderland exhibit, children travel down the rabbit hole to a 2300-square-foot world of Lewis Carroll to play croquet, attend a tea party and try to figure out who stole the tarts. Other activities include "driving" a real Philadelphia SEPTA bus and exploring how boats work in "Move It!" Maurice Sendak fans will enjoy seeing Where the Wild Things Are, with an interactive glimpse into the author's settings. Admission. ~ 210 North 21st Street; 215-963-0667; www.pleasetouchmuseum.org.

Next up is the **Academy of Natural Sciences**, the destination for dinosaur lovers and natural history buffs. Dinosaur Hall displays the skeletons of a tyrannosaurus rex, gigantosaurus and the chicken-sized compsognathus. Activities for children include the Big Dig, where kids can pretend they're archaeologists making the next big discovery, and a time machine they can enter to see

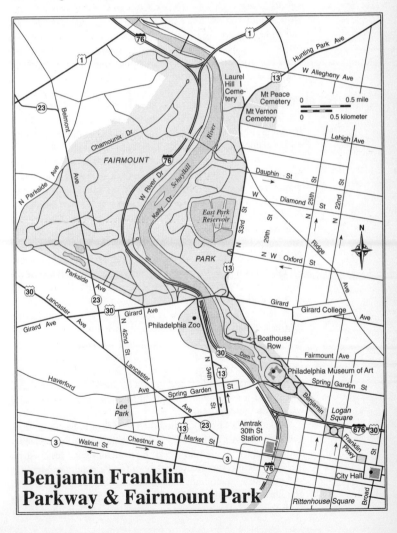

**Benjamin Franklin
Parkway & Fairmount Park**

if they get eaten in the Mesozoic Age. The Academy, which was founded in 1812 and continues as an active research center, also has dioramas showing animals in their natural habitat and a section devoted to extinct and endangered animals. There are live animal exhibits and a nature museum as well, where children learn through games, exhibits and hands-on experience. ~ 1900 Benjamin Franklin Parkway; 215-299-1000; www.acnatsci.org.

Across the street from the Academy is the splendorous **Swann Fountain**, a magical creation of water, statuary and stone built in 1920, designed by Alexander Stirling Calder. In the Swann, water shoots 25 feet high while turtles, frogs and fish spray water from their mouths. Three American Indians, representing the Schuylkill and Delaware rivers and Wissahickon Creek, adorn the center tier. The gardens were revamped in 2005 to better display the works of art, including the Philadelphia Shakespeare Memorial *Hamlet and the Fool*, by Alexander Stirling Calder. (Erected in 1928, it celebrates Philadelphia's Shakespearian scholars and actors, including John and Louisa Lane Drew.) Logan Circle, where the fountain sits, is one of William Penn's original park squares. It has an ominous history, having been used as a burial ground and execution site; the last hanging here occurred in 1823.

Step into the magnificent **Cathedral Basilica of Saints Peter and Paul** and you'll instantly feel like you've landed in Rome. A magnificent Roman Corinthian church, the cathedral is modeled after that city's San Carlo al Corso, and it features the architectural details you'd find in Italy, including the cross-shaped form, massive dome and multiple altars. The brownstone church was constructed between 1846 and 1864. The fresco of St. Peter and St. Paul was painted by Constantine Brumidi, the artist responsible for painting *The Apotheosis of George Washington* in the U.S. Capitol dome. ~ 1723 Race Street; 215-561-1313.

The **Rodin Museum** houses the largest collection of the artist's work outside of Paris. Originally the dream of Philadelphia movie theater magnate Jules Mastbaum, the museum features castings of Rodin's most famous works, including *The Kiss*, *The Burghers of Calais* and *The Gates of Hell*. Mastbaum hired two great French architects, Jacques Greber and Paul Cret, to design the beaux arts–style building and gardens. Closed Monday. ~ 22nd Street and the Benjamin Franklin Parkway; 215-763-8100; www.rodinmuseum.org.

Philadelphia's library, called the **Free Library**, has more than 4 million volumes and an additional 3 million items housed in its central facility. The grand Greek Revival building, designed by the same architectural team that built the Philadelphia Museum of Art, features a monumental entrance hall and grand staircase. The library—denoted by the term "free" because it was open to the public and didn't require membership fees—was founded in

1891. Collections include the Music Library, which is reputed to have librarians who can locate nearly any tune you can hum; the Newspaper Room, which subscribes to more than 130 U.S. and international newspapers; the Fine Art Prints and Photographs collection, with works by Ansel Adams, Dalí and Rembrandt; and the Automobile Collection, one of the largest repositories of automotive literature and history in the world. The Rare Books room (open for tours only at 11 a.m. weekdays) houses a fascinating assortment of books printed before 1501, medieval manuscripts, Sumerian cuneiform tablets and first editions and manuscripts of Charles Dickens, Beatrix Potter, Edgar Allen Poe and others. The library will be undergoing a renovation and expansion for the next several years, but will continue to be open to

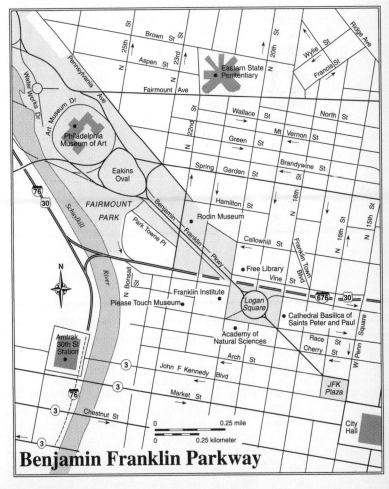

Benjamin Franklin Parkway

the public. ~ 19th Street and Benjamin Franklin Parkway; 215-686-5322; www.library.phila.gov.

A few blocks east of the Benjamin Franklin Parkway is **Eastern State Penitentiary**, the nation's first prison built as a "penitentiary," a place for criminals to learn, through solitude, to be penitent for their crimes. Designed by British architect John Haviland, Eastern State was of a radical design—it resembles a wagon wheel, with cells along the spokes and a central area. A prison until 1971, Eastern State at one time housed Al Capone and bank robber Willie Sutton. The prison became a tourist attraction in 1994, but it is not renovated; instead, its management elected to fix up a few parts and simply prevent the remainder from deteriorating, lending the prison a creepy, sinister atmosphere (so creepy that, in the movie *12 Monkeys*, the penitentiary fills the role of an insane asylum, the home of the character played by Brad Pitt). Guided tours are available, and the audio tour, narrated by actor Steve Buscemi and former inmates, is excellent. Children under seven are not permitted. Closed Monday and Tuesday, and from December through March. Admission. ~ 22nd Street and Fairmount Avenue; 215-236-3300; www.eastern state.org.

FAIRMOUNT PARK   While there seems to be some dispute over which city park is the largest in the United States, Philadelphia's Fairmount Park, at 8700 acres (9200, if you count all the neighborhood parks in the system), is certainly among the biggest. Considered by most Philadelphians to be their backyard playground, Fairmount Park is used for nearly every type of outdoor activity, from running and hiking to cycling, organized sports, rowing, canoeing, kayaking and horseback riding. Fairmount received its name from William Penn's surveyor, Thomas Holmes, who named the green hill overlooking the Schuylkill "Faire Mount" in a 1682 map. Today, the park covers more than six square miles, encompassing 100 miles of trails and bridle paths,

AMERICA'S MOST NOTORIOUS BIRD

Grip, a stuffed raven once owned by Charles Dickens, can be found in the Free Library's Rare Books room. Dickens wrote about a talking raven—Grip—in his mystery *Barnaby Rudge*, written in 1841. Edgar Allen Poe reviewed Barnaby Rudge and apparently was so taken with the idea of a talking raven, he decided to write about one as well. "The Raven," penned in 1845, is Poe's most famous work. Dickens had Grip mounted after the bird died. According to Dickens, Grip's last words were "Halloa, old girl!"

200 acres of waterways, a zoo, botanic gardens, manor homes, playgrounds, boathouses, an amphitheater and a cemetery. Near the art museum, several prominent Fairmount landmarks are within walking distance and easily seen in an afternoon. But to venture farther, you'll need a map and a mode of transportation. Bicycles are available for rent near the boathouses, and Fairmount's windy yet decent road system is perfect for touring by car.

Maps are available of Fairmount Park through the **Fairmount Park Conservancy.** ~ 200 South Broad Street, Suite 700; 215-790-3653; www.fairmountparkconservancy.org.

Near the art museum, the most visible site is the **Fairmount Water Works,** a collection of cute Greek-revival buildings that seem miniature in contrast to the huge art museum that mimics their style. The buildings housed the workings of the city's water system, built in 1801 to provide disease-free water for residents. The water works, once the most sophisticated water system in the world, operated from the early 1800s to 1909. After 1911, when the river became too polluted by industrial development upstream, the water works was transformed into an aquarium. That attraction closed in the 1960s and the water works fell into decay. Today, thanks to a $29 million renovation, the water works are again a scenic attraction—improvements include a restaurant and interpretive signs. ~ 640 Water Works Drive; 215-685-4908; www.fairmountpark.org.

Hidden below the Water Works near the waterline is a little-known statue, park and vista known as the **Schuylkill Esplanade.** ◄ *HIDDEN* Here, you'll find a life-size bronze fisherman and his trusty tackle box perched on a rock overlooking the river. Bronze pavers set in the pathway along the breakwall describe the wildlife in the area, including the river's fish. The bronze statue has been taken away at least twice by floods but has managed to reappear each time without damage. To get to this scenic-yet-noisy space under the bridge, take the concrete steps to the left of the main Water Works building, or walk further to your left until you encounter a Victorian iron spiral staircase.

As you head into Fairmount Park from the art museum, you'll encounter the park's magnificent Azalea Garden on the right and famous Boathouse Row on the left.

The **Azalea Garden** is an incredible conglomeration of more than 2000 azaleas, rhododendrons and evergreen plants that bloom between March and mid-June. Nearby, the fountain in the circular drive is the *Fountain of the Sea Horses*, a replica of the one a the Villa Borghese in Rome. ~ Behind the Philadelphia Museum of Art, between Kelly Drive and Boathouse Row; 215-685-0144.

Boathouse Row is a hub of activity in Fairmount nearly every month of the year. These Victorian buildings house the sculls of

the "Schuylkill Navy," the ten rowing clubs that serve area rowers and university and high school crew teams. Most of the boathouses were built in the 1850s and 1860s and are used by hundreds of clubs, many of which practice on the river nearly
year-round. Philadelphians love their boathouses; at night, they
are outlined in thousands of lights, a picture-perfect sight best
seen from West River Drive, the Schuylkill Expressway or an
HIDDEN ►   Amtrak train. **Lloyd Hall**, a public recreation center and boathouse that opened in 1998, is the newest building on the row,
housing a two-story café, restrooms and a gymnasium. Best of all,
concessionaires run a skate and cycle rental kiosk in good weather.
~ 1 Boathouse Road; 215-685-3936.

The **Ellen Phillips Samuel Memorial Sculpture Garden** has
three terraces of bronze and granite depicting the settlement of
America. Statues include such works as *The
Slave* by Helene Sardeau, *The Poet* by Jose de
Creeft and *The Spirit of Enterprise* by Jacques
Lipchitz. ~ Located on Kelly Drive, south of Girard
Avenue Bridge.

Kelly Drive, once known as
East River Drive, is named
for rower John Kelly, Sr.,
an Olympic gold medal
winner in the 1920 and
1924 games, and father
of actress/princess
Grace Kelly.

The next right after Strawberry Hill Drive is Hunting Park Avenue. Take it to Ridge Road, and you'll find
one of the finest collections of statuary and granite
work in Philadelphia. Sure, **Laurel Hill** is a cemetery, but
how often do you examine the peaceful, if macabre, beauty
of a Gothic burial ground? Laurel Hill is the first U.S. cemetery to
have been designed by an architect. Famous Americans interred
here include Declaration signer Thomas McKean and astronomer
David Rittenhouse. The cemetery contains an incredible selection
of funerary art and house-sized mausoleums. A self-guided tour
is available for a fee. Guided tours are available through the
Friends of Laurel Hill Cemetery. ~ 3822 Ridge Avenue; 215-228-
8200 or 215-228-8817 for the Friends.

When traveling with children, be sure to take them to enjoy
HIDDEN ►   a Philadelphia tradition: the **Giant Slide at Smith Playground**.
The wooden slide, refurbished in 2005, has welcomed Phila-
delphia bottoms for a century and is wide enough to fit ten kids
across. The playground and giant slide are open April through
October. ~ Reservoir Drive; 215-765-4325; www.smithplay
house.org.

Robin Hood Dell is a popular summer venue for jazz, gospel
and blues. The excellent acoustics at this 5800-plus-seat amphitheater are renowned. Past performers include the O'Jays, the
Manhattans and Tito Jackson. Admission. ~ Ridge Avenue and
Huntingdon Drive; 215-685-9717.

Fairmount Park straddles the river, and the western side is
home to such well-known Philadelphia landmarks as the Phila-

delphia Zoo and the Horticultural Center. You'll find other hidden sites here as well.

If you cross the Schuylkill at Strawberry Mansion Drive, head over the river to Belmont Mansion Drive and turn south, toward the zoo, to reach the **Belmont Plateau**, a rise 243 feet above the river that offers a spectacular view of the Philadelphia skyline four miles away.

Heading on down the hill, you will reach the **Horticultural Center**, a 22-acre arboretum and gardens developed originally for the Centennial Exposition in 1876. The current exhibition hall and greenhouse were built for the 1976 Bicentennial celebration on the site of 1876 gardens. Many of the trees featured in the Centennial Arboretum date to 1876. The most popular attraction in this part of the park is the Japanese House, a building originally displayed from 1954 to 1958 at the Metropolitan Museum of Art. The Japanese House, called Shofuso, is a replica of a 17th-century scholar's house. Visitors may walk barefoot on the tatami floors and enjoy the gardens with koi ponds. Ikibana and origami demonstrations often are conducted here, as are tea ceremonies in the adjacent tea house; phone for schedules.

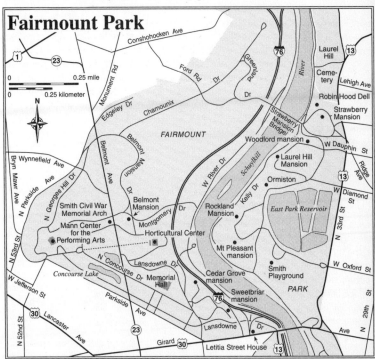

Fairmount Park

Admission. ~ North Horticultural Drive; 215-878-5097; www.shofuso.com.

On Belmont Avenue, you'll pass **Memorial Hall**, built for the Centennial Exposition in 1876 as an exhibit hall. It is one of two buildings from the fair that are still standing; the other is the smaller **Ohio House**, also on Belmont Avenue.

The **Philadelphia Zoo** is the nation's oldest, having opened in 1874 as a Victorian zoological garden, where the landscaping was as important as the animals (some of the original trees survive today). The 42-acre zoo is home to more than 1600 animals, most them in a fairly compact area, making this an ideal trip for families with small children. The zoo has many attractions and fine exhibits. The African Plains feature two open exhibits where antelopes and zebras live side-by-side while, across the way, gazelles and antelopes graze as large African birds strut among them. This section also is home to cheetahs and rhinoceros. The PECO Primate Preserve is a 2.5-acre home for orangutans, gorillas, lemurs and other primates. The Dodge Rare Animal Conservation Center houses several species and educates the public on the importance of their survival to the world. Naked mole rats—the favorite rodent of nearly every little boy I know—can be located here in all their pink, squirmy, ugly glory. Activities in the summer months, include an opportunity to feed Australian lorakeets—a messy yet fun experience—and the chance to take a 15-minute ride in a tethered hot-air balloon. Consider visiting the zoo if you are in Philadelphia in the winter; ten buildings are heated and the animals are more active. Admission. ~ 34th Street and Girard Avenue; 215-243-1100; www.philadelphiazoo.org.

The **Smith Civil War Memorial Arch** is a monument to Pennsylvania's Union generals and includes 14 statues done by 12

sights

AUTHOR FAVORITE

In the northwest part of Fairmount Park, a gravel road runs through one of the prettiest sections of Philadelphia, a wooded gorge carved out by the Wissahickon Creek. **Forbidden Drive**, popular with hikers, mountain bikers and equestrians, meanders more than five miles along the Wissahickon through deciduous forests and past historic ruins and scenic outcrops of granite and blue stone. Two historic buildings occupy this section of the park, as does the only wooden covered bridge remaining in a U.S. city. ~ To reach this section, follow the Schuylkill Expressway west to Exit 32. Take Lincoln Drive to Allen's Lane and turn right. Turn left on Germantown Avenue, take a left at Springfield Avenue and follow to the end.

different artists. Dominating the memorial are likenesses of General George Meade and Major General John F. Reynolds. Other figures include Major General Winfield Scott Hancock and General George McClellan. Oddly, sculptors Alexander Stirling Calder and Daniel Chester French also included a statue of a man wearing a work apron—Richard Smith, the memorial's benefactor—among the great generals of the war.

A war memorial hardly seems like a place for a romantic date, but for many Philadelphians, the Arch is just that, because of the stone benches at the arch's base. The seats are **"whispering benches."** If you sit on one end and have another person sit on the other, you can turn toward the stone wall and whisper; the person on the other end will clearly hear what you say, including "I love you." ~ North Concourse Drive.

◄ *HIDDEN*

Due to the scant amount of lodgings and restaurants near the art museum and Fairmount Park, most visitors to this portion of Philadelphia stay in Center City or elsewhere. However, there are a handful here, including what many consider to be the city's finest hotel, the Four Seasons.

LODGING

On the Parkway, across from Logan Circle, is the **Four Seasons Philadelphia**, a luxurious hotel of incredible opulence and finery. Distinguished for its exemplary service, the the Philadelphia Four Seasons hotel has a reputation as one of country's best. The exterior architecture is less than impressive—a square granite building that looks more like a government building than a four-star hotel—but the interior is sumptuous and elegant, with marble flooring, beautiful rugs, fine draperies and rich upholstery. Rooms are done in relaxing neutrals, but fabrics, bedding, carpeting, artwork and beautiful furnishings combine for a rich, elegant atmosphere. Guest rooms have nearly every amenity you could desire in a hotel room, including mini-bars, twice daily maid service, on-demand video games and comfortable robes. The hotel features a spa and beautiful indoor pool, set in palms and tropical plants. The top-rated Fountain Restaurant is located here. ~ 1 Logan Square; 215-963-1500; www.fourseasons.com/philadelphia. ULTRA-DELUXE.

It's a short walk from the art museum to the **Best Western Center City**, at the edge of Fairmount Park. This traditional low-rise motel has an outdoor swimming pool, fitness center, restaurant and guest laundry. Rooms are decorated in florals and navy, and amenities include hairdryers, ironing boards, coffeemakers and high-speed internet. This hotel is a good buy for those on a budget—parking is free and the hotel is within walking distance of the Phlash trolley, SEPTA buses and a train station. ~ 501 North 22nd Street; 215-568-8300; www.bestwestern.com. MODERATE.

Text continued on page 130.

Mansions of Fairmount Park

Fairmount Park has hundreds of buildings and manor homes that are unoccupied, rented to private organizations or open for public tours. While some of the mansions aren't open to the public, several of these are worth a drive-by. The following drive can be made in and hour without stops. You'll spend more time if you tour some of the homes that welcome visitors.

LEMON HILL   From Boathouse Row on Kelly Drive, turn right off Kelly on to Lemon Hill Drive and follow the road to stately Lemon Hill, once home to wealthy merchant Henry Pratt. The front of the 1880 Federal-style house features large Palladian windows while the rear has a jutting oval to accommodate oval parlors with curved doors and fireplaces. Closed Monday and Tuesday, and from mid-December through March. Admission. ~ Sedgely and Lemon Hill drives; 215-232-4337.

MOUNT PLEASANT   Turn around and return to Kelly Drive. At Kelly Drive, turn right and go under a stone bridge. Take a right at the statue of Ulysses S. Grant, onto Fountain Green Drive. Turn left onto Mount Pleasant Drive to reach Mount Pleasant, a Georgian mansion built in the 1770s by Scottish sea captain John McPherson. It was purchased by Benedict Arnold for his wife-to-be Peggy Shippen, but the couple never spent time here because they were forced to flee the country after Arnold's traitorous actions. Closed for renovations.

ROCKLAND MANSION   Continue on Mount Pleasant Drive and on your left will be Rockland Mansion, an 1801 Federal villa featuring a beautiful elliptical staircase and grand back porch. It has been painstakingly restored for the past four years and is now the home of the Psychoanalytic Center of Philadelphia. Closed to the public.

ORMISTON   At the "T," turn left onto Reservoir Drive. On your left is Ormiston, a lovely brick Federal-style manor home with a beautiful front portico. The land was owned by Tory Joseph Galloway, who served as provost marshal during the British occupation of Philadelphia during the Revolution. It was built in 1798 by a lawyer, Edward Burd, and is named for a country home near Edinburgh, Scotland. Numerous hiking trails wind around Ormiston.

LAUREL HILL MANSION   After passing Ormiston, take a left on Randolph and go to Laurel Hill Mansion. This lovely yellow Georgian country home, built in 1767, was owned by a British loyalist, Rebecca Rawle, and later purchased by Dr. Philip Syngh Physick, the father of American surgery. It is open for tours. Admission. ~ 7201 North Randolph Drive; 215-235-1776.

WOODFORD   North Randolph becomes Edgely, and then turns into Dauphin after Reservoir Drive. Stay on Dauphin until you reach Greenland Drive, a side street that comes before you reach 33rd. Turn left at Woodford manor. This Georgian-style building houses a large collection of antiques and decorative arts. Closed Monday and Tuesday. Admission. ~ 2450 Strawberry Mansion Bridge Drive; 215-228-8364.

STRAWBERRY MANSION   Turn right onto Strawberry Mansion Drive and continue to Strawberry Mansion. The largest home in Fairmount Park, it was built in 1790 and renovated with additions during the 1820s. Its interior reflects the periods in which its owners lived and collected antiques; inside you'll find examples of Federal, Regency and Empire furniture. The attic contains antique toys and a fine doll collection. Closed for restoration. ~ 2450 Strawberry Mansion Bridge Drive; 215-228-8364.

BELMONT MANSION   Follow the signs to Strawberry Mansion Bridge and cross the Schuylkill. Stay on that road, going left at the fork, until you reach Chamounix, and turn left. Stay on this road until you reach Belmont Mansion Drive, which leads to Belmont Mansion. Constructed in the 1700s, it contains some of the nation's oldest original plaster ceilings and incredible views of the city over Belmont Plateau. Franklin, Washington, Jefferson and Madison all enjoyed the breathtaking vista from this home.

CEDAR GROVE   Continue south to Horticultural Drive. Turn left. Follow the road to Landsdowne Drive. Turn left again. Turn left on Sweetbriar and left again on Cedar Grove Drive to Cedar Grove. This 1748 mansion sports a gambrel roof, an unusual feature among the homes in Fairmount. This house, which nowadays would be considered a Dutch Colonial, was moved to its present spot stone-by-stone in the 1930s from the Frankford neighborhood of Philadelphia. Closed Monday. Admission. ~ 1 Cedar Grove Drive; 215-878-2123.

SWEETBRIAR   Backtrack to Sweetbriar Drive and turn left to reach the mansion. Sweetbriar is an elegant neoclassical villa dating to 1797. It was the residence of Samuel Breck, a developer who contributed to the founding of Philadelphia's public school system. Breck enjoyed entertaining; guests at Sweetbriar included the Marquis de Lafayette. Closed for restoration. ~ 1 Sweetbriar Drive; 215-222-1333.

LETITIA STREET HOUSE   After you pass Sweetbriar, continue south on Landsdowne until you reach Girard Avenue. Turn right on Girard and head to 3400 to see a tucked-away, small brick townhouse that looks as if it had been plucked from Philadelphia's wharves and dropped in the country. In fact, that's exactly what happened to the Letitia Street House. Built in 1715 near 2nd and Chestnut streets, the tiny home was located on land owned by William Penn's daughter, Letitia. It was relocated to Fairmount Park in 1883. ~ 3400 Girard Avenue.

Just a block off Logan Square, the **Wyndham Franklin Plaza** has more than 750 rooms in a full-service, highrise setting. This hotel is popular with business travelers, but families will enjoy the hotel's extras as well, including the indoor pool, racquetball courts and in-room movies. Rooms have been recently renovated in neutral tones and light wood furniture. Business travelers who must work during their stay will appreciate the large desks and unbeatably comfortable Herman Miller Aeron chairs. The hotel has two restaurants, including the clubby steak house Shula's, with its menus painted on footballs signed by the Miami Dolphins' Super Bowl–winning coach. ~ 17th and Race streets; 215-448-2000; www.wyndham.com. MODERATE TO DELUXE.

An all-suites hotel favored by business travelers, the **Hotel Windsor** was once an apartment complex. The hotel has 110 studio and one-bedroom suites, with fully equipped kitchens, full-size desks, cable television, hairdryers, ironing boards and high-speed internet. Rooms are decorated in traditional American style, with comfortable plaid overstuffed chairs, Chippendale dining sets and cherry desks. Amenities include a 24-hour fitness center and rooftop pool in season. Two restaurants are on location, and the hotel is two blocks from Logan Circle. ~ 1700 Benjamin Franklin Parkway; 215-981-5678, 877-784-8379; www.windsor hotel.com. ULTRA-DELUXE.

HIDDEN ▶

There's always someone interesting hanging around the front porch of the **Chamounix Mansion**, a hostel that caters to students, international travelers and families. The manor home, built in 1799, has been operating as a hostel since 1964. Accommodations are in air-conditioned dormitory rooms, although some smaller rooms are available for families and couples. Guests can bring their own linens and towels or rent on-site; blankets and pillows are provided gratis. Amenities include two common rooms filled with antiques, a television lounge, internet kiosk, full kitchen and recreation rooms. The hostel also has a collection of bikes for use by guests. For adventurous travelers on a budget, this is a place to consider, as it costs less than $20 a night. ~ 3250 Chamounix Drive; 215-878-3676, 800-379-0017; www.phila hostel.org. BUDGET.

DINING

The choice of restaurants in this part of the city is limited. But there are a number of cafés and concession stands in museums and in the park.

The Philadelphia Museum of Art offers several dining options, including a full-service restaurant, a café and a balcony café that is open weekends only. The **Art Museum Restaurant** is tucked in the museum's west wing, overlooking the Schuylkill River. White tablecloths and sparkling dinnerware provide neutral table settings in a room adorned with original art. The restaurant, which is known for tailoring its menu according to the latest exhibit, features basic American fare tweaked to resemble cuisine from artists' homelands. The museum restaurant stays fairly busy; reservations are recommended. The restaurant sometimes stages special events, including brunch and wine tastings. ~ 26th Street and the Benjamin Franklin Parkway; 215-684-7990. MODERATE.

The **Art Museum Café** and the **Balcony Café**, which is open on weekends, offer lighter fare. The former has a comprehensive menu, including a salad bar, hot entrées, soups and sandwiches, while the latter features sandwiches and pastries in the spectacular setting that overlooks the West Entrance Hall. ~ 26th Street and the Benjamin Franklin Parkway; 215-684-7990. MODERATE.

> The World's Fair was held as the Centennial Exhibition of 1876 in West Fairmount Park. Among the attractions at the fair were the unveiling of Alexander Graham Bell's telephone and Thomas Edison's telegraph.

The **Fountain Restaurant** at the Four Seasons consistently tops the lists of Philadelphia's best restaurants; it has been rated by Zagat as having the best food and decor in the city. The setting is romantic: dark paneled walls and exquisitely set tables overlooking Logan Circle and the beautiful Swann Fountain. Chef Martin Hamann's "spontaneous taste" menu is the top order, a six-course meal of savory and sweet offerings. Surprises on the taste menu have included sauteed red mullet and prosciutto-wrapped figs. Entrées include a trio of Maine lobster dishes—a sautéed tail with celery root and capers; lobster ravioli with truffle in a lemon and cognac sauce, and a ragout with shiitakes, snow peas and ginger. Desserts are fanciful and rich. ~ 1 Logan Square; 215-963-1500; www.fourseasons.com/philadelphia. ULTRA-DELUXE.

The cash-only **Figs** is within walking distance of the art museum and is a popular local spot for Mediterranean fare. Chef Mustapha Rouissiya is Moroccan, and his menu reflects his heritage, rich with seafood, cheeses, olives and couscous. The hummus and applewood smoked–salmon appetizer mixes two delightful tastes and is served with olives and red onions. The pan-seared tuna is served with rock shrimp risotto and accompanied by an unusual banana-coconut curry sauce—ingredients I wouldn't have mixed, but it works for an unusually zippy, sweet meal. ~ 2501 Meredith Street; 215-978-8440. DELUXE.

◄ HIDDEN

The **Valley Green Inn** is a Philadelphia treasure, a 150-year-old roadhouse beside a lovely creek nestled in Fairmount Park's Wissahickon Valley. Serving both traditional and new American fare, Valley Green is popular with those using the park, including cyclists, hikers, horseback riders and day-trippers seeking a relaxing, delicious meal in a lovely setting. Diners can hear horses clip-clop past the windows and enjoy the sounds of the nearby creek. Menus change seasonally. Autumn offerings include the

Colonel's Drunken Catfish, a flavorful cornmeal-encrusted pan-fried catfish served with a sweet bourbon and pecan sauce, and a pork chop coated in garlic and herb–sourdough pretzel crumbs. Sunday brunch is a big draw, as are the Inn's holiday spreads, available on major days except Christmas. Call for reservations and call again if it snows—sometimes the road is impassible and the inn is closed. ~ Valley Green Road at Wissahickon; 215-247-1730; www.valleygreeninn.com. DELUXE.

NIGHTLIFE Cramped, cozy but always fun, **Mace's Crossing** is a hangout for conventioneers and former rowers who seek libations after cheering their alma maters on the Schuylkill. Mace's is homey—the type of bar you'd like to be your neighborhood watering hole. The owner refused to sell when developers built offices and high-rises around it, which is why this brick building is so distinctive among the towers of the commercial district. Mace's has five beers on tap and an extensive bar, including a good selection of vodkas. ~ 1714 Cherry Street; 215-564-5203.

The **Bishop's Collar** is a favorite neighborhood bar that's not far from the art museum. It's a narrow, dark pub that has live music some nights. It gets its name from the white head on a perfectly poured pint of Guinness. This is a great hangout where the bar food is pretty good and the servers friendly. ~ 2349 Fairmount Avenue; 215-765-1616.

All lawn seats at the **Mann Center for the Performing Arts** used to be free, and for some performances they still are. Nonetheless, this amphitheatre is one of the neatest places in Philadelphia to enjoy a concert. Built as the summer home for the Philadelphia Orchestra, the amphitheatre now stages performances of contemporary artists, musical theater, drama, jazz and more May through September. Those with lawn tickets can spread out their blankets and bring a picnic, or purchase food at various kiosks. ~ 5201 Parkside Avenue, West Fairmount Park; 215-878-7707; www.manncenter.org.

SIX

Philadelphia's Neighborhoods

Philadelphia is a cluster of neighborhoods, a microcosm of the country with nearly every socioeconomic group and ethnicity represented. There are more than 150 neighborhoods, and residents closely identify with these communities. Ask a Philadelphian where he's from and he'll tell you "Philly," but then he'll probably clarify that he's from South Philly, North Philly, Germantown, Passyunk, Logan, Roxborough, Eastwick or elsewhere. In Philadelphia's neighborhoods, you'll meet blue-collar workers, young families, professionals and blue-haired ladies who wear hats and gloves. Don't be surprised if they show an interest in you and your origins; Philadelphians tend to stay close to home, growing up and remaining in the neighborhoods. Many never leave Pennsylvania or venture farther than the Jersey shore.

In South Philadelphia's Italian Market, you're as likely to haggle with a Vietnamese merchant as you are a beefy Italian butcher. In Southwark, south of Society Hill, you'll encounter young professionals who have renovated the city's oldest waterfront neighborhoods. Across the Schuylkill in University City, you'll encounter hordes of students heading to class or enjoying themselves at busy restaurants and pubs. In Chestnut Hill and on the Main Line, you'll find the vestiges of high society, tucked neatly in grand estates behind stone walls and manicured lawns.

South Philadelphia

South of South Street is South Philadelphia, a sprawling neighborhood that includes the communities of Southwark, Queen Village, Bella Vista and the Italian Market. Portions of South Philadelphia contain the city's oldest sections, having been settled by Swedes starting in the 1640s. Southwark received its name in 1762 by city decree; it was named for a similar area in London. The name Queen Village, a part of Southwark, relates the area's Swedish heritage, honoring Queen Christina, who actively promoted the settlement. Immigrants who moved to this area included Irish, German, English and Dutch, many of whom worked in the shipbuilding and shipping industry. While it is not as well-known as Society Hill, Queen Village has similarly charming streets, and boasts some of the city's oldest houses. Although some were destroyed when Route 95 was built through the city in the early 1960s, many homes have been snatched up and renovated by urban professionals. Front Street, the first street in Philadelphia, was among the roadways that were spared, a hidden, quaint byway worth touring.

South Philadelphia has produced a number of famous Americans, and not surprisingly, most are of Italian descent, including actor and crooner Mario Lanza, singer Bobby Rydell, and his actor/singer cohorts Frankie Avalon and Fabian. Other famous South Philadelphians include Chubby Checker (raised, but not born there); artist Man Ray; and Larry Fine of the Three Stooges.

SIGHTS   Head south of South Street along 4th Street and you'll find **Fabric Row**, the nation's oldest garment district with more than 20 shops selling upholstery and clothing fabric, notions, beads, ribbons and baubles. Even those who don't sew can appreciate the rich textures of the textiles available here, and there's plenty of inspiration for fashionistas and home decorators. ~ Located on South 4th Street between South and Catherine streets.

To view the oldest homes in the city, head over to **2nd Street**, also called Two Street by old-timers and residents. Many of the small homes in this section date to the mid-1700s, and the area's oldest courtyard, **Workman Place**, is located between Pemberton, Fitzwater, Front and 2nd streets (it now has fallen into private hands, but you can still sneak a peak). **Kenilworth Street** has the oldest homes, dating to the 1740s. This thoroughfare was developed by the Shippen family, whose members included Philadelphia's second mayor and Peggy Shippen, the wife of Benedict Arnold. ~ Along Front and 2nd streets between Bainbridge and Christian streets.

For a lovely sampling of early Colonial architecture, meander along **Monroe, Catharine, Hancock and Queen streets**—Hancock is a tiny cobblestone alley of quaint rowhouses, including two remarkable clapboard homes built in the mid-18th century by a sea captain. On Queen Street, you'll find a distinctive Victorian-era firehouse that has found new life as a rowhouse; it's marked by large gas lanterns and the 1996 sculpture **The Firefighter**, by Colorado artist Joseph Kinkel. ~ Queen Street between Front and 2nd streets.

The **door knocker** at 109 Queen Street in Queen Village is particularly unusual and somewhat creepy.

At Front and Carpenter streets, you'll encounter a neighborhood landmark, the **Shot Tower**. Built in 1808 to produce hunting shot, this is just one of eight shot towers left in the United States. Later, it was used to manufacture military ammunition for the War of 1812 and continued to produce lead shot until 1903.

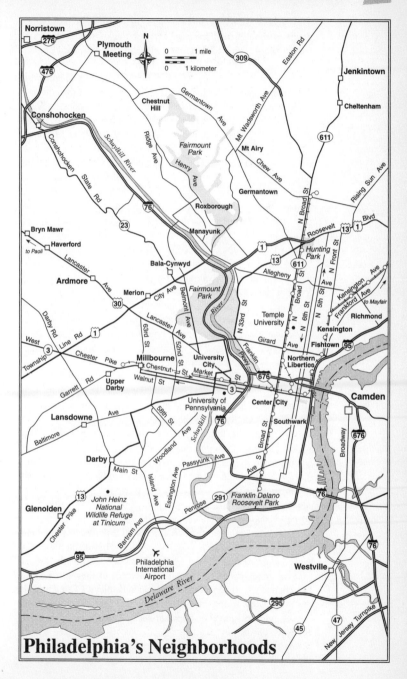

Philadelphia's Neighborhoods

The ammunition production was ingenious: manufacturers dropped molten lead from the top of the towers into vats of water below; the lead droplets cooled as they fell, forming perfect orbs. ~ Front and Carpenter streets.

New Orleans has its Mardi Gras krewes; Philadelphia has Mummers, who celebrate New Year's Day in one of the country's liveliest, most colorful parades. The **Mummers Museum** on Washington Avenue highlights this unique Philadelphia tradition, showing costumes, films and photos of the city's 30-plus Mummers clubs. The city's Mummer tradition can be traced to its early settlers: Swedes visited neighbors at Christmas, ringing bells and pounding pots to frighten evil spirits; the British masqueraded silently ("mum's the word") door-to-door in powder and paint around New Year's Day; Irish immigrants enjoyed celebrating the new year by making merry noise; and the Italians added costumes to the mix. The first official Philadelphia Mummers Parade was held in 1901, although the Mummers had been gathering on New Year's Day since 1876. At the museum, you can attempt to strut like a Mummer to their anthem "Oh, Dem Golden Slippers." Visitors also can create their own master-jam of Mummer music using a push-button medley of banjos, brass and xylophones. During the summer, the museum hosts free outdoor concerts on Tuesday evenings, weather permitting. Closed Monday, and closed Sunday in July and August. Admission. ~ 1100 South 2nd Street; 215-336-3050; www.riverfrontmummers.com.

South Philadelphia is most famous for its **Italian Market**, a stretch of five blocks on 9th Street marked by neighborhood stores, street carts and sidewalk tables loaded with seasonal produce, fresh-caught fish, meats, game and cheeses. Many visitors still associate the Italian Market with the movie *Rocky*, even though Sylvester Stallone made his famous jog along 9th Street 30 years ago. (Of course, 9th Street reappeared in *Rocky II* and *Rocky III*—it would be impossible to film a movie about an Italian in Philadelphia without featuring this section of the city.) Stallone also spent some time in the Italian Market for the filming of *Rocky Balboa*, the sixth movie in the series.

Bring your hungry stomach and wallet if you're heading here, and prepare to purchase your take-home gifts in the market as well. Consider making the market your last stop in the city so you can stock up on its incredible selection of meats, fresh pastas, cheeses, fruits, vegetables, seafood and spices. Closed Sunday and Monday. ~ Along 9th Street between Wharton and Fitzwater streets, with most of the shops between Washington Avenue and Fitzwater Street.

At the end of the Italian Market, where 9th Street intersects Passyunk Avenue is Philadelphia's cheesesteak "showdown." On this street corner, **Pat's King of Steaks** faces **Geno's Steaks**, with each restaurant competing for cholesterol-craving customers around-the-clock. Some locals will say the best cheesesteaks aren't found here, but the dueling restaurants are a Philadelphia must-see, both for the sandwiches and the archetypical South Philly families who run them. ~ Pat's: 1237 East Passyunk Avenue; 215-468-1546. Geno's: 1219 South 9th Street; 215-389-0659.

The **Mario Lanza Museum** pays tribute to the famous tenor and movie star, born just four blocks east of the museum at 634 Christian Street. Lanza, whose real name was Alfredo Arnold Cocozza, grew up in South Philly listening to opera records owned by his parents, immigrants Antonio Cocozza and Maria Lanza Cocozza. He took voice lessons and eventually landed auditions, propelling him toward stardom. Although scorned by some critics, many consider Lanza to have been one of the finest vocalists of the 20th century and he remains popular with countless fans

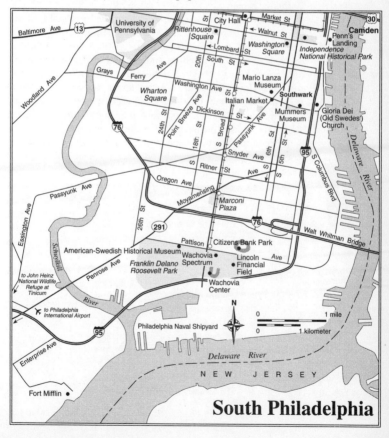

South Philadelphia

today. Lanza died in 1959 in Rome, Italy, at the age of 38. The museum contains photos, memorabilia and movie clips, and its gift shop carries the widest selection of Lanza CDs around. Closed Sunday. ~ 712 Montrose Street; 215-238-9691; www. mario-lanza-institute.org.

HIDDEN ▶ Since 1898, more than a half-million Philadelphians have taken courses at the **Samuel S. Fleisher Art Memorial**, the nation's oldest tuition-free community arts school. Founded as the Graphic Arts Sketch Club, the school has molded such students as Frank Gasparro (the 10th Chief Engraver of the United States) and renowned architect Louis I. Kahn. The Memorial is housed in a former boys school, a Romanesque-revival structure, and a former church. The church structure, called the Sanctuary, continues to be used for art classes and as a performance space. The Fleisher, administered by the Philadelphia Museum of Art, holds several art shows each year in its galleries. Closed Sunday. ~ 719 Catherine Street; 215-922-3456 ext. 318.

In the southernmost reaches of South Philly, you'll find the city's sports arenas—the Wachovia Center, the Spectrum, Lincoln Financial Field and Citizens Bank Park. The area around the stadiums is devoid of attractions and restaurants, but it is home to **HIDDEN ▶** a nine-foot bronze **Rocky**, a statue that once graced the steps of the Philadelphia Museum of Art. The sculpture, Rocky Balboa in boxing shorts with hands raised in victory, was commissioned by Sylvester Stallone in 1982 to commemorate the making of *Rocky III*; he later bequeathed it to the city. It sits near the north entrance of the Wachovia Spectrum. Although Stallone is a New Yorker, it seems he'll forever be considered one of Philadelphia's most famous sons. ~ Broad Street and Pattison Avenue.

AUTHOR FAVORITE

Philadelphia's oldest church, **Gloria Dei** (also called Old Swedes' Church) is of Flemish bond construction, a simple square church that has changed little since it was built. The congregation, founded by Swedish settlers, originated in 1642; the current structure was erected in 1698. The interior is clad in wainscoting and double-hung windows, which were added later. Artifacts here include an 18th-century baptismal font as well as models of the ships that carried the Swedes to the New World, the *Key of Kalmar* and *Flying Griffin*. The sacristy holds Queen Christina's 1608 Bible, and there are historical plaques throughout, including one that pays tribute to singer Jenny Lind, who performed at Old Swedes' in 1851, and another that honors Betsy Ross, who married her second husband, Joseph Ashbourn, at Gloria Dei in 1777. The church is an active Episcopal congregation. ~ 916 Swanson Street; 215-389-1513; www.nps.gov/glde.

Near the stadiums, tucked away in Franklin Delano Roosevelt Park, is the **American-Swedish Historical Museum**, a celebration of the city's first settlers. Modeled after a 17th-century Swedish manor, this stunning museum houses numerous artifacts that belonged to the Swedish colonists, including furniture, silver and handmade dolls. The museum also pays tribute to famous Swedish Americans, including singer Jenny Lind, author Carl Sandberg and John Ericsson, who designed the first ironclad ship, the USS *Monitor*. Closed Monday. Admission. ~ 1900 Pattison Avenue; 215-389-1776; www.americanswedish.org.

◄ HIDDEN

Along the waterfront, you'll see the former **Philadelphia Naval Shipyard**, a base closed by the Defense Department in 1996. This shipyard continues to function as a civilian enterprise, producing commercial vessels under an agreement between the city and Aker American Shipping. The yard is closed to the public, but its mothballed Navy fleet—dwindled down to a few frigates—can be seen from side roads and Route 95. ~ 5100 South Broad Street.

South of the shipyard, near the airport, lies **Fort Mifflin**, a favorite site for area history buffs for its important role in both the Revolutionary and Civil wars. Construction of this fort began in 1771 by the British; later, when conflict arose between the British and the colonies, the Continental Congress authorized construction of a fort across the way, and eventually both became American defenses. Fort Mifflin was the sight of a siege conducted by the British in October 1777 to rout out all Continental troops from the area. Less than 90 years later, the fort housed Confederate prisoners of war and Union wrongdoers. Much here is restored; history buffs will enjoy the cannons, soldiers' quarters, offices and defenses. Open Wednesday through Sunday from May through November. Admission. ~ Fort Mifflin Road; 215-685-4167; www.fortmifflin.com.

◄ HIDDEN

Some of southeastern Pennsylvania's prettiest coastal wetlands have been preserved at the **John Heinz National Wildlife Refuge at Tinicum**, south of the city near the airport. It was named for the late Senator John Heinz, who worked tirelessly to preserve the marsh. An excellent spot for bird-watching, the refuge consists of roughly 200 acres of freshwater tidal wetlands. Wildlife found here include nearly 300 species of birds, fox, deer, muskrat and the endangered red-bellied turtle and southern leopard frog. The informative Cusano Environmental Education Center offers exhibits on the marsh, watersheds and wetlands. ~ 8601 Lindbergh Boulevard; 215-365-3118; heinz.fws.gov.

Most visitors to South Philly stay elsewhere since this is mostly a residential neighborhood with few lodging options. However, the **Shippen Way Inn** just off South Street continues to draw clients for its convenience to the historic areas and reasonable

LODGING

While discussing a recent visit to Philadelphia, tourist Mary Withers from Roanoke, Virginia, described the city as "a little rough." If she only knew. Philadelphia is tough—and not simply because of its blue-collar roots. The city has been a hotbed of organized crime since the early 1900s, with the Mafia dominating the city's crime scene in South Philadelphia and southern New Jersey (although the 1990s saw an increased presence of Russian and Polish mobsters in north Philadelphia as well).

The Italian Mafia rose to power in the city during Prohibition, and Philadelphia's mobsters, closely linked with New York's crime families, have been involved in gambling, racketeering, drug trafficking and other heinous activities. Their history is complex and intriguing; during the early 1980s, there was a shakeup among warring factions, resulting in an all-out war between the groups. In the 1990s, numerous wiseguys turned informants, resulting in arrests and crackdowns. Mob hits continue to occur in Philadelphia each year, although in the words of veteran *Philadelphia Inquirer* reporter George Anastasia, "the business is bankrupt." Still, the city bears the scars of its violent past, and this nine-mile tour takes you through neighborhoods that have witnessed some of the city's darkest moments.

6TH AND CATHERINE STREETS   Michael Ciancaglini and his best friend Joey Merlino were walking near this intersection on August 5, 1993, when rivals attacked. Ciancaglini, 33, was shot in the chest and killed, Merlino was wounded by gunmen from the Stanfa family.

900 BLOCK OF CATHERINE STREET   Continue down Catherine Street to the 900 block. Italian Market florist and mob associate "Frankie Flowers" D'Alfonso, 55, was shot five times on July 23, 1985, as he stopped to light a cigarette while walking down this sidewalk.

TAKE A BREAK   For a bite to eat, head west on Catherine and turn left on 10th Street. At Wharton Street, cut east to 9th Street, where you'll see Pat's King of Steaks and Geno's Steaks (page 143), cheesesteak champs.

934 SNYDER AVENUE   Return to 10th Street and turn left to continue the tour. At Snyder Avenue, make a left. Angelo Bruno, a longtime boss still

prices. Furnished with antiques and reproductions, this set of Colonial rowhouses is within walking distance to Society Hill, Penn's Landing, shopping and South Philly. Some rooms feature pencil-post beds and fireplaces, and the common areas have cozy fireplaces and hand-hewn timbered ceilings. A hearty continental breakfast is served each morning, to be eaten in the dining room or with the squirrels on the small patio in nice weather. The remembered as the "Gentle Don," was assassinated on March 21, 1980, in his car outside his home after eating dinner at Cous' Little Italy on South 11th Street. His death began a chapter of extreme violence in Philadelphia's mob history.

MELROSE DINER, 1501 SNYDER AVENUE   Head west on Snyder Avenue and cross Broad Street. Fankie Baldino, 51, was shot ten times here on September 17, 1993, for his allegiance to Mob boss Joey Merlino during a battle over trade with boss John Stanfa.

NORTH OF THE STADIUMS   Backtrack to Broad Street and head south on Broad. Turn left on Packer Avenue and right on South Juniper Street; drive until you get to Curtin Street. Frank "Chickie" Narducci, 49, was shot ten times after coming home from a court date for a racketeering charge on January 7, 1982.

2117 PORTER STREET   Head west on Curtin Street to Broad, then turn left on Broad. Turn left on West Shunk Street and another left on Carlisle Street. Turn right on West Oregon Avenue. Make a right on 22nd Street and a right on West Porter Street. Here, Bruce Springsteen's song "Atlantic City" immortalized the grisly death of Philip "Chicken Man" Testa, 56, who was killed March 15, 1981, when a nail bomb exploded on his front porch. It's thought that Nicky Scarfo ordered the hit so he could take over operations, starting an era of intimidation, murder and mayhem among organized crime factions from New York, Atlantic City and Philadelphia.

SCHUYLKILL EXPRESSWAY WEST   Return to Oregon Avenue and head west. Turn right on West Passyunk Avenue and follow signs for the Schuylkill Expressway. Head east or west, depending on your next destination after the tour. The year 1993 was busy in Philadelphia for mob hits or attempts. In one blatant attack, boss John Stanfa and Joseph Stanfa were ambushed in rush-hour traffic on the Schuylkill. The younger Stanfa, 23, was shot in the face but lived. Police found an abandoned van at 29th and Mifflin Streets that was used in the attack.

For more information on Philadelphia's sordid crime history, check out books by George Anastasia, an award-winning reporter who has covered Philadelphia's Mafia for nearly 20 years.

common fridge, which holds cheese and wine for evening snacks, is a terrific bonus, especially after a long day of walking or driving. ~ 418 Bainbridge Street; 215-627-7266. MODERATE TO DELUXE.

This part of the city boasts some of the best restaurants and delis around. As you'd imagine, many are Italian restaurants, serving

DINING

either sophisticated northern fare or southern favorites loaded with red sauce (called "gravy" by many in this neighborhood).

A deli that always draws a crowd, **Sarcone's** is famous for its sandwiches, served on the locally renowned Sarcone's Italian bakery rolls. The flavor of these soft, chewy long rolls adds oomph to the loads of meats, cheeses, oil, vinegar and herbs on these sandwiches, making Sarcone's hoagies some of the city's most popular. The Italian hoagie, with thin prosciutto, sopresseta and coppa salami, and provolone, will bring you back for more. ~ 734 South 9th Street; 215-922-1717. BUDGET.

Tony Luke's menu features a variety of cheesesteaks, including such variations as pizza steak and steak with cream cheese and tomatoes. But many flock here for the pork sandwiches with greens, a lesser-known favorite Philly sandwich. The pork is slow-roasted with Italian spices and piled on an Italian roll. Tony Luke's location, just off Exit 19 on Route 95, makes it a popular lunch stop. ~ 39 East Oregon Avenue; 215-551-5725; www.tonylukes. com, e-mail tonylukejr@tonylukes.com. BUDGET.

Mamma Maria is another homespun Italian favorite found in South Philly. It's a top recommendation for business travelers so you're more likely to see non-Philadelphians here other than natives, but the place is authentic South Philly nonetheless. Mamma Maria's serves an all-inclusive seven-course Italian meal: antipasto, soup, pasta, meat or fish dishes, greens, desserts and cordials, including homemade limoncello. The decor is similar to what you'd find in Italy; simple tables, plaster walls, dark walnut molding and accents, and an accordion player sets the mood in the evenings. Bring your appetite; the portions are huge. ~ 1637 East Passyunk Avenue; 215-463-6884. DELUXE.

AUTHOR FAVORITE

If you're looking for an Italian restaurant with flair, try **Franco and Luigi's Pastaria**. Between the accordion player and the singing waiters, including crooning co-proprietor and chef Frank Borda, you'll have more fun than imaginable, especially if you enjoy hearing passable interpretations of Puccini, Caruso and Lanza with your meal. Franco and Luigi's menu is loaded with Italian favorites such as fried calamari, rabe and hot sausage, and shrimp scampi. The *core'ngrato* isn't listed as a "house favorite," but it should be—scallops, crab meat and spinach served with a light vodka sauce over gnocchi. Bring your own bottle of wine to complement the flavors. Dinner only. Closed Monday. ~ 1549–47 South 13th Street; 215-755-8900; www.francoandluigis.com. DELUXE.

If you want to find out what the cheesesteak hype is all about, travel down 9th Street at any time of the day to check out Pat's King of Steaks and Geno's Steaks. Both are open 24 hours a day and you're welcome at any time, but be aware that after about 1 a.m., the neighborhood can seem pretty rough. **Pat's King of Steaks** has a wider menu than Geno's, offering a variety of steak sandwiches as well as roast pork, hot dogs and fish cakes (great on Fridays!). The cheese fries are a meal by themselves. Open 24 hours. ~ 1237 East Passyunk Avenue; 215-468-1546. BUDGET.

The menu at **Geno's Steaks** is simple yet greatly greasy: steak sandwiches, roast pork and fries. They also have Italian hoagies for customers looking for a cold sandwich. Line up, get your order straight and don't forget the napkins. Open 24 hours. ~ 1219 South 9th Street; 215-389-0659. BUDGET.

Fans of big breakfasts will love the **Sam's Morning Glory Diner**, a lovely little restaurant that seems more upscale than its name implies. Coffee flows into your bottomless cup as you choose from egg dishes, homemade waffles or hotcake selections. Morning Glory's frittatas are a menu favorite and vegetarians will appreciate the tofu scrambler, sautéed with spinach, mushrooms, peppers and a touch of curry. Open for breakfast and lunch. ~ 735 South 10th Street; 215-413-3999; www.morning glorydiner.com. BUDGET.

◀ HIDDEN

Upscale steakhouse chains have their formulas, and they never seem to falter, regardless of what city you're visiting. But if you'd like to experience an authentic "boys' club" atmosphere that's pure Philadelphia, try **The Saloon**, a dark, paneled, manly restaurant that caters to Philadelphia businessmen and locals. Families and couples come here to celebrate big events and dates, sometimes saving for a month to splurge on the Saloon's huge salads, baked potatoes and steaks. Businessmen like it for the chummy atmosphere and cute, friendly waitresses. The menu is simple American—large salads, huge steaks and chops—with several delicious Italian dishes as well, including stuffed veal chops and lobster pasta. Closed Sunday. ~ 750 South 7th Street; 215-627-1811. ULTRA-DELUXE.

Step into **Southwark** and you'll feel instantly at home in this warm atmosphere that leaves the craziness of South Street at its threshold. A bistro of dark mahogany woods, amber walls and a painted punched-tin ceiling, Southwark draws a professional crowd looking for a relaxing drink and something to eat that's not a hamburger. The menu is inspired, with a selection of appetizers that includes tasty crab beignets as well as escargots mixed with shaved garlic and shallots. Among the hearty entrées is roast pheasant with rosemary polenta. Save room for desserts as well; try the chocolate *pot de crème*. Southwark does not take

◀ HIDDEN

reservations for parties of more than six; the dining room is petite, as is the outdoor seating area in good weather. ~ 701 South 4th Street; 215-238-1888. MODERATE TO DELUXE.

SHOPPING   In South Philadelphia and Southwark you'll find clusters of neighborhood shops, such as those on Fabric Row, at the 600 and 700 blocks of 4th Street, and the dynamic Italian Market.

Pushcarts and stalls crowd the streets and sidewalks of the **Italian Market,** just as they do in courtyards across Italy Tuesdays through Saturdays (some vendors are open Sundays, although the Sabbath is not the liveliest time to visit). At the market, you'll find beautiful produce, including avocados, exotic fruits, root vegetables and everyday favorites; hand-carved meats; homemade cheeses and sausages; and flowers, all at reasonable prices. Also like an "Old World market," you'll find vendors selling other merchandise, hawking trinkets, T-shirts, DVDs and compact disks. The Italian Market has a number of large family-owned bakeries, butcher shops and stores.

DiBruno Bros. has great gifts, with a wide selection of cheeses, gift baskets, olive oil and more. You'll find other wares as well, including T-shirts, bootleg videos, DVDs and CDs. On one recent visit, a vendor tried to sell passers-by a house! Closed Monday. ~ 930 South 9th Street; 888-322-4337; www.dibruno. com. **Fante's Kitchen Wares** carries beautiful dishes and pans, teapots and gourmet coffees, mixes and more. Closed Monday. ~ 106 9th Street; 800-443-2683.

Tucked among the Fabric Row storefronts of upholstery and dress fabrics is **Baldwin Leather and Fabric,** which carries a wide selection of hides, leathers, exotic skins and furs. Baldwin has the materials you won't find at your local fabric shop. It's a must-stop if you have leather upholstery, furniture or apparel needs. ~ 755 4th Street; 215-627-7668.

HIDDEN ►   If you're feeling adventurous and want a new look, consider making an appointment at **Jean Madeline Aveda Institute**—a beauty school where you can get a salon-quality cut and color

AUTHOR FAVORITE
D'Angelo Bros. Meat Market is a glorious assault on the senses, its glass cases stocked with slabs of deep red beef, whole pigs and freshly ground sausages. Salamis, sausages, rabbits and more hang from the ceiling. Crowds jostle to get their order in for fresh cuts or hand-prepared meat mixes. D'Angelo's features 10 types of pâté and 20 types of sausages, including an eye-watering Four Alarm Sausage of pork and habanero pepper. Closed Monday. ~ 909 South 9th Street; 215-923-5637.

for a fraction of upscale salon prices. Yes, the beauticians are students, but they're closely supervised and aren't even allowed to touch a real head until they've practiced on hundreds of mannequins. The products are top-quality and service is friendly. If you are getting your hair cut, bring a picture; most students are still learning the art of judgment. And if you'd like a manicure, bring your own polish because the salon doesn't carry any. ~ 315 Bainbridge Street, Suite A; 215-574-0334.

▼▼▼▼▼▼▼▼▼▼▼
University City

During a recent advertising campaign, University City billed itself as "Left of Center," a creative play on words for this West Philadelphia neighborhood that's home to the University of Pennsylvania, Drexel University, the University of the Sciences in Philadelphia and several internationally renowned think tanks. Bounded by the Schuylkill, Powelton Avenue and 44th Street, West Philadelphia traces its roots to the pre-Penn days, when Puritan William Warner purchased 1500 acres of land in the area and built an estate here in 1677. The first permanent bridge across the Schuylkill was constructed in 1805, opening the area for development as a country getaway for Philadelphia's city dwellers. University City was incorporated into the city in 1854. The University of Pennsylvania, founded as a Colonial college in 1740, moved to the neighborhood in 1872.

SIGHTS

Philadelphia's **30th Street Station** is a grand memorial to the golden era of train travel, a renovated neoclassical monolith built in 1934 that features 90-foot ceilings and art deco lighting. The Pennsylvania Railroad War Memorial dominates the Main Concourse's east end, a bronze sculpture installed in 1952 that commemorates railroad employees who died serving their country. You may recognize parts of the station from the 1985 movie *Witness*—it figured prominently in the movie as the setting where a young Amish boy sees a gruesome murder. ~ 30th and Market streets.

The prestigious **University of Pennsylvania** is the fourth oldest institution of higher learning in the United States, an Ivy League school with a student body of nearly 20,000 undergraduate and graduate students. Penn—the preferred short-form—is a leader among the nation's schools, noted for its graduate and professional programs in business, law and medicine. The school has a number of interesting sites, including its buildings, bookstore and shops. ~ 3541 Walnut Street; 215-898-5000.

The **University Museum of Archaeology and Anthropology** holds a treasure trove of rare domestic and international artifacts, most collected during expeditions by University of Pennsylvania scientists. The collection includes Egyptian, Chinese, Roman, African, Polynesian and Southwestern antiquities, including an

Egyptian palace with 12-ton Sphinx, a mummified cat, the world's largest cloisonne temple lions, a 19th-century rock crystal ball owned by China's Dowager Empress, and the world's oldest wine vesicle from Mesopotamia. Older children who have studied ancient cultures will find this museum's environs and artifacts fascinating. The museum shop features a unique selection of books, jewelry and reproductions for sale. Closed Sunday and Monday from Memorial Day through Labor Day. Admission. ~ 3260 South Street; 215-898-0657.

HIDDEN ▶ Engineers and computer scientists can call ahead to see the computer that started it all, ENIAC, the world's first all-electronic digital computer. ENIAC, an acronym that stands for electronic numerical integrator and computer, was developed to calculate artillery firing tables for the U.S. Army during World War II. Although it wasn't operational until 1946, it was used for its original purpose, winnowing the average calculation time from 12 hours to 30 seconds. It also was used for weather predictions, atomic-energy calculations and number studies. ENIAC filled a room the size of a squash court, weighing 30 tons and containing 17,500 vacuum tubes. Roughly 10 percent of ENIAC is on display in this basement where it was created, at the Penn's Moore School of Engineering and Applied Sciences. A portion also is on display at the National Museum of American History in Washington, DC. By appointment. ~ 200 South 33rd Street; 215-898-2492.

Housed in the University of Pennsylvania's original library at the West Philadelphia campus, the **Fisher Fine Arts Library** is one of the best known works of Philadelphia architect Frank Furness, whose credits include the magnificent Pennsylvania Academy of the Fine Arts, the sprawling clubhouse of the Merion Cricket Club near Haverford, and an addition and interiors for St. Stephen's Church in Philadelphia. The Fine Arts Library was the first to separate its reading room from the stacks; the three-story reading room features massive columns, arched windows and beautiful natural light to study by. Closed weekends during summer break. ~ 220 South 34th Street; 215-898-8325.

The **Institute of Contemporary Art** at the University of Pennsylvania aims to promote the works of emerging and established artists. Exhibitions focus on paintings, photography, sculpture, performance art and film. Past exhibitors include Andy Warhol and performance artist Laurie Anderson. Closed Sunday through Tuesday. Admission. ~ 118 South 36th Street; 215-898-7108.

HIDDEN ▶ An urban oasis tucked among the University of Pennsylvania's historic buildings, the school's **Biopond** is a hidden gem, enjoyed by students, faculty members, couples and local residents for its beautiful trees and gardens, wildlife and ambiance. The pond is maintained by the university's biology department, hence the nickname, and the area is formally known as the James G. Kaskey Memorial Garden. In this secluded greenspace you'll encounter sunbathing turtles, hopping frogs, toads, egrets and other forms of wildlife under a canopy of magnolia, gingko, horse chestnut and Kentucky coffee trees. The garden has benches for studying and resting. ~ Hamilton Walk, near 38th Street behind the Richards Medical Research Building.

North of Penn is **Drexel University**, a college whose founders pioneered the concept of cooperative education, a learning method that combines classroom study with on-the-job experience. Drexel has nearly 17,000 undergraduate and graduate students and was established in 1891 as a school for practical arts and sciences. The third floor of the university's Main Building, at 32nd and Chestnut Streets, holds the Westphal Picture Gallery, a fine arts gallery that houses one of the city's treasures, the **Rittenhouse Clock**. This complex timepiece was designed by astronomer David Rittenhouse. Not only does it tell the time of day in hours, minutes and seconds, it plays ten tunes and shows the date, phases of the moon, the lunar orbit, the earth's orbit and the signs of the zodiac. Closed weekends. ~ 32nd and Chestnut streets; 215-895-0480.

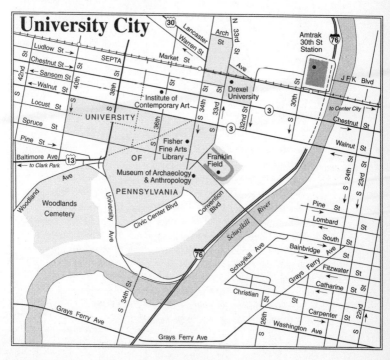

Beyond the universities, West Philadelphia has a number of parks and other sites of interest. In **Clark Park**, you'll find a statue of Charles Dickens—the only one in the world (Dickens apparently had willed that he be remembered by his writing; the statue, commissioned for the Chicago World's Fair in 1893 was to be given to Dickens' family, who refused to accept it). ~ South 43rd and Baltimore Avenue.

On Woodland Avenue is the **Woodlands Mansion and Cemetery**, a neoclassical manor home built in 1787 that features interesting indoor spaces and a cemetery that holds a number of famous Americans, including artists Rembrandt Peale and Thomas Eakins, university founder Anthony Joseph Drexel, physician Samuel Gross and architect Paul Cret, who designed the gates to his final resting place and the Rodin Museum, as well as other works throughout Philadelphia. ~ 4000 Woodland Avenue.

LODGING Like South Philadelphia, West Philadelphia is a neighborhood with few lodging choices. However, a number of known hoteliers operate businesses here, a plus for those visiting or working at the universities.

The Inn at Penn is located at the heart of the university campus, convenient for parents, academics and those with business at the school. The hotel has an on-site fitness room and amenities for business travelers, including a center for computers and faxing. The hotel's restaurant, Penne, has won accolades for its wine list, as well as its northern Italian fare. Renovations of the inn's 238 rooms began in November 2005 and will be completed in 2006. ~ 3600 Sansom Street; 215-222-0200; www.innatpenn. com. ULTRA-DELUXE.

AUTHOR FAVORITE

The Gables is a remarkable Victorian structure now serving as a B&B in West Philadelphia. Built in 1889 for a prominent Philadelphia physician, this home has been painstakingly restored—no small feat for a building that has served as a residence for the elderly, and for Jesuits. Its ten bedrooms are each furnished with antique beds, period furnishings and Victorian stenciling or period wallpaper. The Blue Willow Room, in the turret, is a cozy getaway with brick corner fireplace and a decorating theme that echoes the delicate porcelain of the same name. Leave time to enjoy sitting on the welcoming front porch if the weather is good. And be sure to schedule your day to begin after breakfast. You wouldn't want to miss this rich meal of hot dishes, breads and fresh fruit. ~ 4520 Chester Avenue; 215-662-1918; www.gablesbb.com. MODERATE TO DELUXE.

The **Sheraton University City**'s 316 guest rooms feature contemporary furniture with dark blue bedspreads and walls, and gold and taupe accents. The hotel's common areas are more traditional in style, with Federal- and Philadelphia-style furniture, including camelback sofas, wing chairs and brass chandeliers. Amenities include an on-site restaurant, a florist and coffee kiosk, a well-equipped fitness center and a seasonal swimming pool. ~ 3549 Chestnut Street; 215-387-8000; www.philadelphiasheraton.com. ULTRA-DELUXE.

A grand Victorian manor home built in 1907, **Spruce Hill Manor** is convenient for those wanting to stay in West Philadelphia. Spruce Hill is a large, imposing Edwardian structure with huge interior rooms, including a vast dining room with dark wood wainscoting and plaster walls, and an elegant parlor with Victorian antiques and Oriental carpets. Bedrooms are large and decorated with Victorian antique bedding. Many have fireplaces and a separate seating area. The Family Suite features a master bedroom, sitting room, elegant library and kitchenette. Innkeeper Janet Reitano will make every attempt to pamper you; she's also willing to drive you to an appointment on request. Two-night minimum stay. ~ 331 South 46th Street; 215-472-2213; www.sprucehillmanor.com. MODERATE.

For budget-minded travelers who don't mind a few rules—including the separation of men and women by floor, no smoking, no alcohol nor food in rooms, and no blasphemy or cursing—the **Divine Tracy Hotel** might fit the bill. Clean, with a friendly staff and a communal dining room, the Divine Tracy offers small rooms, some with air-conditioners—but none with televisions—for about $50 a night. The Divine Tracy is staffed by volunteers who follow the teachings of the Peace Movement Mission, a religious group founded by Philadelphia preacher Father Divine. The Tracy is popular with students and university guests; it's got an 85 percent occupancy rate, despite all its rules. ~ 20 South 36th Street; 215-382-4310. BUDGET.

◀ HIDDEN

West Philadelphia's restaurants are jammed with students most nights during the school year, but its fun to sit alongside these young, brainy people and enjoy a meal and a drink. If you don't like crowds and want to dine in the area, consider traveling during winter or summer break for a quieter experience.

DINING

In a town where the competition among Italian restaurants is tough, **Penne**, a hotel restaurant popular with students whose parents are in town, stands up to the rest with a fine selection of pastas, seafood and chicken dishes. Located in the Inn at Penn, Penne's menu favorites include gargenelli—pasta with lobster and roasted artichokes in a saffron sauce—and a satisfying gnocchi

Text continued on page 152.

Old Maids Never Wed and Have Babies, Period

Overbrook, Merion, Narberth, Wynnewood, Ardmore, Haverford, Bryn Mawr, Paoli. These are the towns along Philadelphia's Main Line; the mnemonic about old women is how Philadelphians remember where these villages lie along what is now the R-5 SEPTA commuter rail line. The Main Line was immortalized in the 1940 movies *The Philadelphia Story* and *Kitty Foyle*, the home of some of the nation's wealthiest magnates. The towns in the region initially were founded in the 1700s and 1800s, but the area took off as a suburb in the 1800s, when Philadelphia's rich railroad executives built enormous estates along their "main line." Today, this area continues to serve the well-to-do, with gracious estates, country clubs and private high schools flanking the tracks and Route 30, the road that passes through much of the region.

The Main Line is home to a number of nationally recognized colleges and universities, including **Bryn Mawr**, a women's college founded in 1885 that is one of the elite "Seven Sisters" schools. **Haverford College**, a top-rated private school, is the oldest college in the United States with Quaker origins. **Villanova** and **St. Joseph's** universities, two schools founded by Roman Catholic groups, are frequently recognized for their students' contributions to sports and academia.

While there's not much to do along the Main Line other than drive, gawk at the houses and eat (Wayne has a number of fine restaurants), there are a few points of interest. **Chanticleer Garden** is an inspiration to any homeowner, a 31-acre "pleasure garden" of beautiful bedding plants, winding paths and ruins. The Spring Garden comes alive in May with the delicate blue blooms of quamosh; the Teacup Garden features tropical plants; and the beautiful Asian woods present a delicate balance of American deciduous forest with Japanese, Korean and Chinese native plants. Open Wednesday through Saturday from April through October. Admission. ~ 786 Church Road, Wayne; 610-687-4163; www.chanticleergarden.org.

For a real treat, arrange a tour of **Woodmont**, one of America's great castles that now serves as home to the Peace Mission Movement of Father Divine. Woodmont was built in 1892, a French Gothic house built for steel magnate Alan Wood. The limestone castle took four years to complete, and its incredible interior features carved banisters and balconies, a grand staircase and enormous fireplaces. Modest dress is required for the tour—no shorts or sleeveless tops, and no profanity please. Woodmont continues to serve as the home of Mother Divine, the second wife of Peace Mission Movement founder Father Divine, who died in 1965. As of 2005, at the age of 80, Mother Divine remained the leader of the movement. Open Sunday and by appointment. ~ 1622 Spring Mill Road, Gladwyne; 610-664-4210.

Need to do some shopping to keep a little one happy? Consider ducking into **Pun's,** an independent toy store with a great selection of handmade and unique toys as well as items from all over the world. Kids will love the train that loops around the store. ~ 839½ Lancaster Avenue, Bryn Mawr; 610-525-9789.

with seared sea scallops. Particularly nice is the menu's flexibility, allowing diners to choose appetizer-sized portions of entrée selections. The menu features wine suggestions, and a wine-tasting offers a sampling of three varieties. ~ 3600 Sansom Street; 215-222-0200. DELUXE.

When you step into **Pod**, you'll feel like you've landed inside the set of *2001: A Space Odyssey*. This sushi and adult beverage-concoctions bar is one of Stephen Starr's themed Philadelphia restaurants, this one featuring Japanese food in a trendy, funky setting. The most popular way to dine at Pod is to reserve a "pod," an enclosed dining space designed for a large group, where you can change the color of your pod by moving a switch. This is a great place to eat appetizers and order drinks, including sake. Large plates of sushi travel along the sushi bar by conveyer belt. Be prepared for high noise levels, however; despite its fairly high prices, Pod often is packed with students enjoying a good time. ~ 3636 Sansom Street; 215-387-1803; www.podrestaurant.com. DELUXE.

The **White Dog Café** wears its heart on its menus, its website and newsletters. This homegrown Philadelphia institution donates up to 20 percent of its profits to the White Dog Café Foundation, which supports such causes as workplace justice, anti-war movements and demonstrations, and youth education. The White Dog's menu relies heavily on organically grown vegetables and "humanely raised" ingredients. (Just how lamb ended up on this menu-with-a-cause, however, I'll never understand.) The fish dishes are tops, especially the horseradish brioche–crusted Alaskan King salmon with crème fraîche. ~ 3420 Sansom Street; 215-386-9224; www.whitedog.com. DELUXE.

HIDDEN ► **Mad Mex** is Tex-Mex, not authentic Mexican, but it's got all the right features of a top-notch student destination—dim lighting, tacky decor, waitresses whose shirts say "Practice Safe Mex," and half-price food between 2 p.m. and 4 p.m., and 11 p.m. and 1 a.m. The frozen margaritas are terrific, especially with the never-ending baskets of chips and salsa. Try the fajitas or surprisingly good thai curry burrito—but not if you are drinking a margarita; there's something about mixing curry and tequila that doesn't quite work. ~ 3401 Walnut Street; 215-382-2221; www.madmex.com. BUDGET.

An ever-popular BYO for the locals, **Nan** features Thai-French fusion fare in a quiet atmosphere of light woods and green trees. You can't go wrong with traditional picks of escargots or chicken lemongrass soup for starters. The entrée list pleases a variety of tastes, with everything from delicious pad thai to a rich filet mignon with goat cheese or salmon with lemongrass. ~ 4000 Chestnut Street; 215-382-0818. DELUXE.

If you're looking for something slightly out of the ordinary, try dining at the **Restaurant School at Walnut Hill College**. The ◀ HIDDEN school runs four eateries; diners can choose from the Great Chefs of Philadelphia Restaurant, with menus developed by Philly's renowned chefs and executed by the students; the European Courtyard; the Italian Trattoria; and the American Heartland. With all the fine restaurants in Philadelphia, why risk dining at a restaurant school? Two reasons—one, the fixed prices are reasonable, and two, where else would you get a chance to do this? The restaurants have full bars and extensive wine lists (although drinks are not included in the fixed prices) and are open for dinner. For a quick bite to eat or mid-morning snack, the school's Pastry Shop and European Market serve breakfast and lunch fare as well as pastries and breads. ~ 4207 Walnut Street; 215-222-4200; www.therestaurantschool.com. MODERATE TO DELUXE.

Once again, as a residential area, West Philadelphia has little in **SHOPPING** the way of shopping. However, store selection is improving, with the opening of **University Square**, adjacent to the University of Pennsylvania. This set of shops includes Urban Outfitters and **Eastern Mountain Sports**. EMS sells a complete line of hiking and camping gear, as well as clothing for your outdoor needs. Top brands include North Face, Teva, Thule, Patagonia and Kelty, as well as EMS's own house brand. ~ 130 South 35th Street; 215-386-1020; www.ems.com.

If you'd like to take any mementos home from the nation's fourth oldest university, you'll find them at the **Penn Bookstore**, which carries sweatshirts, T-shirts, hats, coats, rain gear, bumper

SWEET SOUNDS OF PHILLY

Philadelphia's music scene has always been hip and fresh. *American Bandstand* originated from the WFIL studios at 46th and Market streets, and Philadelphia rock stations WMMR and WYSP have been responsible for boosting many careers in their 40-plus years. Today, WXPN, 88.5, the University of Pennsylvania's public radio station, leads the adult alternative-music scene, devoting its airtime to singer/songwriters and contemporary artists not usually heard on commercial stations. It's unfortunate that so few major American cities have stations like WXPN, which can be heard in many stores and restaurants throughout Philadelphia. A sampling of WXPN programming can be heard nationwide on NPR stations that air *World Café*, a program hosted in the WXPN studios that showcases contemporary music, folk, rock, blues and jazz.

stickers, blankets, jewelry and more. ~ 3601 Walnut Street; 215-898-7595; www.upennbkstore.com.

NIGHTLIFE Nightlife in this part of the city mainly revolves around students, with the area's bars and pubs catering to a young crowd. To experience the student scene, a visit to **Smokey Joe's** is a must. The bar is a venerable Penn institution; in a commencement speech in 1975, President Gerald Ford told graduates "There are 16 institutions of higher learning at the University of Pennsylvania—17 if you include Smokey Joe's." Smokey Joe's usually crowded bar features pub fare, live music and a boisterous, happy—albeit clique-y—clientele. ~ 210 South 40th Street; 215-222-0770.

HIDDEN ► The Bridge Cinema de Lux movie house features six screens and a cocktail lounge under one roof; patrons can eat dinner or sip a martini before or after their show. This upscale theater offers a number of special events and features, including a Silver Screen Classics series, where, once a month, patrons can enjoy a movie from the 1930s through 1980s, a drink and popcorn for a dollar. ~ 40th and Walnut streets; 215-386-3300.

▼▼▼▼▼▼▼▼▼▼▼▼▼▼

Northwest Philadelphia

Accessible by bus, car and commuter rail, the northwest portion of Philadelphia has much to offer, including unique neighborhoods, historic sights, shopping and nightlife. Each neighborhood has a distinct flavor, and it would be difficult to visit all in a day, or even two. Depending on your interests, however, you're likely to find a favorite that you'll want to visit time and again.

SIGHTS In 1683, a group of Germans received a land grant from William Penn to settle in the northwest section of Philadelphia, where they planned to build one of the first industrial towns in the United States. A paper mill was constructed in 1707, and by the mid 1700s, their village, called **Germantown**, had become a thriving community of businesses, schools, churches and a firehouse. Tradesmen and professionals, including weavers, carpenters, doctors and tanners, set up shop in the area and built homes, some of which still stand today. During the Revolution, Germantown was occupied by the British, and in 1777, the British used it as a stronghold to turn back an American advance. In 1793, when Philadelphia was struck by a yellow fever epidemic, Germantown flourished as city dwellers fled to escape the city's close quarters. In the 1800s, Germantown served as a hotbed for abolitionism; the first written protest against slavery was drafted by its residents. Today, this neighborhood thrives as a community of mostly middle-class families who enjoy its proximity to Center City and Fairmount Park. Germantown features numerous historic buildings and landmarks, which can be visited individually or grouped as part of a scheduled tour. For information on tours, contact the **Germantown Historical Society.** ~ 5501 Germantown Avenue; 215-844-0514.

Sixteen years after losing to the British at Cliveden, George Washington returned to Germantown, this time to escape the yellow fever epidemic that raged in the city. During the summer of 1793, Washington stayed at the **Deshler-Morris House**, a stone Colonial on Germantown Avenue about a mile from Cliveden. Washington conducted government business while at the home, holding meetings with his cabinet, including Thomas Jefferson, Alexander Hamilton and Edmund Randolph. Open by

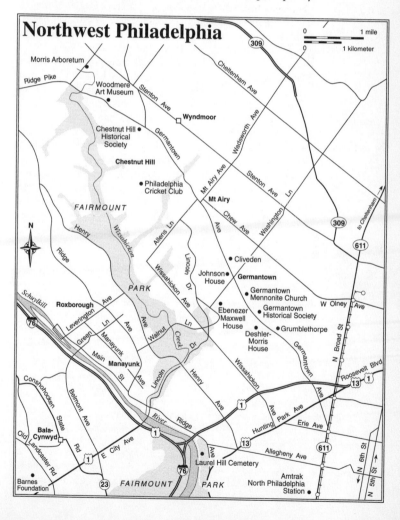

Northwest Philadelphia

appointment mid-December through March. Other times, closed Monday and Tuesday. Admission. ~ 5442 Germantown Avenue; 215-596-1748.

The tiny **Germantown Mennonite Church**, built in 1770, relates the story of the Mennonites and their arrival in the region. Its exhibits include bibles and books printed in Germantown in the 18th century, as well as a desk that was used in 1688 while members penned the first written protest against slavery in the colonies. Open by appointment. Admission. ~ 6133 Germantown Avenue; 215-843-0943.

A comfortable, cozy stone home with an unusual name, **Grumblethorpe** was built in 1744 as a country getaway for wine importer John Wister. This fine example of Pennsylvania German architecture was constructed of stones from the Wister property and locally harvested oak. It was referred to as Wister's "big house" until the 1800s, but was later renamed Grumblethorpe by a family member who took a fancy to the name after finding it in a book. Before the Battle of Germantown, British General James Agnew established his headquarters here. During the battle, Agnew was shot and his soldiers carried him to the parlor of Grumblethorpe, where he died. More than 200 years later, Agnew's bloodstains remain visible on the room's wide-planked flooring, despite attempts over the years to clean them. Today, the bloodstains are as much a part of Grumblethorpe as the walls— caretakers wouldn't think about trying to remove them. The house contains numerous antiques, including the desk where descendent Owen Wister penned the Western novel *The Virginian*. Open Tuesday, Thursday and Sunday from April to mid-December. Admission. ~ 5267 Germantown Avenue; 215-843-4820.

AUTHOR FAVORITE

A magnificent Georgian mansion constructed in 1763, **Cliveden** is one of Germantown's finest buildings. Built as a summer residence for wealthy attorney and justice Benjamin Chew, Cliveden (rhymes with "lived in") was the site of the Battle of Germantown during the Revolutionary War. British troops in Germantown sought protection from the charging Continental Army within the manse's 18-inch-thick walls. The troops deflected Washington's charge, and 77 American soldiers died in the battle. The scars of that event are still visible both outside and inside the house; there are cannon holes in the façade and a bullet hole in one of the offices. The home contains significant antiques and a number of Chew family heirlooms. Closed Monday through Wednesday and from January through March. Admission. ~ 6401 Germantown Avenue; 215-848-1777; www.cliveden.org.

The large stone **Johnson House** was completed in 1768 by Quaker Dirck Jansen, who built it as a gift for his son John Johnson. During the Battle of Germantown, the home was in the thick of things; it bears the scars of musket shot and cannonball fire. After the battle was over, the victorious and hungry British pilfered the Johnsons' food and trashed the home. But the home is most significant for the role it played in history more than 80 years later, when it served as a stop on the Underground Railroad. The third generation of Johnsons were very active abolitionists and helped win the freedom of many slaves. Harriet Tubman led slaves through the Johnson House on their way to the home of abolitionist Lucretia Mott in nearby Cheltenham. Open Thursday, Friday and Saturday. Tours by appointment on Thursday and Friday; on Saturday, tours are offered at 1:30 p.m., 2:30 p.m. and 3:30 p.m. ~ 6306 Germantown Avenue; 215-438-1768; www.johnsonhouse.org.

The **Ebenezer Maxwell House** bears a passing resemblance to the Addams Family's house, an imposing Second Empire structure sometimes referred to as "Victorian Gothic." But on the inside, this 1859 house is pure Victorian finery, with elaborate Philadelphia-made furnishings, draperies, hanging lamps and chandeliers. Built by cloth merchant Ebenezer Maxwell, the house sits among other Victorian-era homes on a quiet street. This Gothic manor can be visited April through December on weekends, and the gardens are open year-round. Admission for house. ~ 200 West Tulpehocken Street; 215-438-1861.

East of Germantown is **Cheltenham**, another neighborhood in Northwest Philadelphia. Here lies a Philadelphia oddity, the **Ryerss Museum**, an Italianate mansion filled with an eclectic collection of objects belonging to a wealthy globe-trotting family. Much of the bric-a-brac was acquired by Mary Anne Reed Ryerss, a former housekeeper who married Robert Ryerss, heir to the home. The collection includes Asian art, ship models, costumes, armor and glassware. There also are photos and memorabilia dedicated to the families' pets, as well as a pet cemetery. Closed Monday through Thursday. ~ 7370 Central Avenue; 215-685-0544 or 215-685-0599.

Back at Germantown, head north and you'll come across **Mount Airy**, a community that sprang up after train service arrived here in 1882. Long in the shadow of Chestnut Hill, its ritzy neighbor to the north, Mount Airy has regained popularity as a neighborhood that cherishes diversity and promotes community spirit. While there are few historic sights here, consider visiting one of Mount Airy's popular nightlife venues, either North by Northwest or McMenamin's Tavern.

Chestnut Hill is the highest point in the city at 446 feet above sea level. It was named for the trees that once dominated this ridge and is now known for its quaint shopping district and grand homes. Cobblestone Germantown Avenue is lined with boutiques, galleries, specialty shops and restaurants and is a favorite destination for weekend lunches or dinners after a day spent in Fairmount Park. Chestnut Hill has been a community for the well-to-do since it was developed in the 1880s. Architects and builders, drawn here by the completion of the area's commuter rail terminus, designed and marketed the area's large homes for high-income wage earners. Today Chestnut Hill possesses some of the city's finest homes, in a variety of architectural styles, including Tudor, Queen Anne, Victorian and neo-Colonial. For information on touring Chestnut Hill, check out the **Visitors Center** for maps and assistance. ~ 8426 Germantown Avenue; 215-247-6696; www.chestnuthillpa.com.

The **Chestnut Hill Historical Society** has information on the area's history, and volunteers will steer you toward hidden sights and destinations. ~ 8708 Germantown Avenue; 215-247-0417.

The **Woodmere Art Museum** spotlights Pennsylvania talent, including the works of Benjamin West, Frederick Church, N. C. Wyeth, Edward Redfield and Daniel Garber. In a Victorian mansion with mansard roof, the collection is presented in a charming setting that includes tapestries, sculpture and Oriental rugs. Closed Monday. Admission. ~ 9201 Germantown Avenue; 215-247-0417.

To find some of Philadelphia's oldest and largest trees, head for the **Morris Arboretum**, a Victorian garden landscape that encompasses 92 acres in Chestnut Hill. The arboretum, run by the University of Pennsylvania, features thousands of rare plants, a collection of garden ornaments, a G-scale outdoor garden railway and a fernery—a Victorian greenhouse that contains hundreds of lush ferns in an indoor woodland environment. The arboretum is especially notable for its collection of historic trees, including the largest Japanese Katsura in the United States, and Chinese dawn redwoods. Admission. ~ 9414 Meadowbrook Avenue; 215-247-5777; www.business-services.upenn.edu/arboretum.

WHERE WE GO FOR DRINK

Originally known as Flat Rock, Manayunk received its distinct name (pronounced man-E-yunk) in 1824, when community elders chose the Leni Lenape word *manaiung*, meaning "where we go for drink." The name was meant to highlight the existence of the town's canal, which made the river passable for commerce and travel. Today, it's considered even more apropos because this former mill town has become a favorite destination for shopping, dining and celebrating.

Located west of Wissahickon Creek and Fairmount Park lies the neighborhood of **Manayunk**. Manayunk's spirit can best be described as adaptable—the area grew as a cotton and paper mill town populated by English, Irish, German, Italian and Polish immigrants. But as the Civil War drew near and the South stopped sending cotton to the North for processing, the mills began manufacturing woolens, including blankets and textiles, to support the Union. Some mills closed but others survived, and the town managed to escape the economic collapse that many mill towns in Pennsylvania experienced. In 1983, Manayunk was named a National Historic District, and the town reinvented itself again, transforming into a trendy shopping and dining destination. There are more than 80 stores and restaurants here, most of them locally owned or exclusive to Philadelphia. Parking can be a challenge, especially on a sunny summer weekend. Consider taking the SEPTA commuter train to avoid parking hassles.

Cycling fans will probably know Manayunk for the **U.S. Pro Cycling Championship**, held every June. Renamed the Philadelphia International Championship in 2006, this prestigious race features 130 riders who complete a circuit throughout Philadelphia, including a climb up Manayunk's steep roadway from river level ten times. "The Wall," as the climb is called, is the most famous portion of the course, where spectators root, holler and toast the cyclists as they grind up the steep incline. ~ 2550 Eisenhower Avenue, Building B, Suite 206, Norristown; 610-676-0390.

West of the Schuylkill River in Merion is the **Barnes Foundation**, established in 1922 by Albert C. Barnes to promote education of the arts. This expansive collection boasts modern and Asian art, Greek, Roman and Egyptian antiquities, African artifacts and an arboretum. Among the pieces are 175 Renoirs, 66 Cezannes and 44 Picassos, displayed in collages or ensembles alongside other items and paintings. These cluttered displays are designed to illustrate that certain elements and traditions are common to art and everyday items across time and geography. Barnes, a great friend and collaborator of education reformer John Dewey, believed that art and education should be accessible to all regardless of income. Today, the collection is mostly viewed by students—the city of Merion has limited the number of visitors to 400 per day—but reservations can be made 45 to 60 days in advance to see it on weekends and Wednesday through Friday in July and August. Admission. ~ 300 North Latch's Lane, Merion; 610-667-0290, option 5 for reservations; www.barnesfoundation.org.

Simple and elegant, the 36-room **Chestnut Hill Hotel** is conveniently located at the heart of the suburb's shopping and dining district. A Victorian inn built in 1864, the hotel is furnished in

LODGING

Colonial-style decor. Rooms are bright and airy, with pencil post beds, Sheraton-style nightstands and dressers, and pale tones of beige and primary colors. The hotel features three on-site restaurants. Continental breakfast is included in the room rate. ~ 8229 Germantown Avenue; 215-242-5905; www.chestnuthillhotel. com. MODERATE TO DELUXE.

The imposing **Silverstone Bed and Breakfast** has a beautifully decorated Victorian interior, with romantic soft pastels, floral accents, Oriental rugs and sparkling woodwork. Rooms are spacious; most have queen beds, sitting areas and private baths. The home also has a small luggage elevator. Guests have use of the gardens, a private kitchen, the porch and backyard—access that gives the sense of being at a close friend's house. ~ 8840 Stenton Avenue; 215-242-3333; www.silverstonestay.com. MODERATE.

DINING

For a quick meal, the **Metropolitan Bakery** offers a selection of breads, rolls, soups and salads as well as sweet treats and coffee. This bakery, which has several stores throughout the city, is known for its French berry roll—a chewy, tasty sourdough roll packed with dried berries—and its delectable brownies, which are moist and sinful. ~ 8607 Germantown Avenue; 215-753-9001; www.metropolitanbakery.com. BUDGET.

On a beautiful day in Chestnut Hill, you'll be hard-pressed to get a seat at the **Chestnut Grill and Sidewalk Café**, a first-come, first-seated eatery that has a comfortable, cozy dining room and wraparound terrace. The grill offers a menu in the realm of a traditional country club grill, featuring crabcakes, large sirloin hamburgers and salads. But it also has a few surprises like spicy

AUTHOR FAVORITE

Middle Eastern restaurant **Al Dana II** has a large, loyal and discriminating customer base who travel to Chestnut Hill just to dine on the offerings of lamb shanks, kebabs or the "Holy Land Special"—grilled chicken served on flatbread and topped with onions, sumac and pine nuts. The proprietor is a Palestinian native of Jordan who moved to the United States when he was ejected from Kuwait following the Gulf War in 1991 (a half a million Palestinians were ordered to leave Kuwait after the government regained power). He began his business out of a food cart in Center City. Today, Al Dana II serves a delicious selection of Lebanese and Middle Eastern favorites at reasonable prices. House specials include chicken curry and salmon Casanova, a sautéed filet prepared in a lemon, garlic and cognac reduction. ~ 8630 Germantown Avenue; 215-247-3336; www.aldana2.com. MODERATE.

grilled catfish and California rolls. ~ 8229 Germantown Avenue; 215-247-7570. MODERATE.

For ice cream, cookies and other sweets, **Bredenbeck's Bakery** **and Ice Cream Parlor** in Chestnut Hill is a local institution, serving hand-dipped cones, shakes and sundaes in a variety of exotic homemade flavors. Bredenbeck's has been in Chestnut Hill since 1983, but the business dates to 1889, when Bavarian immigrants set up shop in the Northern Liberties section of the city, north of Old City. ~ 8126 Germantown Avenue; 215-247-7374; www. bredenbecks.com. BUDGET.

◄ HIDDEN

Manayunk boasts roughly 30 restaurants, which may seem like overkill, but if you travel here on a summer weekend in good weather, you'll be lucky to find a seat. **Bourbon Blue**'s menu pays fleeting homage to the city of New Orleans with a few blackened dishes and jambalaya—surprising, considering it touts itself as "an inspired N.O. experience." But three things make Bourbon Blue cool: the nightly live music in the Canal Lounge, the casual atmosphere in a historic mill and the location—on the canal in Manayunk. Bourbon Blue offers some of the best nightlife in Manayunk; good drinks and great Cajun fries, enjoyed while listening to jazz, blues or contemporary music. ~ 2 Rector Street; 215-508-3360; www.bourbonblue.com. DELUXE.

If you want to enjoy Manayunk at its funkiest and most fun, spend the morning window shopping and drop by the **Couch Tomato Café** for chili, a wrap, salad or slice of pizza—among Philadelphia's best. You decide whether you want your fixin's with lettuce or in a white, wheat, spinach or tomato-basil wrap. Choices range from tuna or chicken salad to salmon perricone, served with roasted red peppers, cucumbers and fresh spinach, or pomodora, with grilled eggplant, roasted red peppers, fresh tomatoes and mozzarella. The eggplant parmesan calzone bursts with chunks of breaded eggplant and cheese. ~ 102 Rector Street; 215-438-2233; www.thecouchtomato.com. BUDGET.

The **Chestnut Hill Cheese Shop** has been in business since the early 1960s. This family-owned store sells a wide selection of aromatic imported and domestic *fromage* and gourmet gifts, including chocolates, caviar, jams, jellies and coffee. The store's website also features an excellent encyclopedia of cheese and information on serving it and pairing it with other foods. ~ 8509 Germantown Avenue; 215-242-2211; www.chcheeseshop.com.

SHOPPING

The **Chestnut Hill Farmer's Market** is held Thursday through Saturday off Germantown Avenue behind the Chestnut Hill hotel. At the market, you can purchase meals-to-go, fresh produce, meats, seafood, flowers, coffee and chocolates. To indulge your favorite pooch, check out the booth manned by the

Chestnut Hill Dog Bakery. ~ 8229 Germantown Avenue; 215-242-5905.

HIDDEN ▶ Drop by **Kilian Hardware** just to enjoy the feel of a small-town hardware store. This is a great place to go for that hard-to-find widget you might need if you own a vintage house. Wish you hadn't tossed your rotary dial phone when Trimlines hit the market? You'll find a wide selection of antique phones here, plus vintage guitars as well as the usual selection of paints, tools, garden ware and supplies. ~ 8450 Germantown Avenue; 215-247-0945.

The latest chick fashions are done uniquely by a trio of Manayunk designers at **Bias**, a fabulous boutique of T-shirts, trousers, glittery sweaters and well-cut dresses in the heart of the shopping district. The service is great, with salespeople who really know their fabrics, and can offer advice about what works for you and what doesn't. The store changes merchandise with the seasons; great sales occur at the end of each. ~ 4442 Main Street; 215-483-8340; www.biasfashion.com.

Manayunk's only independent music store—make that only music store—is **Main Street Music**, a great supplier of cutting-edge CDs. The staff is helpful, and like the big-name stores, Main Street has listening kiosks so you can preview their wares. You can pick up a copy of something you heard on WXPN that morning or take a gamble on a large selection of used CDs. Main Street also sells DVDs. ~ 4444 Main Street; 215-487-7732.

Country meets style at **Pompanoosuc Mills**, a Vermont furniture company with a store in Manayunk. Pampanoosuc specializes in well-designed hardwood furniture with clean lines, including beds, armoires, dressers, desks and nightstands that have Shaker, Mission or country overtones. Every piece is built to order, and crafted from a selection of hardwoods that includes cherry, oak, maple and birch. ~ 4120 Main Street; 215-508-3263; www.pompy.com.

NIGHTLIFE One of the top spots in Northwest Philadelphia for live music and dancing, **North By Northwest** is a large venue—a former **HIDDEN ▶** furniture store—that packs in patrons with its eclectic menu and entertainment. Dining options include soul food favorites catfish and pickled beets, as well as Middle Eastern dishes and Tex-Mex *quesadillas*. The music menu is diverse as well; each night features different genres: dance music or jazz on Tuesdays, salsa on Wednesdays, and soul and jam bands on weekends. The second Tuesday of every month is singer/songwriter night. Closed Monday. ~ 7165 Germantown Avenue; 215-248-1000; www.nxnw.com.

A great place to mingle with the locals after a day of sightseeing, **McMenamin's Tavern** has 17 beers on tap and great fried pub fare. The place is small and comfortable with a mixed clientele that could be straight from the set of *Cheers*—doctors, lawyers, construction workers, and probably a postman or two. Try the fish and chips with a pint of Newcastle. ~ 7170 Germantown Avenue; 215-247-9920.

There's no shortage of places to go in Manayunk at night; it's one of the city's most popular watering holes. The **Manayunk Brewery**, set in a centuries-old mill, draws big crowds every night for its home brews, including pale ale and pilsner. Equipped with a rotisserie, pizza oven and sushi bar, the brewery, offers a variety of foods to go along with the cold beer. For great evening entertainment, don't miss the dueling pianos on Thursday nights. They play—and compete—by request. ~ 4120 Main Street; 215-482- 8220.

The **Bayou** is another lively Manayunk joint, open from lunch to late-night. This is a vintage-style neighborhood bar, with Naugahyde bar stools, a jukebox and numerous TVs for ardent Eagles, Flyers and Phillies fans. Located right on Main Street, it's always crowded. The bar menu is tinged with Cajun- inspired offerings such as buffalo wings and Cajun fries—popular with the beer-drinking crowd. ~ 4245 Main Street; 215-482-2560.

Bourbon Blue, set in a historic mill, has quickly become a popular place to see and be seen, drawing fashion-conscious 20- and 30-somethings for the atmosphere and the live music. Tuesday and Thursday, Bourbon Blue hosts duos; Wednesday has acoustic soloists and Saturday rocks with bands. The music varies, ranging from jazz and blues to contemporary. The exception to "live" is Friday, when a deejays spins tunes. ~ 2 Rector Street; 215-508-3360; www.bourbonblue.com.

SEVEN

Bucks County

The young couple in the Rose Bank Winery's tasting room didn't know much about wine. They weren't too sure about the heftier cabernets or *chambourcins*. But pourer Dave Fleming didn't mind. He spoke with these South Philadelphian day-trippers patiently, instructing them through the wine-making process. Then, after discussing the 15-plus varieties, he let them pour samples at their own pace.

At one's own pace—that is the essence of Bucks County. Bucks is not so much for *doing* but for *savoring*. A countryside of rolling fields and agricultural estates, Bucks has fostered a culture of relaxation, and though there's plenty to do, one never feels rushed or hurried here. Bucks County encompasses 600 square miles and is less than an hour's drive from Center City. Its northern reaches, consisting of woodlands and several large lakes, are dotted with villages, including Perkasie, Riegelsville, Erwinna, Uhlerstown, and the larger Quakertown. The central area—mainly rolling farmland, historic structures and small creeks—includes the well-known artist and antiques havens of New Hope, Doylestown and Lahaska. Bucks' southeastern part, sometimes called the "Heritage Region," contains historical sites such as William Penn's estate and Washington Crossing Historic Park, as well as suburbs and industrial areas bordering North Philadelphia.

Penn founded Bucks County in 1682, choosing to build a country estate here on a cliff overlooking the Delaware River. Aptly named for Buckinghamshire, England, the county resembles its bucolic namesake, with large stone houses, tended fields, hedgerows and villages. New Hope, the county's most well-known town, was settled as an industrial area in the late 1700s. The Delaware River Canal, which runs through New Hope and Bucks' eastern border, is part of a system of canals that was used for transporting coal to New York and Philadelphia, and its construction led to much of the county's development. Today, its towpath and waterway continue to be a large part of Bucks County's appeal, drawing visitors to its trails and bike paths, as well as water recreation opportunities.

Despite its popularity, Bucks County has managed to retain its agricultural and rural atmosphere, capitalizing on its beauty as a tourist destination. However, in the past ten years, Bucks' attractiveness—and its vast amounts of available land—has drawn developers, and today, residents, government and commercial interests continue to battle over the county's vision for the future as both a Philadelphia suburb and a farming community. It is a battle that could wipe out what Bucks County is famous for, its charm.

Most visitors begin their Bucks County experience at New Hope, taking in the antique meccas of Lahaska and Lambertville, New Jersey, while in the area. This is where we'll begin our tour. From Lahaska, we'll take U.S. Route 202, which bisects the county, heading west to the county seat of Doylestown. We'll meander northward on various roads into the Lakes Region, exploring its state parks and small towns. Then, for a scenic, unforgettable trip south toward Philadelphia, we'll return by River Road, a 60-mile scenic byway that parallels the Delaware and skirts numerous small villages, running past area parklands and outdoor recreation opportunities and through historic sites.

Touring this area, you'll understand why many visitors return to Bucks County year after year, and why it has inspired so many creative works. Sure, there's shopping and unique stores and art shows and great bars. But it's Bucks' golden glow of sunlight on the soybean fields, the morning mist hanging over its field-stone barns and hayfields, and the gentle ripples of fish or turtles peeking from above the silvery Delaware that brings visitors back. Bucks is an all-inclusive spa package for body and soul, to be shared for a day, a weekend or more.

New Hope is Bucks County's favorite day-tripper destination, for its more than 180 art galleries, gift shops, antique stores, restaurants and quaint inns, grouped around its compact Main Street. New Hope was settled initially in 1719 as a ferry stop, and many of its early buildings date to the mid-1700s. The town later received its name after mill operator Benjamin Parry rebuilt two mills after the originals burned in 1790. Parry called his new buildings the new "New Hope Mills," and the name stuck. The downtown bustles on weekends with shoppers, tourists, hikers, bikers and motorcyclists. In fact, traffic can back up substantially in town, so it's wise to arrive early if you plan to spend the day.

SIGHTS

There is much to see in New Hope, including shops, historic sites and restaurants, but one of this town's prime forms of entertainment is its people. New Hope attracts a diverse crowd; many visitors simply like finding a good sidewalk table and parking themselves to enjoy the parade for an afternoon.

The Delaware Canal provides recreational opportunities to New Hope visitors, its towpath serving as a popular trail for hikers, bikers and equestrians. A refurbished lock and the fully re-

HIDDEN ▶ stored **Locktender's House** offers a glimpse of what life was like along the Delaware in the 1800s. It also serves as a visitor's center for the area, providing information on local sites and activities. Closed weekends from November through March. ~ 145 South Main Street, New Hope; 215-862-2021; www.fodc.org.

Before the railroads were able to move raw materials across Pennsylvania and the country, freight was moved along the Delaware Canal, on barges pulled by mules. Though this practice ceased officially in 1931, visitors can still enjoy the experience of boating along the straight, narrow waterway. The **New Hope Canal Boat Company** provides tours on the canal. Closed October through April. Admission. ~ 145 South Main Street, New Hope; 215-862-0758.

House tours of the **Parry Mansion**, former home of mill owner Benjamin Parry, are popular with historians. This 18th-century house contains an amalgam of American decorating tastes spanning 150 years. Each of the eight rooms is furnished in a distinctive period, ranging from Colonial to late Victorian. Admission. ~ 45 Main Street, New Hope; 215-865-5652; www.parrymansion.org.

HIDDEN ▶ For those who'd like a faster trip through Pennsylvania's countryside, the **New Hope and Ivyland Railroad** offers 50-minute rides on one of four antique steam locomotives or two diesels. Young train lovers will enjoy the special holiday events; in December, the company puts on a Polar Express ride and meet-and-greet with Santa. Admission. ~ 32 West Bridge Street, New Hope; 215-862-2332.

The **1870 Wedgwood Inn**, a Victorian-style bed and breakfast, was built on the foundation of the former headquarters building of George Washington's Army. This historic underpinning, containing rooms and tunnels for storage of goods and arms, was used as a hideaway on the Underground Railroad. ~ 111 West Bridge Street, New Hope; 215-862-2570.

A walk across the Delaware River to Lambertville on a half-mile bridge between the towns affords visitors a spectacular view of both towns and the river. The stroll along the **New Hope–Lambertville Bridge**, a turn-of-the-20th-century steel truss bridge, is a thrill in itself, as you watch the Delaware's murky waters swirl at least 30 feet below, next to the circa-1814 bridge abutments. ~ East Bridge Street, New Hope.

Lambertville, New Jersey, is much like New Hope, in that it offers a panoply of antique stores, art galleries and restaurants, but Lambertville tends to be less crowded, and on weekends, it serves as a respite for those tired of New Hope's mob scene. Many of New Hope's finest antique dealers have opened stores in Lambertville or have relocated there completely, as New Hope's shops have become increasingly focused on fine arts, crafts and

One-day Getaway

New Hope Adventure

- Plan to visit on a Tuesday or Saturday, heading first to **Rice's Sale and Country Market** (page 188), a 30-acre bazaar that features nearly 500 tables and stalls filled with antiques, crafts, Amish goods and new and used collectibles.

- Head into New Hope and stroll the assortment of stores, shops and galleries along Main Street. If you pass an interesting restaurant, consider making a reservation for the evening; on Saturdays, New Hope's eateries fill quickly.

- Dine at one of New Hope's historic restaurants like the **Logan Inn** (page 185), one of the country's oldest stage stops.

- If the weather is nice, head north on River Road to **Point Pleasant** (page 174), to rent a canoe, or **Lumberville** (page 174), to rent a bicycle. If the weather is poor, cross the river to Lambertville, NJ, to take in more shopping and antiquing, or head to the **Parry Mansion** (page 166), an 18th-century house filled with 150 years worth of furniture. Or you may want to hop on the **New Hope and Ivyland Railroad** (page 166) for a steam-train ride through the Pennsylvania countryside.

- Catch dinner in a church—**Marsha Brown** (page 184)—and a piano bar serenade or cabaret show afterward at **Odette's** (page 190). Marsha Brown features a unique Cajun-inspired menu. Odette's is New Hope's favorite nightspot, with nightly sing-alongs.

- To complete your day, enjoy a moonlight stroll along the Delaware and the canal along the towpath.

giftware. Lambertville also has a rich history of its own. The **Marshall House,** home to the Lambertville Historical Society, is the boyhood home of James Wilson Marshall, instigator of the California Gold Rush. Closed October through March. ~ 62 Bridge Street, Lambertville, NJ; 609-397-0770; www.lambert villehistoricalsociety.org.

Antique browsers, if traveling by car, should drive across the bridge from New Hope to Lambertville, continue to River Road

HIDDEN ▶ and head south two miles to check out the **Golden Nugget Antique Flea Market.** This antiques flea, nearly 40-years-old, boasts more than 200 outdoor vendors and 60 indoor shops. Like any flea market, this one has its "junque," but many New Hope area antique dealers frequent the Golden Nugget in search of hidden gems. Open Wednesday, Saturday and Sunday. ~ 1850 River Road, Lambertville, NJ; 609-397-0811; www.gnmarket.com.

Heading back through New Hope and "south" on U.S. 202 (if you have a compass, you'll realize you're actually traveling northwest), you'll encounter several area antique stores and eateries before arriving in Lahaska, home to **Peddler's Village,** a Colonial-themed shopping and dining area that contains a fully restored, 1922 carousel, a bed-and-breakfast inn and more than 70 specialty stores. Events held at this shopping village include a Scarecrow Festival in September and a Strawberry Festival in May. ~ 5927 Lower York Road, Lahaska; 215-794-4000.

Continue along 202 and you'll end up in **Doylestown,** the county seat. It was named for Edward Doyle, a settler who arrived here in 1692 after receiving a land grant from William Penn. Once home to some of Bucks County's most famous residents, including Michener and the pop singer Pink, Doylestown is remarkable not only for its famous sons but also for the variety of architectural styles found here. The city's residential architecture includes Colonial and Federal styles, Queen Anne, Italianate and revival. On a walking trip through town, you'll notice elaborate gingerbread-laden porches standing door-to-door with staid Federal porticos and asbestos-sided Victorians. Doylestown's Historic District itself is listed on the National Register of Historic Places for the town's contributions to Pennsylvania's commerce, government and architecture.

Without eccentric millionaire, tile maker, architect and archaeologist Henry Mercer, Doylestown may have ended up just another blip on the map, a Main Street destroyed by outlying shopping malls and the interstate. But Mercer's legacy—three one-of-a-kind reinforced concrete buildings that served as a home, a museum and a tile factory—continues to attract visitors here.

The son of a naval officer and Philadelphia socialite, Mercer moved to Bucks County as a child, and after studying abroad and at Harvard, he settled into a life of eccentricity in Doyles-

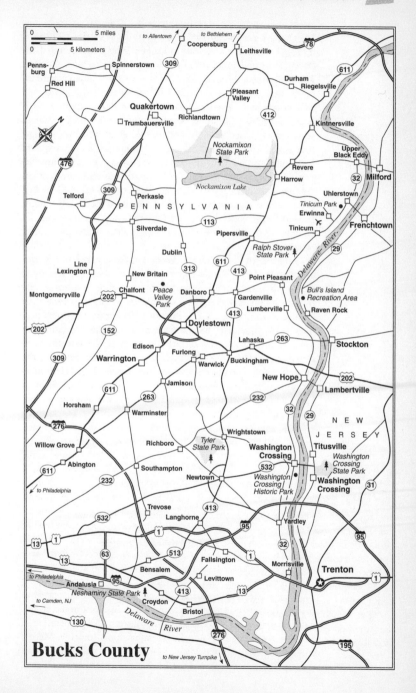

Bucks County

town. A lawyer, archaeologist, and self-studied architect, Mercer built three colossuses, Fonthill, his home built between 1908 and 1912; the Moravian Pottery and Tile Works, constructed between 1911 and 1912; and the Mercer Museum, built in 1916.

Fonthill is a 44-room castle built entirely of concrete. Based on the design of a 13th-century Rhenish castle, Fonthill was built as a testament to the sturdiness of concrete and its fireproof character. When it was under construction, many area residents watched with concern, believing that the structure, built without blueprints, would implode. The house contains 18 fireplaces, five bedrooms and ten bathrooms. It also features an early Otis elevator and steam heat—unusual for a home built in this period. Adding to Fonthill's weirdness are dead-end halls, walk-in fireplaces, turrets, a mansard roof and elaborate tile work, some fired at Mercer's nearby factory and many purchased abroad, including 33 antiquities from Babylon. Admission. ~ East Court Street, Doylestown; 215-348-9461.

Adjacent to Fonthill is the **Moravian Pottery and Tile Works**, another of Mercer's concrete monoliths. The building resembles a Spanish mission, with arched doorways and buttresses embellished by minarets. Mercer built the tile works to preserve the hand-crafted art of pottery making. His decorative tiles, produced in Arts and Crafts and European styles, adorn numerous building façades as well as interiors; Mercer tiles are found in nearby Bucks County homes and inns as well as the Pennsylvania State Capitol. The tile works continues to operate today, run as a museum and gift shop by the Bucks County Department of Parks and Recreation. A self-guided tour is available. Admission. ~ 130 Swamp Road, Doylestown; 215-345-6722.

Ask anyone who attended elementary school in the Philadelphia suburbs what they remember from school, and they're

AUTHOR FAVORITE

sights   The oldest building in Doylestown is a tavern constructed by the Doyle family in 1752. Originally called the Doyle Tavern or Doyle's Town, this former Colonial inn has been modified several times, most notably in 1873 with an addition of a French mansard roof. The inn became the **Fountain House**, a hotel frequented by Henry Ford and Katharine Hepburn. Although Doylestown has mostly managed to avoid turning itself into a quaint conduit for retail chain stores, this historic structure is now a Starbucks. However, it is the coolest Starbucks you'll ever drink a latte in, with fireplaces and games indoors, and comfortable rockers along the front porch outside. ~ At the crossroads of Route 202 and State Route 611.

likely to cite their field trips to the **Mercer Museum**. The third of Mercer's concrete structures, this four-story castle is filled with items your grandparents likely tossed once electricity made their lives easier. The museum, open since 1916, displays seemingly every hand tool made before the Industrial Revolution. Nearly 50,000 artifacts hang in its cavernous center court or are tucked away in rooms, dormers and along hallways. If you've ever played in an old attic or barn, you'll feel at home among the salmagundi. There are sleds, boats, carriages, medical implements, caskets, baskets, picks, axes, saws, cigar store Indians and more. Admission. ~ 84 South Pine Street, Doylestown; 215-345-0210.

Across the street from the Mercer Museum is the **James A. Michener Art Museum**. An imposing stone structure that was once home to the Bucks County Jail, the museum includes the works of 18th-, 19th- and 20th-century American artists, including a vast collection of Pennsylvania Impressionists' works. A portrait of George Washington painted by Rembrandt Peale also hangs here. The museum's lobby contains a number of artifacts, including a desk, typewriter and manuscript, complete with editorial comments from Michener. Those with extra time may want to bring along a book to the museum and enjoy the **George Nakashima Reading Room**, a Japanese-style room designed by Nakashima's daughter, Mira Nakashima-Yarnall, to showcase her father's furniture. Nakashima, an artist and woodworker, is a former resident of New Hope. Closed Monday. ~ 138 South Pine Street, Doylestown; 215-340-9800.   ◄ HIDDEN

The **National Shrine of Our Lady of Czestochowa** is a place of pilgrimage for Polish Americans. It was visited twice by Pope John Paul II, in 1983 and 1991, and by Lech Walesa in 1989. This is the final resting place of the heart of Ignace Jan Paderewski, pianist and the first prime minister of Poland. (Paderewski's body, once buried in Arlington National Cemetery, was returned to Poland in 1992.) The facility features a modern church building, several retreat centers and a cafeteria that serves Polish food on Sundays. ~ 654 Ferry Road, Doylestown; 215-345-0600.

Traveling south of Doylestown, between Warwick and Buckingham is the **Eight Arch Bridge**, the last remaining stone   ◄ HIDDEN
bridge with eight arches in Pennsylvania. This hand-laid bridge, which spans 218 feet, was built in 1803 and was used until the 1960s when a new bridge was constructed to accommodate traffic on York Road. ~ York Road (Route 263) at Neshaminy Creek, Warwick.

Roads north from Doylestown head to "lake country," an expanse of hilly woodlands containing several small and one large body of water. The Delaware River and numerous recreation areas provide opportunity for outdoor recreation and water sports.

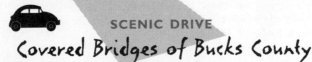

Covered Bridges of Bucks County

There are only six remaining bridges of the nineteen that used to be in Madison County, Iowa, but Bucks County has twelve and many are easy to find. This tour will lead you to five. If you start out from Philadelphia, expect to take five hours with stops; from New Hope, it's roughly a two-hour drive without stops.

WASHINGTON CROSSING HISTORIC PARK   Leave Philadelphia early. Head north on Route 95 to Exit 51A, heading north on Woodside Road. Cross east to River Road along any right hand turn to enjoy a slower, scenic drive on the Delaware. Stop at Washington Crossing Historic Park (page 175) to tour the buildings and lands. Allow an hour.

LOUX BRIDGE   Continue north through New Hope. At Point Pleasant, head west on Point Pleasant Pike to Carversville-Wismer Road. Go north to the Loux bridge, an 1874 span made of hemlock that is the second shortest covered bridge in the county. A sign calls it the Cabin Run Bridge, but that bridge is found downstream. Allow half an hour to get from Washington Crossing to the first bridge.

CABIN RUN BRIDGE   Pass through the bridge to Dark Hollow Road. Turn right. Then turn right on Covered Bridge Road to Cabin Run Bridge. It was built in 1871 and named for the log cabins and stone houses that once lined the creek banks. Take a nature hike at nearby **Ralph Stover State Park** (page 192). Allow an hour.

Nearby **Perkasie** captures the dream of small town America, featuring historic and new buildings, a lively main street area and a creek-side city park with carousel, covered bridge and hiking trail. ~ Borough of Perkasie; 215-257-5065; www.perkasie.org.

The **Pearl S. Buck House and Historic Site** is an 1835 stone farmhouse belonging to the Nobel Prize–winning author. Preserved as Buck owned it, it includes a vast collection of Pennsylvania and Chinese furniture and decorative arts, as well as several pieces of her work and awards. Buck lived at Green Hill Farm for nearly 40 years, moving to the area after penning *The Good Earth*. She wrote more than 100 works here and is buried on this 60-acre estate. The humanitarian organization Pearl S. Buck International, also has its headquarters here. Closed Monday. ~ 520 Dublin Road, Perkasie; 215-249-0100, 800-220-2825 ext. 170.

FRANKENFIELD BRIDGE   Reverse course on Covered Bridge Road and cross onto Dark Hollow Road, passing Stover Myers Mill. Turn left onto Cafferty Road and go to Frankenfield Bridge. At 130 feet in length, it's one of the longest in the county. Allow half an hour.

BREAKTIME   Go through the bridge until you reach Hollow Horn Road. Turn right and head toward **Erwinna** (page 173). At this point, you'll probably want to lunch in Erwinna or cross the Delaware at Uhlerstown to dine in **Frenchtown, New Jersey** (page 174), taking in that village's antique stores and gift shops. The **Frenchtown Inn** (7 Bridge Street; 908-996-3300), set in an 1805 hotel, has an upscale lunch menu and an extensive wine list. Allow an hour and a half.

ERWINNA BRIDGE   From Erwinna, turn left on Hill Road and follow it to the right to the Erwinna Bridge, a span listed on the National Register of Historic Places as having been built in 1871. However, county records suggest a bridge was originally constructed here in 1832. It is the shortest bridge. Allow half an hour.

UHLERSTOWN BRIDGE   Return to Erwinna the way you came and turn left on River Road. Go two miles and turn left on Hill Road to reach the Uhlerstown Bridge. This span, built of oak, has windows and is the only covered bridge that crosses the Delaware Canal. Allow half an hour.

NEW HOPE   Head south on River Road to New Hope (page 165). In New Hope, stroll across the bridge to **Lambertville** (page 166) or window-shop in New Hope. There are a number of fine restaurants here that will make a perfect end to your tour.

For those traveling to the area in May, **Peonyland**, a farm   ◀ *HIDDEN* with more than 60 varieties and 60,000 tree peonies, is worth the stop. Drexel graduate Michael Hsu and his family have cultivated one of the country's largest collections of these plants, which bear China's national flower. Open in May by appointment. ~ 475 Church Road, Richlandtown; 215-536-9388.

Along the Delaware River, the towns of **Upper Black Eddy**, **Uhlerstown** and **Erwinna** provide lodgings and rest stops for outdoor enthusiasts along the Delaware River. The aptly named **Ringing Rocks Park**, two miles west of Upper Black Eddy, con-   ◀ *HIDDEN* tains a seven-acre boulder field, which, when its rocks are struck with a hammer (or another rock), sings. Not all the rocks ring, and scientists have yet to determine why, because the boulders are all made up of diabase, a common ingredient in the Earth's crust, but only about a third of the rocks ring. This geological phenomenon draws families and music makers year round; don't be frightened by the hikers carrying ball peen hammers. ~ Ringing Rocks Road, Bridgeton Township; 215-757-0571.

HIDDEN ▶ Along the Delaware, also near Upper Black Eddy, is the 126-acre **Tinicum Park**, a county park containing ball fields and recreation areas for use by local residents. But contained within the park boundaries is the **Erwin-Stover House**, an 1800 Federal-style home built by Irish immigrant Arthur Erwin and later purchased by a miller, Henry Stover. The grounds are lovely for picnicking, and nearby is a well-preserved, stone and frame bank barn typical of those built in Bucks County in the mid-1800s. House tours by appointment only. ~ River Road, Erwinna; 215-757-0571.

Across the river from the upper Bucks County villages are the towns of **Milford** and **Frenchtown,** New Jersey—quaint whistle stops where you'll find antiques stores, restaurants and gift shops. Use the bridges at Upper Black Eddy or Uhlerstown to reach these destinations.

While in Lumberville, be sure to notice the Black Bass Hotel, a 1740s inn and restaurant favored by President Cleveland. ~ 3774 River Road, Lumberville; 215-297-5770.

River Road, or Pennsylvania State Route 32, is a scenic touring road that connects northern Bucks County to New Hope and points south. This byway winds through small villages and along high cliffs overlooking the Delaware. The speed limit is 35 m.p.h., and drivers should take care to watch for cyclists as well as artists, who like to set their easels along the stony, narrow edge to paint the river views.

Point Pleasant, another River Road hamlet, developed as a way station for rafters and canalmen who worked the Delaware River and Canal. The first gristmill was built here in 1748, an operation that provided grain for Revolutionary War soldiers. A number of inns and taverns were constructed in Point Pleasant, some of which still exist. Today, the village is known as an embarkation point for paddlers, kayakers and fishermen on the Delaware River.

HIDDEN ▶ Farther south on the river lies **Lumberville**, a small village favored as a country retreat by President Grover Cleveland. The **Lumberville Store**, in business since 1770, rents bicycles and sells sandwiches for picnics on the Delaware Canal. ~ 3741 River Road, Lumberville; 215-297-5388.

The town also serves as a trailhead for those hiking to Bull's Island, a recreation area in New Jersey. The **Lumberville–Raven Rock Footbridge** leads over the Delaware River here. A bridge has been at this site since 1856; following a flood in 1903 that washed away one of its spans, it deteriorated to such a state that it was closed during World War II. The footbridge that now carries hikers and cyclists was built in 1946. ~ Bull's Island Recreation Area, 2185 Daniel Bray Highway, Stockton, NJ; 609-397-2949.

River Road heads south through New Hope toward Philadelphia, linking several more small villages, towns and historic sites. Two and a half miles south of New Hope lies the **Bowman's** ◄ HIDDEN **Hill Wildflower Preserve**, a 100-acre refuge containing more than 1000 native plant species and wildlife. The last two weeks of April are ideal for wildflower sightings, but the park's variety ensures that something is almost always in bloom between early March and mid-October. Wander along the preserve's meadow and woodland trails, take guided tours or sit in the forest gazebo sanctuary. Birders shouldn't miss the Sinkler Bird Observatory, a sunroom with picture windows that overlook the preserve and numerous bird feeders. Lucky bird-watchers may catch sight of an owl or pileated woodpecker, the largest of the North American woodpeckers. The Platt Collection, an exhibit of 100 stuffed birds, nests and more gathered by local ornithologist Charles Platt, never fails to interest children. The collection features nearly every type of bird in the Delaware Valley Region. Daily tours are offered April through October. Admission. ~ 1635 River Road; 215-862-2924.

On the preserve's grounds stands **Bowman's Hill Tower**, a 110-foot stone lookout built in the 1930s to mark the promontory where George Washington's men monitored the Delaware. The brief elevator trip to the top rewards visitors with unobstructed views; the scenery is at its most spectacular in fall, when the leaves burst into shades of scarlet, gold, cinnamon and titian.

Local lore says that the land on which the tower was built is linked with Dr. John Bowman, a British surgeon who allegedly ventured to catch the pirate Captain William Kidd but ended up joining forces with him instead. Legend suggests Bowman settled in Bucks County after Kidd was captured and later asked to be buried on the high hill. For years, fortune hunters sought pirate treasure here, but there's no proof Bucks County has ever been linked to pirates or booty. Still, it makes for a good story. Today, digging or removal of artifacts, plants or animals is prohibited in the park. ~ Two miles south of New Hope on River Road.

Washington Crossing Historic Park is where General Washington and his army of 2400 so famously braved high water, snow and frigid cold on Christmas Day 1776, to surprise British and Hessian troops in Trenton, New Jersey. Whether Washington stood in his boat defiantly, as portrayed in Emmanual Leutze's famous work, we'll never know, but a reproduction of the famous painting hangs alongside other memorabilia at the Memorial Building and Visitor's Center (the original hangs in New York's Metropolitan Museum of Art). Each Christmas, local history buffs attempt to re-create the crossing—a spectator event that has become a holiday tradition for many area residents. Washington's feat must have been difficult—high water canceled the re-enactment from 2002 to 2004. ~ 1112 River Road, Washington Crossing; 215-493-4076.

HIDDEN ▶

Not to be missed on the grounds of Washington's Crossing is the **McConkey Ferry Inn**, where Washington and his staff ate Christmas dinner before traveling to New Jersey. The **Mahlon K. Taylor House** is a completely restored 1817 residence trimmed with the furnishings of a well-landed gentleman. The **Taylorsville Store** is a working general store once run by Mahlon Taylor. In this Federal structure, you'll find a cache of colonial merchandise, including traditional toys, souvenirs and bricks of tea similar to those tossed overboard at the Boston Tea Party. Visitors center closed Monday. ~ River Road, Washington Crossing; 215-493-4076.

HIDDEN ▶

For those with an hour to spare, on the New Jersey side lies the 2009-acre **Washington Crossing State Park**, where Washington landed and regrouped before marching to Trenton. A collection of Revolutionary War artifacts, housed at the park's museum, makes history come alive. Display cases hold soldiers' letters, doctor's notes, prints, swords, muskets and more. To reach the park, cross the river at New Hope or Route 95 to the south. Admission. ~ 355 Washington Crossing-Pennington Road, Titusville, NJ; 609-737-0623.

Traveling south of Washington Crossing on River Road leads visitors past lovely riverfront mansions, the most notable of which were owned by William Penn and Nicholas Biddle, president of the Second Bank of the United States.

Pennsbury Manor is Penn's country estate, reconstructed on 43 acres of the 8400 that Penn once owned near Morrisville. The Georgian-style mansion and outbuildings portray life as it was along the Delaware River in the 17th century. The manor house was built on the original home's foundation and contains both original and period furnishings—the largest collection of 17th-century furnishings in Pennsylvania. The formal and kitchen gardens, bake and brew house, vineyard and barn that houses Red Devon cattle and Arabian horses, demonstrate that Penn, a Quaker, enjoyed a lifestyle befitting an accomplished and wealthy gentleman. Tragically, Penn died penniless due to mismanagement of his estate. He is buried in Jordans, England. Closed Monday. Admission. ~ 400 Pennsbury Memorial Road, Morrisville; 215-946-0400; www.pennsburymanor.org.

The **Glen Foerd Mansion** is a circa-1850s home currently being restored to Victorian elegance. The house, built originally by Philadelphia financier Charles Macalester—founder of Macalester College in St. Paul, Minnesota—has undergone several renovations, including transformation into an Edwardian summer home at the start of the 20th century. The home is lav-

Bucks County Wine Trail

It's not Napa Valley, but Bucks County has a cottage wine industry based on the region's capacity for growing native American grapes such as concord and catawba, as well as hybrids and vinifera like riesling and chardonnay. Pick a sunny day and enjoy the free tastings.

Buckingham Valley Vineyards has an ambitious wine list that includes chardonnay, chambourcin, vidal blanc and riesling. It is one of the few wineries in Bucks County that sells sangria as well. Closed Monday. ~ 1521 Route 413, Buckingham; 215-794-7188; www.pawine. com.

Despite the challenges of growing such varietals in this climate, **Crossing Vineyards and Winery** has crafted some excellent cabernet sauvignons, and its chardonnay has taken home state honors. ~ 1853 Wrightstown Road, Washington Crossing; 215-493-6500; www. crossingvineyard.com.

New Hope Winery has a selection of whites and reds but historically, its specialty is fruit wines, including apple, cherry and peach. ~ 6123 Lower York Road, New Hope; 215-794-2331; www.newhopewinery.com.

Peace Valley Winery features several specialty whites, including riesling and gewurztraminer, as well as those made from table grapes such as Fredonia and Niagara. Closed Monday and Tuesday. ~ 300 Limekiln Road, Chalfont; 215-249-9058.

Fans of sweet wines will enjoy the wide selection at **Rose Bank Winery**, including blush, American fruit wines and spicy, fruit-based wines. Closed Monday through Thursday. ~ 258 Durham Road, Newtown; 215-860-5899.

The Ullman family, in the area since 1968, grows a tidy grouping of chardonnay, cabernet franc, and chambourcin grapes at **Rushland Ridge Vineyards**. Open weekends March to December. ~ One mile from Almshouse Road on Rushland Road, Rushland; 215-598-0251.

Sand Castle Winery specializes in several complex whites, including riesling and chardonnay, although it also produces pinot noir and cabernet sauvignon. Fee for tour. ~ 755 River Road, Erwinna; 800-722-9463; www.sandcastlewinery.com.

ishly decorated, containing an art gallery, pipe organ and elaborate stained-glass skylights. Grounds include a lily pond, cottages, carriage house and the remnants of a boathouse destroyed by vandals in the 1980s. The home's conservation corps aims to restore the boathouse for enjoyment by visitors and make the facilities available to rent for special events. By appointment only or scheduled monthly tours. Admission. ~ 5001 Grant Avenue, Philadelphia; 215-632-5330; www.glenfoerd.org.

A third elegantly restored mansion on the Delaware is **Andalusia**, the grand home of Nicholas Biddle, director of the Second Bank of the United States. At Andalusia, Biddle cultivated grapes, mulberry trees (his attempt to jump-start the silk industry in the United States), race horses and Guernsey cattle. The magnificent main house, designed by U.S. Capitol architects Thomas U. Walter and Benjamin Latrobe is distinguished by its colossal Doric-columned porch. Outbuildings include a grotto, a billiard room and "graperies"—hothouse vineyards now home to rose gardens. Those who have seen the Second Bank of the United States building at Independence Park will recognize the similarities between its façade and Andalusia's; both show Biddle's fondness for classic architecture. By reservation only. Admission. ~ 1237 State Road, Andalusia; 215-245-5479; www. andalusiahousemuseum.org.

HIDDEN ►

Fallsington is a hard-to-find historic village that serves as a time capsule to the past 300 years. This quaint old village contains the Quaker meeting house where Penn worshipped, a log cabin and several stone houses and commercial buildings constructed between the 1600s and early 1900s. Historic Fallsington, Inc., sponsors numerous activities, including open houses, Colonial fairs and a Christmas tree–lighting ceremony during the year, and guided tours are available for a fee. Tours offered Tuesday through Saturday from mid-May to mid-October; other

PLAYTIME ON SESAME STREET

For those with young children in tow and a day to spare, **Sesame Place** is a must-visit for the ten and under crowd. Located in Langhorne, just north of the Bucks–Philadelphia border, Sesame Place has been a local favorite for more than 25 years. Now owned by Anheuser-Busch, it features rides, shows, playgrounds and chance meetings with familiar *Sesame Street* puppet characters like Elmo, Big Bird and Cookie Monster. The extensive water park is a popular swimming hole during the summer months. Memorial Day through Labor Day, open daily; weekends early May through October. Admission. ~ 100 Sesame Road, Langhorne; 215-752-7070; www.sesameplace.com.

times tours by appointment only. ~ 4 Yardley Avenue, Fallsington; 215-295-6567; www.historicfallsington.org.

If you head back to Philadelphia on Route 1, you may be intrigued by a creepy set of abandoned buildings at Byberry Road and where Route 1 becomes East Roosevelt Boulevard. This facility is the **former Philadelphia State Hospital**, a nearly 100-year-old asylum that closed in 1990. The place has a tragic history of abuse, neglect and mistreatment of patients, and its 50-odd buildings exude a sinister aura. Much of the tract has been sold to developers, but development has been hampered by the presence of asbestos and other hazardous materials.

Bucks County is replete with country inns, historic hotels and romantic getaways. What it lacks is a good selection of moderately priced hotels and family-friendly lodgings. A few can be found in the southeastern part of the county, near the towns of Langhorne, Bristol and Bensalem, and along the interstates in the county's northern section. Most of these locales are just a short drive to New Hope, Lambertville, New Jersey, and Doylestown and other Bucks County attractions.

LODGING

For a country getaway, Bucks County offers an astonishing selection of more than 30 historic hotels, lodges and bed-and-breakfast inns. Most places provide breakfast with the rate, even if they lack the word "breakfast" in their title. Choices include a rustic one-room 17th-century cottage, grand Victorian mansions, Empire-era, New York–style boutique hotels and Colonial farmhouses. Fussy and fine, sleek and modern or comfy-cozy— it's here. Those hoping to visit during spring blooms or fall foliage must plan ahead; hotels often are booked three or more months in advance for weekends.

Many inns require a two-night minimum stay, so be sure to inquire about restrictions. And if you're visiting with children, ask about age limits. Some B&Bs allow children over 12, but others won't allow anyone under 16. Few allow young children. Smokers should note that many are non-smoking facilities.

The following is a sampling of some of Bucks' best inns. For more information, **The Bucks County Bed and Breakfast Association of Pennsylvania** offers information on 41 area inns. ~ 215-862-2570; www.visitbucks.com.

New Hope boasts several top-rated inns and beds and breakfasts, including the ever-popular **Porches on the Towpath**, a former granary where guests can sit on the front porch and watch cyclists, hikers and mules pass by on the main trail through town. This ten-bedroom home is tastefully decorated with English and French antiques. Several rooms have canal views, and the recently renovated carriage house offers private entrances and its own balcony. All rooms have their own bathrooms and showers.

Some feature antique clawfoot tubs. Most rooms feature queen beds; room 11 is a gem, with two queens, gleaming beige and white walls, elegant wainscoting, a fine collection of paintings and a private courtyard with fountain. A full country breakfast is served at 9:15 a.m. each day. ~ 20 Fishers Alley, New Hope; 215-862-3277, fax 215-862-1833; www.porchesnewhope.com, e-mail info@porchesnewhope.com. MODERATE.

The **Logan Inn,** in the middle of New Hope, is one of the five oldest inns in the United States. While many area inns boast that "Washington slept here," it's thought that he actually did stay at what was once known as Ferry Tavern, at least five times. The Logan Inn's 16 rooms are beautifully appointed with Colonial and Victorian antiques and reproductions; several feature romantic canopy beds. Each has its own bathroom, and a few have river views. Complimentary breakfast. Closed January and early February. ~ 10 West Ferry Street, New Hope; 215-862-2300; www.loganinn.com, e-mail loganinn@verizon.net. DELUXE.

The **1870 Wedgwood Inn** is a colorful Victorian-era farmhouse furnished in an eclectic mix of antiques, modern furnishings and artwork. The eight guest rooms are hand-stenciled or painted by a local artist and feature gas fireplaces or electric Franklin stoves. Two have king-sized beds; the rest have queens. Several have their own porches and all have private bathrooms. Breakfast can be eaten in the dining room or delivered to your room. The friendly staff also will make arrangements for special services, including an in-room massage, day spa appointments or carriage and hot-air balloon rides. Children who "sleep through the night and respect antiques, fine linens and other things delicate" are welcome—a rarity for Bucks County inns. ~ 111 West Bridge Street, New Hope; 215-862-2570; www.wedgwoodinn. com, e-mail stay@wedgwoodinn.com. DELUXE TO ULTRA-DELUXE.

ARTISTS IN RESIDENCE

In 1898, artists came to New Hope after Pennsylvania painters William Lathrop and Edward Redfield bought property there, giving rise to the Penn-sylvania Impressionist movement. Later, in the 1930s, Bucks County was "discovered" by a range of talented Americans, including Dorothy Parker, S. J. Perelman and Oscar Hammerstein II. Pulitzer and Nobel Prize–winning author Pearl Buck settled here in her 40s and is buried on her beloved estate, Green Hills Farm, near Perkasie. Pulitzer Prize winner James Michener is a Bucks County native raised in Doylestown, and he returned there to write after many adventures overseas.

The proprietors of the 1870 Wedgwood Inn also operate the **Aaron Burr House,** an 1873 Queen Anne Victorian B&B named for the third vice president of the United States who, up until February 2006, was the only vice president to have shot another person. The inn's stone foundation is what remains of the pre-Revolutionary home where Burr fled after killing Alexander Hamilton in 1804. The present-day retreat has seven bedrooms, each with private bath. All are decorated with beautiful Victorian or Colonial furniture, lacy bedspreads and swag curtains; some have ceiling fans and fireplaces. Breakfast is served fresh daily, and the inn shares recreational facilities, including swimming pools, tennis courts and a clubhouse, with other inns in the area. ~ 80 West Bridge Street, New Hope; 215-862-2343; www.aaronburrhouse.com. MODERATE TO DELUXE.

A unique blend of Federal and Victorian architecture, the **1833 Umpleby House** is another B&B property run by the owners of the 1870 Wedgwood Inn. The six lovely suites and two guest rooms are each individually painted and stenciled by a local artist; they feature antiques and original art, and are adorned with fresh flowers year-round. All have a private bathroom; some have jacuzzi tubs, their own porches or fireplaces. Like the Aaron Burr House, guests can access recreational facilities such as swimming pools (in season) and tennis courts. Bonus amenities include a guest refrigerator and pantry and wireless internet throughout the hotel. ~ 111 West Bridge Street, New Hope; 215-862-3936; www.umplebyhouse.com. MODERATE TO DELUXE.

For family-friendly digs, the **Best Western New Hope Inn** is a 152-room, modern hotel located just outside downtown New Hope. Guest rooms are furnished in typical hotel style, with desks, nighstands and chairs. Each is wired for Internet access and offers video games, coffeemakers, irons and ironing boards. The grounds include a playground, tennis court (racquets can be borrowed at the front desk, if needed) and an exercise room. The heated outdoor swimming pool is open seasonally. ~ 6426 Lower York Road, New Hope; 215-862-5221; www.bwnewhope.com. DELUXE.

The grand **Mansion Inn** is an ornate Second Empire Victorian set in manicured gardens behind a hand-crafted, scrolled wrought-iron fence. Its five suites and two bedrooms are decorated with antiques, including four-poster beds, upholstered headboards or antique wrought-iron beds. Many have fireplaces, and all have private bathrooms with bath or shower. The Ashby Suite, in the adorable garden cottage, has its own front porch entrance. Suites come equipped with robes and fruit baskets; all rooms offer complimentary sherry and turn-down service, and a full breakfast served in the dining room. A romantic, vine-decked gazebo is a hallmark on the grounds; there's also an awarding-winning restaurant on-site. ~ 9 South Main Street, New Hope; 215-862-1231; www.themansioninn.com. ULTRA-DELUXE.

New Hope prides itself on its diversity, and **The Raven** is the hotspot among gay visitors for nightlife, food, hospitality and dining. The motel has 12 rooms, two lively bars, a restaurant, pool and a cabaña bar that hosts well-attended Sunday bashes. Rooms are decorated in a functional, almost monastic style, with two queens or a king bed and a chair. All have private baths. Although the Raven is *the* center for New Hope's gay dining and nightlife, proprietors Rand Skolnick and Terrence Meck, who recently bought and renovated the property, say they "welcome all." ~ 385 West Bridge Street, New Hope; 215-862-2081, fax 215-862-3868; www.theravenresort.com, e-mail info@theraven resort.com. MODERATE.

For an indulgent getaway beautifully set on the river, **Bridgeton House on-the-Delaware** draws weekenders with peaceful surroundings and an Arts and Crafts decor. An 1836 home that has been used as a bakery and general store, Bridgetown House has been lovingly restored by its owners and furnished to please the most discriminating tastes. Most rooms have French doors that lead to balconies overlooking the river. Each room has a private bath and comes with luxury linens, terry robes and toiletries. Rates include a two-course breakfast, served in the dining room or a continental breakfast delivered to your door. Afternoon tea with warm cakes and fragrant tea or sherry is particularly gratifying after a day of adventuring. ~ 1525 River Road, Upper Black Eddy; 610-982-5856, 888-982-2007; www.bridgetonhouse.com, e-mail info@bridgetonhouse.com. DELUXE TO ULTRA-DELUXE.

AUTHOR FAVORITE

The **Bucksville House** in Kintnersville wraps around you like a country quilt. This five-bedroom bed and breakfast, which has served in the past as an inn, tavern and Prohibition-era watering hole, is decorated with American country furnishings, reproductions and antiques. Rooms are fresh and cheery, decorated with quilts, painted country furniture and antiques such as spinning wheels and ladderback chairs. The common rooms include a breakfast area that once served as a blacksmith shop. Guests who are keen on the paranormal will appreciate innkeepers Barb and Joe Szollosi's stories of the numerous ghosts who live here. ~ 4501 Durham Road, Kintnersville; 610-847-8948; www.bucksvillehouse.com. DELUXE.

A 2001 renovation of the historic 1902 **Doylestown Inn** linked the inn's two original buildings architecturally by a large sunny atrium and center hallway, allowing the inn to be served by an elevator and each room to have its own heating and air conditioning. This hotel, located conveniently at the heart of Doylestown, beckons visitors with its comfortable front porch rockers and well-appointed lobby. Each of the 11 rooms has a four-poster or sleigh bed, a minibar and whirlpool tub. A typical room might have a king-sized four-poster cherry bed, nightstands, two upholstered Boston lolling chairs and luxurious window treatments. Rates include complimentary breakfast and a newspaper. ~ 18 West State Street, Doylestown; 215-345-6610, fax 215-348-9940; www.doylestowninn.com, e-mail info@doylestowninn.com. ULTRA-DELUXE.

Around the corner from the Doylestown Inn is the **1814 House Inn**, a new bed and breakfast featuring rooms named for famous Bucks County residents. The seven rooms and suites have Colonial-style furnishings and offer satellite television, high-speed internet access and a complimentary fruit basket. Several have fireplaces or Franklin stoves and jacuzzi-style bathtubs. The Mead Suite features a four-poster bed with ball-fringe canopy, a corner fireplace and comfortable chaise, and an oversized whirlpool tub. Afternoon tea is served on request, and there's a cozy courtyard and comfortable common room for reading or playing board games. ~ 50 South Main Street, Doylestown; 215-340-1814, 800-508-1814, fax 215-340-2234; www.1814houseinn. com, e-mail info@1814houseinn.com. ULTRA-DELUXE.

◄ HIDDEN

The stone **Weisel Hostel**, a former country estate, is one of Bucks County's most popular bargain lodging sites, with 20 beds and one family room. The common area features a stone fireplace and comfortable couches. Lodging is dorm-style, and houseparents live on-site. The eight-acre grounds, which boast a wealth of wildlife, have trails that connect to Nockamixon State Park. ~ 7347 Richlandtown Road, Quakertown; 215-536-8749. BUDGET.

The **Golden Pheasant Inn** is a well-known dining destination for its award-winning French cuisine and six bedrooms that offer romantic lodgings with canal and river views. The rooms, which are available for dining customers, are appointed in French provincial style and contain French, American and English antiques. Each has its own bath. This family-run restaurant and inn was built in 1857 and is located in quiet Erwinna, on the towpath. Chef Michael Faure, a native of France, studied in Paris and honed his skills at the Hotel du Pont in Wilmington and Le Bec Fin in Philadelphia before he and his wife, Barbara, purchased the property in 1986. On-site is a guest cottage that is pet- and family-friendly, with some restrictions. Dining and lodging packages are available. ~ 763 River Road, Erwinna; 610-294-9595; www.goldenpheasant.com. MODERATE TO DELUXE.

Across the river from Erwinna and Uhlerstown lies the New Jersey village of Frenchtown, a rural community that offers antiquing, art galleries, fine dining and shopping. If you seek a hotel that offers something besides Victorian or Federal furnishings, **HIDDEN ►** the **National Hotel** in Frenchtown, is an 11-room boutique inn cleanly outfitted with furnishings that suggest the West Indies, Africa or turn-of-the-20th-century Manhattan. All guest rooms have private baths, some with whirlpool tubs. A few have private porches as well. The hotel's restaurants are excellent places to relax after a bike ride on the towpath or a day of shopping. ~ 31 Race Street, Frenchtown, NJ; 908-996-4500, fax 908-996-3642; www.frenchtownnational.com, e-mail info@frenchtown national.com. DELUXE.

DINING   The restaurant choices in Bucks County range from sophisticated to diner menus that offer hundreds of choices. The area lacks a specific regional cuisine; however, many restaurants use locally grown ingredients and serve game in season. Several world-renowned chefs own restaurants in the county, which boasts beautiful scenery and a well-heeled clientele. Atmosphere is a priority for Bucks restaurants; here, you'll find cozy dining nooks; elaborately set tables with fine linens, china and crystal; and simple country kitchens. Settings include a former church, pre-Revolutionary taverns and inns, Victorian manor homes, barns, mills and more.

In the northeastern United States, diners are ubiquitous, earning loyal fans for their all-inclusive menus and 24-hour break-**HIDDEN ►** fasts. The **Eagle Diner**, with two locations in Bucks County, is a local family favorite, featuring fresh baked goods, comfort foods, Italian specialties and deli choices. The food is not fancy, but service and preparation are consistent, with hearty portions dished up promptly and courteously. The selection of home-baked goodies and delicious bread keeps locals coming back. ~ 739 Street Road, Warminster, 215-672-8228; and 6522 Lower York Road, New Hope, 215-862-5575; www.eagledinerpa.com. BUDGET.

New Hope offers a medley of dining options, with new restaurants coming onto the scene every year. The eponymous **Marsha Brown** made a splash when it opened in 2003 in a refurbished Methodist church. Restaurateur Brown, who owns several area Ruth's Chris steakhouses, has created an eatery that celebrates her Louisiana roots. The food is southern with an emphasis on Creole, and selections include an extensive raw bar, seafood, chicken and beef. The Eggplant Ophelia is a delightfully stacked casserole of crabmeat, shrimp and vegetables with a spicy kick. For dessert, the crème brûlée is divine. Marsha Brown's atmosphere is dramatic, featuring a stained-glass window and choir loft. The 40-foot painting over what used to be the altar, however, is unnerving and likely to detract from the first-time diner's experience. The frightening depiction of warriors fighting off lions is by artist Valeriy Belenikan, a Russian native who now lives across the bridge in Lambertville, NJ. ~ 15 South Main Street, New Hope; 215-862-7044; www.marsha brownrestaurant.com, e-mail marshabrown1012@comcast.net. ULTRA-DELUXE.

For casual dining and family fun, **El Taco Loco** has just the   ◄ *HIDDEN* right menu. The *quesadillas* are gooey and fresh, and the fajitas satisfying. Vibrant walls, Mexican pottery and colorful tablecloths complete the package. ~ 6 Stockton Avenue, New Hope; 215-862-0908; www.el-taco-loco.com, e-mail eltacoloco@veriz on.net. BUDGET.

For more than 200 years, **Odette's** has been a mainstay of the New Hope dining and entertainment scene, first operating as an inn, starting in 1794. Later, it was transformed into a country French restaurant in 1961 by Ziegfield Follies girl Odette Mytril Logan. Today, Odette's is known as a cabaret, piano bar and restaurant popular for its nightly sing-alongs, especially with the weekend visitor set. Nationally recognized performers frequently take the stage at Odette's as well. Some tables offer excellent river views, so be sure to request one when making reservations. The menu sticks to its French and Continental roots with selections such as braised short ribs, grilled pork chops and bouillabaisse. ~ 274 South River Road, New Hope; 215-862-2432; www.odet tes.com, e-mail info@odettes.com. DELUXE TO ULTRA-DELUXE.

Gerenser's Exotic Ice Cream is a New Hope one-of-a-kind   ◄ *HIDDEN* shop, with ice cream flavors you won't find elsewhere. Lines

---

AUTHOR FAVORITE

The **Logan Inn**, established in 1727, is one of the five oldest inns in the United States. The facility offers several dining options, including a Colonial room, a garden dining room and a tavern. The glass-enclosed front porch is one of the best in New Hope for dining and people-watching. Fare is American with a smattering of Italian thrown in. The crabmeat and shrimp pasta, prepared with a white wine cream sauce, makes a colorful, delectable meal. In the tavern, the gooey baked brie complements the beer selection. Closed January and early February. ~ 10 West Ferry Street, New Hope; 215-862-2300; www.loganinn.com, e-mail loganinn@verizon.net. MODERATE TO DELUXE.

often are down the sidewalk on summer nights. The Caribbean Spicy Tree Bark is a popular sample flavor, rich with cinnamon. Other flavors include Ukrainian Rose Petal and Banana Brandy. ~ 22 South Main Street, New Hope; 215-862-2050. BUDGET.

The formal dining rooms and parlors of the **Mansion Inn** are among the most popular romantic dining spots in Bucks County. The inn features a seasonal menu heavy on meats and game in the winter, enlivened with seafood in the summer. Entrées include rack of lamb prepared with a cherry demiglaze, and venison wrapped with bacon. Closed Tuesday from May through November; closed Monday through Wednesday from mid-November to May. ~ 9 South Main Street, New Hope; 215-862-1231; www.themansioninn.com. DELUXE.

Country French cooking tops the menu at **The Inn at Phillips Mill**, a farmhouse located at a bend in River Road north of New Hope. This warm dining room provides a sweet setting for dining on simple French fare. Highlights include the lamb chops and veal. Leave room for dessert; the lemon meringue pie is worth a splurge. And be sure to bring along your favorite wine; the inn is a BYOB facility. ~ 2590 River Road, New Hope; 215-862-9919. DELUXE.

The **Golden Pheasant Inn**'s restaurant dishes up French favorites in a cozy, historic atmosphere of plaster walls, exposed beams and painted woodwork. Menu selections include appetizers such as escargot and frog legs, and entrées such as grilled petite lamb chops and filet mignon topped with a delicate béarnaise. Closed Sunday through Tuesday. ~ 763 River Road, Erwinna; 610-294-9595; www.goldenpheasant.com. ULTRA-DELUXE.

To celebrate with a group or enjoy an intimate dinner, **Evermay on the Delaware** is the place for a special occasion, serving a six-course fixed-price dinner in the elegant setting of an 18th-century estate. Chef Andrew Little draws ingredients from his kitchen garden and local suppliers—not the least of the lessons Little took away from working for a year at the five-star Inn at Little Washington in Washington, Virginia. Servings include delicate soups; tantalizing appetizers, such as seared scallops dressed in bacon; fresh greens; snappy duck or fish; a cheese course; and light desserts, including pound cake or lemon cream. ~ River Road, Erwinna; 610-294-9100; www.evermay.com, e-mail info@ evermay.com. ULTRA-DELUXE.

Meat-and-potatoes types and families will enjoy the **Cock 'n Bull Restaurant** at Peddler's Village in Lahaska. This Colonial-themed restaurant serves hearty dishes like beef bourguignon in a fresh bread bowl and chicken pot pie. On Thursdays, the all-you-can-eat buffet overflows with carved roasts, potatoes, soups and pies. ~ Peddler's Village, Route 202 South and Street Road, Lahaska; 215-794-4000; www.peddlersvillage.com. DELUXE.

Café **Arielle**, a French restaurant in Doylestown's former   ◀ *HIDDEN* agricultural works, often gets overlooked in a county dominated by fine French restaurants. But Chef Jacques Colmaire serves a simple yet well-prepared selection of entrées, including sweet-breads in a demi-glaze, marinated ostrich filet and veal scaloppini with wild mushrooms. Candles on the table and fresh linens add to the romantic ambience. ~ 100 South Main Street, Doylestown; 215-345-5930. DELUXE.

North of Doylestown, in Quakertown, lies a favorite desti-nation for locals and college students, **Bubba's Potbelly Stove**.   ◀ *HIDDEN* This restaurant offers generous portions of proteins and carbo-hydrates at bargain prices, in a log-cabin adorned with steer horns and wagon wheels. James "Bubba" Barry passed away in March 2005, but his family-run restaurant remains a thriving hotspot. The French onion soup is topped with more cheese than a pizza, and the burgers are huge. ~ 1485 North Route 309, Quakertown; 215-536-8308. BUDGET.

In Lumberville, a British flag hangs outside the **Black Bass Hotel**, an inn and restaurant that features seasonal menus pre-pared in "new American style" (ironic, considering the place was a Tory hangout during the Revolutionary War). Menu selections include a lobster bouillabaisse, duck with pear-ginger chutney and roasted sea bass served with a gumbo-type sauce. The lunch menu, with entrées at only half the price of dinner selections, fea-tures some of the same choices as the dinner menu. The setting is Colonial, rich with heavy English furnishings, and there are awesome views of the river and pedestrian footbridge. ~ 3774 River Road, Lumberville; 215-297-5770; www.blackbasshotel. com, e-mail info@blackbasshotel.com. ULTRA-DELUXE.

The phoenix **Café Marcella** is a sunny Italian bistro that has   ◀ *HIDDEN* survived a fire and two floods—the latter occurring within a year's time of one another. Still, this dinner-only BYOB continues to please its flock of loyal patrons. Salads are fresh and generous, and the pastas are light and satisfying. Start with an order of the

A FUSION OF FLAVORS

In Doylestown, **Siam Cuisine at the Black Walnut** fuses not only Thai and French cuisine, but Eastern and Empire culture as well. This eatery, in an 1846 townhouse, operates under two chefs, one French and one Thai, allowing you to mix courses or combine flavors into one presentation. The Chilean sea bass, served in a tamarind ginger sauce, is piquant, and the lemon tart, with coffee, tops off a perfect meal. ~ 80 West State Street, Doylestown; 215-348-0708, fax 215-348-8395; www.siamcuis inepa.com. MODERATE.

whole wheat garlic bread and try the *fradiavolo* as an entrée. This dish of shrimp, clams, scallops, fresh fish and mussels prepared in white wine and served over pasta is a house specialty. ~ 1253 River Road, Washington Crossing; 215-321-8789. MODERATE TO DELUXE.

HIDDEN ▶

What's not to like about a restaurant that recommends you eat dessert first? The **Goodnoe Dairy Bar and Family Restaurant** in Newtown is a local favorite featuring fresh-made pies, cookies and cakes; ice cream made on the premises; and hot cinnamon buns. The restaurant's comfort foods are among its menu standouts, including fried flounder, liver and onions, shepherd's pie and turkey dinners. The "black cow"—a rootbeer float with three scoops of ice cream—is a meal in a glass. ~ 298 North Sycamore Street, Newtown; 215-968-3875; www.goodnoe.com. BUDGET TO MODERATE.

HIDDEN ▶

Close to Philadelphia, in Bensalem, is an outlet of a local Philadelphia chain, **Nifty Fifty's**, a (what else?) 1950s-themed restaurant that serves fresh-cut French fries, homemade milkshakes and made-to-order cheeseburgers. This noisy, splashy eatery could double as Arnold's diner from *Happy Days*—head here after school and you'll find students squeezing into booths and lining up at the counter. Breakfast is served here as well, with frosty glasses of fresh-squeezed orange juice and cups of steaming coffee. ~ 2555 Street Road, Bensalem; 215-638-1950. BUDGET.

SHOPPING

Bucks County is known for its antiques and art galleries, although you'll find a wide selection of crafts, books, linens and clothing shops throughout the area. New Hope and Lambertville, New Jersey, are the epicenter of the county's antiques trade, with stores that sell the gamut, from formal and country American to French, English and Asian.

HIDDEN ▶

Known to locals and shop dealers, and visited rarely by tourists, **Rice's Sale and Country Market** is a Tuesday-morning tradition in New Hope, featuring antiques, produce, Amish-made baked goods and delicatessen fare. This country market has been

◆◆

FORM, FUNCTION AND SPIRITUALITY

For handmade furniture that doubles as artwork, the **George Nakashima** workshop and gallery is open Saturdays for tours. The Japanese-American woodworker and artist moved to New Hope after living with his family at an internment camp during World War II. Nakashima, who also was an architect, is world-renowned for melding form, function and spirituality into his creations. Open Saturday. ~ 1847 Aquetong Road, New Hope; 215-862-2272; www.nakashimawoodworker.com.

held since the Civil War, and is open year-round Tuesday, and March through December on Saturday. Also open on major holidays. ~ 6326 Greenhill Road, New Hope; 215-297-5993; www.ricesmarket.com.

A Mano Galleries in New Hope and Lambertville offers stylish American crafts, furniture, hand-made jewelry, Judaica and decorative accessories. ~ 128 South Main Street, New Hope, 215-862-5122; and 42 North Union Street, Lambertville, NJ, 609-397-0063; www.amanogalleries.com.

For art deco lighting and accessories as well as European furniture and 1950s memorabilia, there's **Cockamamie's** in New Hope. Owners Herb Millman and John Dwyer also are terrific resources for all things deco, providing decorating advice and help finding unique pieces. Closed Tuesday. ~ 6 West Bridge Street, New Hope; 215-862-5454; www.cockamamies.com.

Night Owl Vintage Clothing carries '60s and '70s threads as well as items from the 1940s, 1950s and 1980s. ~ 19B Bridge Street, New Hope; 215-862-9685.

The Golden Door Gallery spotlights Bucks County artists, sculptors and printmakers, and carries a decent selection of works by artists from around the United States. Closed Monday. ~ 52 South Main Street, New Hope; 215-862-5529.

Farley's Book Shop is an independent bookstore once owned by playwright John Kenyon Nicholson. This store is jammed with popular novels, books of local interest and children's literature. ~ 44 South Main Street, New Hope; 215-862-2452.

A vast selection of antiques and arts can be found on both sides of the river, in Pennsylvania and New Jersey. In New Hope, **Ingham Springs Antiques, Inc.**, offers a discriminating selection of 18th-century furnishings. The store is pricey, but owners Richard and Alyce Sandor have scoured the East Coast looking for superlative examples of early American formal and country furnishings. ~ 6319 Lower York Road, New Hope; 215-862-2145.

Hobensack & Keller, Inc., specializes in Oriental carpets, accessories and antique and reproduction garden items, including urns, statues and fencing. ~ 96 Bridge Street, New Hope; 215-862-2406.

Another delightful antique store that features garden items is **Peter Wallace, Ltd.** This tiny townhouse, jammed with paintings, porcelain, chandeliers, sconces, European and American furniture, and engravings also features a back patio, overlooking the Delaware, that contains fountains, urns, statues and more. ~ 52 North Union Street, Lambertville, NJ; 609-397-4914.

Across the street from Peter Wallace is **Jim's of Lambertville**, a gallery that carries a selection of paintings and sculptures by local artists including an abundant collection of Pennsylvania

Impressionists, such as Edward Redfield and William Lathrop. Closed Monday and Tuesday. ~ 6 Bridge Street, Lambertville, NJ; 609-397-7700.

For brand names at discount prices, **Penn's Purchase Factory Outlet Stores** feature such well-known labels as Jones New York, Nautica, Waterford and Orvis. There are 37 stores and services, including a Tupperware shop for those who don't know any Tupperware ladies. ~ Route 202, Lahaska; 215-794-0300; www.pennspurchase.com.

Across the street from Penn's Purchase is **Peddler's Village**, a group of more than 70 specialty stores in a Colonial setting. You'll find clothing, housewares, shoes, jewelry, handcrafted accessories, garden lighting, Christmas ornaments, cookware and French country fabrics. Stores like **Knobs 'n Knockers** (215-794-8045) sell unique and hard-to-find accessories to personalize your home. ~ Route 202, Lahaska; 215-794-4000; www.peddlersvillage.com.

Back in Northeast Philadelphia, just a hop, skip and a jump from County Line Road, **Franklin Mills** continues to be a top shopping destination. A discount outlet center with more than 200 shops and 1.7 million square feet of retail space, the Mills has warehouse stores like Burlington Coat Factory and Bed, Bath and Beyond, as well as designer outlets like Anne Taylor Loft, Guess and Kenneth Cole. Pennsylvania has no tax on clothing, which makes Franklin Mills especially enticing for out-of-state and international visitors. ~ 1455 Franklin Mills Circle, Philadelphia; 215-632-1500; www.franklinmills.com.

NIGHTLIFE Odette's piano bar and cabaret remains one of New Hope's most popular places to chill in the evenings, with local and national stars taking the stage in the cabaret nearly every night. Past performers include New York stars Margaret Whiting, Karen Akers and Andrea McArdle. Cover. ~ 274 South River Road, New Hope; 215-862-2432; www.odettes.com.

BROADWAY—BUCKS COUNTY STYLE

Don't be surprised if, while strolling through Doylestown, church bells peal out Broadway hits from shows like *The Sound of Music, Oklahoma* or *West Side Story*. Doylestown is proud of its links to Broadway: Oscar Hammerstein II penned "Oh, What a Beautiful Morning" on his front porch at nearby Highland Farm, and Stephen Sondheim spent a portion of his childhood here. Additional notable residents include Margaret Mead, seed king W. Atlee Burpee and playwright Moss Hart.

The **Bucks County Playhouse**, one of Pennsylvania's official state theatres, was built in the original New Hope mills and began as a summer stock venue. Many big-name stars have performed on this stage, several before they were famous, including Alan Alda, Liza Minelli, George C. Scott and Merv Griffin. Today, the playhouse mainly produces musical revivals. ~ 70 South Main Street, New Hope; 215-862-2041; www.buckscountyplay house.com.

For gay and lesbian visitors, **The Cartwheel** danceclub has five bars and a large dancefloor with a deejay spinning throbbing techno. The club also hosts drag show contests. Cover. ~ 437 Old York Road, New Hope; 215-862-0880.

In Doylestown, jazz and blues are the headliners at **Maggie's Place**, a small nightclub for live acts. Top artists as well as newcomers perform here. Cover. ~ 812 North Easton Road, Doylestown; 215-489-3535; www.maggiesplace611.com.

The **Comedy Cabaret at Poco's Restaurant** features stand-up from nationally recognized comedians in a setting above a Mexican restaurant. Arrive early, enjoy a margarita and catch a show. Cover. ~ 625 North Main Street, Doylestown; 215-345-5653.

The **County Theatre** is a nonprofit in Doylestown that shows independent and lesser-known films in a restored 1938 movie house. The theater also hosts special events. ~ 20 East State Street, Doylestown; 215-345-6789

NOCKAMIXON STATE PARK 🧍 🚲 🛶 ⚓ 🐟 🚤 ⛵   **PARKS**
Rugged hills and deciduous forest draw thousands of visitors each year to Nockamixon State Park. At Nockamixon, 5283 protected acres surround a 1450-acre lake, used for sailing, canoeing and kayaking and motoring, although there's a 20 horsepower limit. In winter, hiking trails are popular for Nordic skiing and sledding, while the adventurous can ice fish on the lake. A marina has docking space for 648 boats, plus more storage on dry land. If you don't own a boat, you can rent one, in season. Choices include sailboats, paddleboats, canoes, rowboats and pontoons. You also can fish from a pier or the shoreline. Roughly 3000 acres of this park are open to hunting in season, and game species include deer, rabbit, pheasant and turkey. There are picnic facilities throughout the park, a swimming pool, a youth hostel and cabins for rent. Around the lake, there are three miles of moderate hiking trails. For steep, more strenuous hikes, inquire at the ranger stations about the trails in the environmental study area. Swimming is not allowed in the lake. Some activities require fees. Restrooms are available, as are picnic areas and charcoal grills. ~ 1542 Mountain View Drive, Quakertown; 215-529-7300.

▲ There are ten budget-priced modern cabins with two or three bedrooms, bathrooms and heat.

RALPH STOVER STATE PARK 🚶 🚵 ⚓ ⛵ Twenty miles from Nockamixon lies the 45-acre Ralph Stover State Park, a destination for two high-adventure sports—whitewater boating and rock climbing. The High Rocks area—a 200-foot cliff face overlooking Tohickon Creek—presents challenges to experienced rock climbers, while the creek offers Class III rapids and wider pools for novice and expert kayakers. High Rocks' vistas are accessible to hikers by a steep trail. There are shaded picnic pavilions, fireplaces and restrooms. ~ 6011 State Park Road, Pipersville; 610-982-5560.

TYLER STATE PARK 🚶 🚵 🐎 ⚓ ⛵ This 1711-acre setting carefully preserves a portion of Bucks County's woods and farmland from development. The park has an extensive network of hiking, bicycling and equestrian trails, as well as picnic facilities, a nature center and summer canoe rentals. A 27-hole Frisbee golf course stays busy on weekends. The hike to the Schofield Ford Covered Bridge, in the park's northern reaches, is a gentle, meandering walk through deciduous forest to the county's longest covered bridge. The bridge burned in 1991 but was rebuilt on its original stone abutments. To reach it by car, drive west on Swamp Road from Newtown and follow signs. Facilities include restrooms, picnic areas and concession stands. ~ 101 Swamp Road, Newtown; 215-968-2021.

> Tyler State Park is home to a variety of plants and animals, including snapping turtles, eel, water snakes, muskrats and numerous bird species.

NESHAMINY STATE PARK 🚶 🏊 ⚓ ⛵ On the banks of the Delaware River, Neshaminy State Park is a place to see the the tide ebb or flow at a rate of one inch per minute. This 330-acre park features a boat launch for access to the the Delaware River, as well as a 235-slip marina. Two swimming pools (fee)—a main pool and tot "spray"—pool are popular in the summer months. The park has four miles of hiking trails and abuts a 71-acre tidal marsh along the river. The River Walk Trail is a personal favorite, a chance to explore the delicate marshes of the Delaware River. There are picnic areas and restrooms. For a child-friendly brochure on this ecosystem, stop by the park office before heading out. ~ 3401 State Road, Bensalem; 215-639-4538.

PEACE VALLEY PARK 🚶 🚵 ⚓ Lake Galena sparkles in this Bucks County–operated park, beckoning to migratory birds and waterfowl. Bald eagles, osprey and owls are spotted here as well as numerous songbirds. This 1500-acre park is treasured by local residents for its fishing stock, which includes bass, walleye and catfish. A nature center maintains several trails and bird blinds, and park rangers are available for information, maps and educational seminars such as guided nature walks and evening stargazing courses. There are restrooms and picnic areas; boat rentals (fee) are available in season. The six-mile circuit trail is beautiful no matter what season, with views of this pristine lake and its incredible assortment of wildlife. ~ 230 Creek Road, New Britain; 215-822-8608.

Outdoor Adventures

FISHING

Anglers are drawn to Bucks County's lakes, rivers and streams, including Neshaminy Creek, Peace Valley Reservoir and the Delaware River, for the area's stock selection. A Bucks County father-and-son team snagged a three-foot alligator in an area creek in 2005, but this catch is not the norm; it was a case of a pet on the lam. More common in these waters are trout, bass, walleye, catfish, bluegill and carp. Several companies operate full- and half-day guided flyfishing trips, including **Delaware River Fly-Fishing Guide Service.** ~ 877-473-6219; www.flyfishingguideservice.com.

Locally owned and operated **Mainstream Outfitters** also runs trips and sells flyfishing supplies, including those made by Orvis. ~ 1121 North Easton Road, Doylestown; 215-766-1244; www. mainstreamoutfitters.com.

KAYAKING & BOATING

Bucks County boasts a multitude of places to sail, motor, kayak and canoe, including the restful Delaware River, the wide Peace Valley Reservoir and the 1450-acre Lake Nockamixon. At two of the largest area parks, Nockamixon and Peace Valley, boat concession stands offer a selection of boating platforms for rent, from paddle boats, canoes, kayaks, motor boats and pontoons at Nockamixon, to kayaks, canoes, sailboats and rowboats at Peace Valley. Ralph Stover State Park, with whitewater rapids on the Tohickon Creek, is a favorite for advanced kayakers.

◄ HIDDEN

Along the Delaware, at Point Pleasant, another River Road hamlet, is **Bucks County River Country,** where outdoor enthusiasts rent canoes, kayaks and inner-tubes for Delaware River excursions. The company offers two- to four-hour outings as well as full-day and vacation trips aboard canoes and kayaks. Inner-tubes are available for lazy rides downriver. ~ 2 Walters Lane, Point Pleasant; 215-297-5000; www.rivercountry.net.

GOLF

In the southeastern portion of the county lie the **Middletown Country Club** and **Bensalem Country Club,** two courses open to the public that are among the area's original courses. Middletown, in Langhorne, is a tough course built in the 1910s. Its hills and tree-lined fairways can prove frustrating, but if you enjoy trying to figure out the lay of the land, this course presents a mental challenge. Fee. ~ 420 North Bellevue Avenue, Langhorne; 215-757-6953.

Bensalem's first nine holes lure a golfer into complacency with their pleasant layout, but the back nine are more of a challenge. Fee. ~ 2000 Brown Avenue, Bensalem; 215-639-5556.

Bucks County also operates a nine-hole, par-31 course in Fairless Hills called **Oxford Valley**. This course features open fairways and moderately fast greens. Fee. ~ 141 South Oxford Valley Road, Fairless Hills; 215-945-8644.

TENNIS

The county-operated, 1200-acre **Core Creek Park** in Middletown Township has several public tennis courts. Call in advance to make reservations. ~ Tollgate Road, Middletown Township; 215-757-0571.

RIDING STABLES

Several private companies rent horses for trail rides. **Haycock Stables, Inc.**, is near Lake Nockamixon and leases horses for one- to two-hour rides near the state park. ~ 1035 Old Bethlehem Road, Perkasie; 215-257-6271.

Showme Stables, also in Perkasie, offers a trail-riding lesson that includes a half hour in a riding ring and a one-hour trail ride. ~ 3618 Ridge Road, Perkasie; 215-795-2902.

JOGGING

Tyler State Park has 10.5 miles of multi-use trails that are well suited for jogging. These asphalt-paved paths have exercise stops along the way, and the hills of the trails will challenge the fittest. The park also has more than 100 miles of wooded trails for hikers and equestrians. Trails lead past old farms, ruins and creeks.

The **Delaware Canal Towpath** is a scenic, flat 60-mile trail that requires little thought to enjoy. The straight, well-worn path is perfect for finding one's groove and cruising for miles, although runners should watch out for passing cyclists and mules (and mule dung!). Portions of the towpath were closed after Hurricane Ivan and a devastating spring flood in 2005, so check with park officials about the trail's status before heading out. ~ 11 Lodi Hill Road, Upper Black Eddy; 610-982-5560.

BIKING

Bucks' meandering country roads and the **Delaware Canal Towpath** are a cyclist's dream, offering straight, simple trails or hilly terrain. The towpath and River Road, which parallel the river, are crowded with cyclists, joggers and hikers from early spring to late fall. The main trail along the river is the towpath, a flat, hard-dirt, straight trail between the canal and the river. This scenic trail will lead you past historic homes and through dense woodlands. Watch your step or your front wheels, however; mules still use the towpath for pulling barges along the canal.

Popular Tyler State Park has a number of cycling trails as well.

Bike Rentals   Companies that rent bicycles in Bucks County include **New Hope Cyclery**. ~ 404 York Road, New Hope; 215-862-6888.

The **Lumberville Store Bicycle Rental Co.** rents several different types of bicycles and sells picnic supplies to boot. ~ River Road, Lumberville; 215-297-5388.

Freeman's Bicycle Shop, near Nockamixon State Park, rents two-wheelers for use in the park or on area roads. ~ 4105 Durham Road, Ottsville; 908-996-7712.

Bucks County is a hiking paradise, with miles of groomed trails and comfortable paths that lead through southeastern Pennsylvania's prettiest scenery and forests. All distances listed for trails are roundtrip unless otherwise noted.   **HIKING**

While Nockamixon State Park is known mainly for boating and family recreation, it has numerous woodland trails and paths. The most popular is an **asphalt-topped trail** (5.6 miles) that runs along the lake, meandering over small rises and falls along the shoreline.

The **High Rocks Loop** trail (3.5 miles) at Ralph Stover State Park has it all: easy grade, magnificent views and a loop so you never see the same thing twice. The vista on High Rocks is 200 feet above Tohickon Creek, granting you scenery of the surrounding woods—a remarkable sight, especially in the fall as the foliage changes. Another popular hike at Ralph Stover is the moderately strenuous **Tohickon Creek Trail** (7.3 miles), which runs through the park and along the High Rocks area, tracing a gorge and reaching an elevation of 400 feet. It is best hiked in better weather; snow and ice make the path dangerous.

With its vast network of trails, including those for cycling, horseback riding and walking, Tyler State Park is one of Bucks County's most popular destinations. There's an exercise circle with various stations between the Woodfield and Mill Dairy trails west of the creek. For a quiet hike through the woods, consider the **Schofield Covered Bridge trail** (1 mile), a short in-and-out jaunt that passes a rebuilt covered bridge. The trailhead is at the parking lot off Swamp Road, the park's northern boundary.

At Peace Valley Park, the paved **circuit trail** (6 miles) is a scenic, quiet stroll around a crystal reservoir. You're bound to see lots of wildlife, including numerous birds, deer and small mammals. The park also has 14 miles of unpaved nature trails through the surrounding deciduous forest.

Transportation

AIR

The nearest large airport is Philadelphia International Airport, roughly 25 miles from New Hope. For more information, see "Transportation" in Chapter One. A small recreational airport with a grass runway is located in Erwinna. **Van Sant Airport** is home to Sport Aviation, Inc., a company that runs glider and biplane rides and rentals. The airport is open for transient traffic May through November. ~ 516 Cafferty Road, Erwinna; 610-847-8320.

EIGHT

Lancaster County

Traffic jams occur in Pennsylvania Dutch Country, and sometimes they are almost otherworldly. My car was one of several trapped behind a horse and buggy on a two-lane road. Tractor-trailers and cars flew past in the opposite direction. As a break in the oncoming flow appeared, I prepared to pass. Yet as I glanced over my left shoulder, I discovered that *I* was being passed—by a fast-moving horse and buggy, no less! One look at the driver was all it took to figure it out: the speedy carriage was full of teenage Amish boys.

Lancaster County is a dichotomy of cultures: modern America meets pioneer days. Like many Pennsylvania counties, Lancaster is a bucolic locale of rolling fields, farmland, winding creeks and covered bridges. But Lancaster's beauty is enhanced by the presence of the Old Order Amish and Mennonites who have farmed the land for more than 300 years. These religious groups spurn the use of electricity, gas-powered engines and modern technology in favor of preserving a simple lifestyle.

Lancaster County, 65 miles west of Philadelphia, was settled in the early 1700s by German and Swiss Mennonites and the Amish—an offshoot of the Mennonites. The name "Pennsylvania Dutch" is a misnomer—a corruption of Pennsylvania *Deutsch*, meaning German. Other settlers came to Lancaster at the same time as the Amish, drawn here by the area's rich farmland, including the Scots, Irish, French, English and Jews. Later, businessmen and professionals arrived.

In the decades before the Revolutionary War, Lancaster was the colonies' largest inland town. During the Revolution, it made its mark producing wagons and vehicles to support the army, while area iron mongers forged weapons and ammunition for the war. When the Second Continental Congress fled the path of the British Army in 1777, it convened in Lancaster on September 27, making the city the U.S. capital for one day. After the war, Lancaster served as a pass-through for settlers heading west and became a boomtown of textile mills, furniture makers and granaries. With the advent of the turnpikes and later the railroad, Lancaster County served as a launching pad for Western expansion.

Lancaster has been home to several famous Americans, including James Buchanan, the only U.S. president from Pennsylvania. Other famous Lancastrians include abolitionists Thaddeus Stevens and Linda Hamilton Smith, steamboat inventor Robert Fulton, Civil War general John Reynolds, American precisionist painter Charles Demuth and Brigadier General Edward Hand, George Washington's adjutant general during the Revolution.

Today, Lancaster wages a war against development. It has grown significantly in the past 30 years, drawing both businesses and residents to its rural locale and beautiful setting—an attraction that may very well destroy it. Lancaster City's population is more than 60,000; the county has nearly half a million denizens and is growing.

Lancastrians work in small businesses, hospitals, manufacturing and farming. One of the county's largest employers is carpet and flooring megacorp Armstrong. Much of the county's economy, however, is based on tourism. More than $1 billion is spent on tourist attractions and destinations each year by more than 4 million visitors to the county. Most are drawn to its wealth of Amish farms and an abundance of Pennsylvania Dutch food, antiques, handmade furniture, quilts, outlet malls and romantic lodgings in a lovely country setting.

Lancaster has something for any type of traveler. If large commercial tourist operations appeal to you, you'll find them here; nearly all have some type of Amish angle or theme. Those seeking a slow, relaxing weekend of antiquing, shopping, sightseeing and romantic inns, will find it here too. Outdoor enthusiasts will love its remote hiking trails, several lakes and the Susquehanna River. And those who want a working vacation can live on a farm and perform chores if they wish.

I'd always thought it odd that anyone would want to vacation in a place where the people are a tourist attraction. It just seemed too voyeuristic. But once I traveled to Lancaster, I learned the Amish are only a part of this region's appeal. Their presence helps Lancaster retain its charm, and maintain its landscape of rolling farmland, foothills, small villages and historic towns. Here, you'll find fresh country air, expansive views, antiques and furniture shopping, and German food. As a bonus, you'll sometimes encounter the Amish—an opportunity to ponder the fact that people can thrive without PDAs, TV or electric lights.

Most visitors begin their tour of Lancaster County in the county seat, Lancaster. Centrally located, it is a perfect jumping-off point for the rest of the county, including the Amish areas of Bird-in-Hand and Intercourse, the Mennonite town of Lititz and the Victorian-style village of Ephrata to the north, the railroad town of Strasburg to the southeast and the small towns along the Susquehanna River to the west. Farther afield, across the river, you'll find the world-famous chocolate town of Hershey and Gettysburg National Battlefield, a 90-minute drive.

Lancaster

▼▼▼▼▼▼▼▼▼▼ Lancaster (pronounced *lank*-eh-stir) is a busy little city at the heart of Pennsylvania Dutch Country, located roughly in the middle of the county. Lancaster was declared a "townstead" in 1730, mapped out by James Hamilton in a fashion much like Philadelphia with a center square, called Penn Square. Lancaster is a city of courtyards, tree-lined streets, businesses and brick residences; it served twice as the state capital, from 1777 to 1778 and from 1799 to 1812. Today, it remains a thriving community of business owners, shopkeepers, manufacturers and government workers. In Lancaster, you'll find a large number of restaurants, bistros and cafés, shops, galleries and museums to explore and enjoy.

SIGHTS

The **Pennsylvania Dutch Convention & Visitors Bureau** provides maps, guides and brochures for your visit. Helpful staff will send you information before you visit and they will assist in making reservations once you've arrived. ~ 501 Greenfield Road; 717-299-8901, 800-723-8824; www.padutchcountry.com.

At the center of Lancaster is **Penn Square**, home to the 1874 **Soldiers and Sailors Monument**, which honors Pennsylvania's Civil War veterans. Near the square is **Central Market**, a bustling

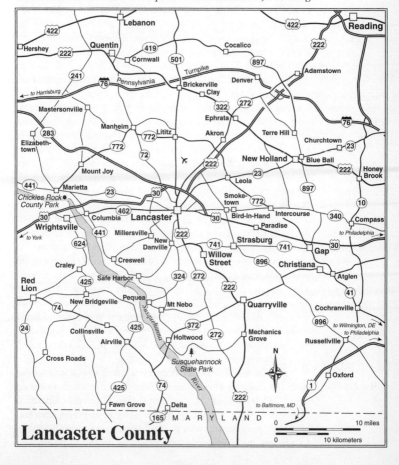

Lancaster County

indoor farmer's market. Held in a Romanesque-revival building constructed in 1889, the market is the nation's oldest farmer's market, in operation on this site since the 1730s. Central Market features more than 80 stalls offering Pennsylvania Dutch specialties such as scrapple, sausages, cheeses, breads and shoofly pie, a Pennsylvania Dutch confection of molasses, corn syrup and crumb topping. You'll also find baked goods, flowers, crafts and produce. Open Tuesday, Friday and Saturday. ~ Off Penn Square; 717-291-4723.

Quilters will appreciate the art behind the workmanship at the **Lancaster Quilt and Textile Museum**. The museum's permanent collection showcases 82 Amish quilts from the 1870s to the 1940s, each with vibrant colors, intricate patterns and complex stitches. The museum rotates them roughly every six months. The museum occupies the vaulted main rooms of the former Lancaster Trust Building, a beaux arts facility constructed in 1912. (Disabled patrons should be aware that the historic building doesn't have an elevator and there are 20 stairs to climb to the exhibit area.) Closed Sunday and Monday. Admission. ~ 37 Market Street; 717-299-6440.

The **Lancaster Cultural History Museum** features art and artifacts that show Lancaster's development from inland city to farming community and tourist destination. Items in the permanent collection include Lancastrian and Amish-made furniture, clocks, toys and folk art. The rotating exhibit changes roughly every six months; in 2005, visitors flocked to the display of the props and costumes used in the 1985 movie *Witness*. The museum is located in the former Lancaster City Hall and a Masonic lodge, both built in the 1790s. Closed Monday. Admission. ~ 13 West King Street; 717-299-6440.

HIDDEN ► The contemporary art collection at the **Lancaster Museum of Art** contrasts sharply with its facility, an 1846 Greek-revival mansion. The museum features contemporary regional artists and contains a variety of works, including sculpture, photography and paint. Past exhibitions have also included weavings, Christmas trees and pottery. The art museum's home is the magnificent Grubb Mansion, a building whose interior is considered one of the finest examples of original woodwork in the Philadelphia area. The drawing rooms sport twin marble mantels and Ionic pilasters along the windows and doors. Closed Monday. ~ 135 North Lime Street; 717-394-3497.

Franklin and Marshall College is a small liberal arts school that was founded as Franklin College in 1787, when it opened on a 200-pound contribution from Benjamin Franklin. In 1853, Marshall College, originally located 40 miles west in Mercersburg, merged with Franklin to form the current institution. The school was the first co-educational college in the United States,

and is a highly regarded educational institution. "F&M's" signature building, the Gothic-revival "Old Main," built in 1856,
was originally called Recitation Hall. It sits on Gallows Hill, the
former site of Lancaster's public executions. The **Rothman
Gallery** at F&M at 700 College Avenue, features fine art, folk art
and decorative arts. ~ 637 College Avenue; 717-291-3911.

The **North Museum of Natural History and Science**, also located at Franklin and Marshall, packs a lot into a little space for
visitors and, especially, for kids. The planetarium wows children
with its stories and explanations of the night sky. The museum
features live animals, including snakes and turtles, and a dinosaur exhibit. Admission. ~ 400 College Avenue; 717-291-3941.

Wheatland was the home of President James Buchanan from
1848 until his death in 1868. This Federal house, built in 1828,
has been furnished as it was when Buchanan lived there, with
many of his own belongings. A 45-minute tour by costumed guide
offers a glimpse into Buchanan's fascinating yet troubled life. It
also includes information about Harriet Lane, Buchanan's niece,
who lived at Wheatland and served as Buchanan's hostess in the
White House. Lane was the first person to bear the title "First
Lady." Open daily April through October, and Friday through
Monday in November; closed December through March. Admission. ~ 1120 Marietta Avenue; 717-392-8721, fax 717-295-
8825; www.wheatland.org, e-mail jbwheatland@wheatland.org.

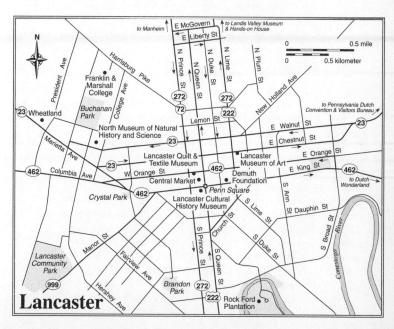

The **Demuth Foundation** operates the 18th-century home, studio, and garden of modernist painter Charles Demuth, whose works include the 1928 *Figure 5 in Gold*, based on a poem by friend William Carlos William. Demuth lived from 1883 to 1935 and moved to the home at age seven. The Victorian gardens are preserved in the manner in which Demuth's mother tended them.

HIDDEN ► Next door is the **Demuth Tobacco Shop**, the oldest continuing tobacco shop in the United States. The Demuth family opened it in 1770, and family members ran it until 1986, when it was deeded to the foundation. It continues to operate as a store and has many fine historic artifacts pertaining to the sale and trade of tobacco. Closed in January. ~ 120 East King Street; 717-299-9940.

The home of Brigadier General Edward Hand, Washington's adjutant general, is **Rock Ford Plantation**, a beautiful 1794 Georgian brick manor home with a welcoming front porch and meticulously preserved interior. This stunning example of post-Revolution construction was saved from demolition in 1957 by the Junior League of Lancaster. It is now operated by the Rock Ford Foundation, Inc., and is open to the public in season. The grounds, on the banks of the Conestoga River, are some of the prettiest you'll see in the county. In nice weather, bring a picnic. Open Thursday through Sunday from April through October. Admission. ~ 881 Rockford Road; 717-392-7223; www.rock fordplantation.org.

Those traveling with young children may want to check out the **Hands-On House** children's museum, especially if the weather is poor. Kids up to age ten will stay busy face-painting, working on an assembly line and exploring nature. Closed Monday from Labor Day through Memorial Day. Admission. ~ 721 Landis Valley Road; 717-569-5437; www.handsonhouse.org.

If you do have young children in tow, you may also want to consider visiting **Dutch Wonderland**, an amusement park for the under-ten crowd. This 45-acre park features 30 gentle rides, gardens and interactive shows. Duke's Lagoon, with fountains and

AUTHOR FAVORITE

Pennsylvania's German heritage comes to life at the **Landis Valley Museum**, a re-creation of rural Pennsylvania village life in the 1700s and 1800s. In a lovely setting, visitors can trek through more than 20 buildings, including a barn, blacksmith shop, country store, farmhouse and others. There are daily demonstrations of spinning, weaving, sheepshearing and tin making. Special events include yearly Civil War re-enactments and German baking demonstrations at Christmas. Admission. ~ 2451 Kissel Hill Road; 717-291-1888; www.landisvalleymuseum.org.

water attractions, is among the park's most popular destinations. ~ 2249 East Lincoln Highway; 717-291-1888, 866-386-2839; www.dutchwonderland.com

LODGING

Lancaster County has lodging to suit any budget, from full-service resorts and family-friendly motels to cabins, romantic inns and campgrounds. Several Lancaster farms operate as "farm bed & breakfasts," where guests stay and share in the chores, if they wish. The **Pennsylvania Dutch Country Welcome Center** has a full listing at www.800padutch.com.

Visitors should expect to pay an 11 percent occupancy and state tax on top of basic room rates in Lancaster County. Be aware that many inns and resorts cater to children, but some do not, especially the bed-and-breakfast inns; if you travel with young-sters, be sure to ask about policies before making reservations.

The city hosts a wealth of name-brand motel franchises, many of which offer suites, swimming pools, playgrounds and game rooms for family fun. Brands you'll find here include the Court-yard By Marriott, Holiday Inn and Hampton Inn, among others.

The **Eden Resort Inn and Suites,** a Best Western property, is a popular spot for families, with guest rooms and suites over-looking well-manicured grounds. Common rooms are tastefully decorated in Colonial and French Colonial–style furnishings; the spacious guest rooms, finished in beige and gold with light cherry furniture, offer in-room games, large televisions, wireless inter-net access, hair- dryers and refrigerators. The extended-stay two-story suites are a "home away from home," with wood-burning fireplaces, full-sized kitchens and dining space. There are two restaurants on site, as well as tennis courts, a fitness center and a game room. ~ 222 Eden Road; 717-569-6444, 800-528-1234; www.edenresort.com. MODERATE.

A B&B that feels like a historic hotel, **King's Cottage,** about a mile from Lancaster's center square, is a 1913 Spanish-revival home listed on the National Register of Historic Places, mainly for its distinctive architecture. The house features a large, invit-ing living room, a sunroom with piano and library, and a slate patio with fish pond. The eight rooms are spacious and contain beautiful Victorian or Colonial furnishings. Some have crystal chandeliers and fireplaces. Each has a spacious private bath, many with period fixtures including stained-glass windows and pedestal sinks. A full breakfast is served in the Chippendale-style dining room. Samson, the owner's bichon frisé, is likely to join you while you relax in the public areas. ~ 1049 East King Street; 717-397-1017; www.kingscottagebb.com. DELUXE.

What kid—or kid at heart—wouldn't love a swimming pool with water slide, fountains and a giant spitting frog? How about a chance to play shuffleboard or participate in a scavenger hunt?

The **Willow Valley Resort and Conference Center** is a full-service facility ten minutes from Lancaster that caters to families. The resort has several restaurants, a chapel, a golf course, a fitness center and three pools, including the atrium pool with all the cool toys. Two restaurants serve the traditional German smorgasbord, and there are optional meal plans. Rooms are furnished in early-American style, with cherry furniture, and hunter, burgundy and gold bedding and walls. Recently renovated rooms feature lighter cherry furniture and floral bedding. No alcohol is allowed on the property since the resort is Mennonite-owned. One floor is reserved for smokers. ~ 2416 Willow Street Pike; 717-464-2711, 800-444-1714; www.willowvalley.com. DELUXE.

DINING

Lancaster County is not the place to visit if you're on a diet, unless it's a high-carbohydrate, high-protein, meat-on-your-bones-type diet. The Amish work between eight and ten hours a day, performing heavy labor, and they take enough steps to walk between eight and ten miles a day. With all this exercise, it's no wonder foods like scrapple, chicken pot pie, shoofly pie, butter noodles, bologna, ham, dumplings, sticky buns and cookies are meal staples. Most of these specialties are featured in Pennsylvania Dutch restaurants, where food could be served family-style (with platters passed around at long banquet tables), or laid out in all-you-can-eat buffets (called smorgasbords in Lancaster).

Of course, not every restaurant in Lancaster serves German fare. The county has a variety of eateries, featuring ethnic selections, Cajun menus and New American or classic European fare. Reservations are recommended for most restaurants, especially on weekends during the summer and fall months.

The **Log Cabin** is known throughout Lancaster and as far away as Philadelphia for its romantic atmosphere and classic Continental cuisine. Over the creek and through the woods, travelers must go through a covered bridge to reach this former speakeasy in the forest. The atmosphere varies, depending on which room you are in; the main dining room, the original log cabin, has open-beam ceilings and dark furniture that is brightened by white table cloths and fine art. The steaks and chops are the big draw, and the tarragon roasted chicken with lemon zest is piquant. ~ 11 Lehoy Forest Drive; 717-626-1181; www.logca binrestaurant.com. ULTRA-DELUXE.

HIDDEN ►

The wine cellar at **Strawberry Hill** is to be celebrated; there are more than a thousand selections at this modern American restaurant set in a brick Victorian townhouse. The interior features exposed brick, rich paneling, funky French poster art and an open arched fireplace. The venison apple sausage, when available, makes a great starter, and the grilled rack of lamb with

Amish
Cuisine

When visiting Pennsylvania Dutch Country, you'll have ample opportunity to sample some signature dishes. Hopefully you'll have worked up an appetite because many of them are laden with fat and calories, necessary for a hard day's work. At breakfast, scrapple is often served as a side dish to eggs and toast. Similar to sausage, scrapple grinds together the meat that's left behind (usually hog head, heart and liver scraps) once the stand-alone pork cuts have been removed. This mixture is then combined with spices and cornmeal and usually fried.

Another staple of the Amish diet is canned and pickled foods. Because the Amish don't like to waste food, they tend to eat fresh fruits and vegetables in season and can and pickle nearly everything for later consumption. For side dishes, you'll see bread-and-butter pickles, pickled Brussels sprouts and chow chow, a pickled salad that contains an assortment of beans, cauliflower, onions and other veggies.

For dessert, there are several sweet treats. Shoofly pie is named after the traditional response from Colonial cooks as they checked their pies cooling on window sills. This "wet-bottom pie" of gooey molasses, corn syrup and egg is topped with a crumb layer of sugar, cinnamon and flour. Funnel cake, now popular nationwide thanks to traveling carnivals and county fairs, is made by squeezing batter into a circular pattern and deep fried. Although you can enjoy it with a variety of toppings, it's usually enjoyed plain with a sprinkling of confectioners' sugar.

fresh mint oil is fragrant and pleasing. Owner and native Lancastrian Dennis Kerik can help with your wine selection. On Sunday, you can enjoy jazz jams at Strawberry Hill from 8 p.m. until midnight. ~ 128 West Strawberry Street; 717-299-9910; www.strawberryhillrestaurant.com. ULTRA-DELUXE.

HIDDEN ►   The Brasserie is a favorite watering hole for Lancastrians, carrying a menu of classic bar fare like burgers and fries as well as pasta and prime rib. Set in a 1925 home, the restaurant has five cozy dining rooms and a deck and front porch for outdoor dining, weather permitting. The bar makes specialty martinis, and the tomato bisque is the best in town. ~ 1679 Lincoln Highway East; 717-299-1694. MODERATE.

The atmosphere is pure romance at the Olde Greenfield Inn, a traditional American restaurant set in a 1780 stone farmhouse. The home has been painstakingly restored; Windsor chairs frame the tables in the cozy rooms. Couples can reserve the wine cellar for an intimate dining experience away from other diners. The menu is fresh and uncluttered; entrée selections include filet mignon, lamb chops and pork tenderloin, served with sautéed vegetables. ~ 595 Greenfield Road; 717-393-0668. ULTRA-DELUXE.

It's hard to believe that news reporters know anything about fine dining establishments; after all, most can barely afford to eat in them. But the owners of Lancaster's local paper have been running a casual American restaurant, the Pressroom, successfully in the city for some time. The Pressroom is located in a former hardware building and features exposed brick, high ceilings and square art deco booths. Food is casual, with overstuffed sandwiches and pizza as well as heftier entrées such as filet mignon and pasta. ~ 26-28 West King Street; 717-399-5400. BUDGET TO MODERATE.

The Amish sell goods from their homes, so as you drive around, be sure to look for small sale signs along roadways—it's one of the best ways to meet the "real" Amish. No sales on Sunday.

It has an oddball name, but Haydn Zug was a real man, a local character who was the last owner of this former general store, built in 1852. The dining rooms are warm and inviting; Colonial touches include pewter tableware. Menu items include steak, crab and stuffed mushrooms. The smoked pork chops with fresh horseradish are zingy. ~ 1987 State Street, East Petersburg; 717-569-5746. DELUXE.

SHOPPING   Much of vacationing in Lancaster is about shopping. The county has farmer's markets and small antique stores, antique malls, reproduction furniture shops and hundreds of outlet stores. Small-town and village roadways are lined with shops, and country roads are pocked with small signs announcing the sale of goods from Amish homes. The Amish sell quilts, crafts, furniture and foodstuffs out of their homes, but you'll also notice as you drive through the county, road signs advertising purebred puppies for sale. Many area farmers consider dogs to be a commodity, and Lancaster is thought to have one of the largest concentrations of puppy mills in the United States. Area humane societies request that you do not support this cottage industry.

Lancaster is a destination for bargain hunters, but the city also has a nice selection of small shops downtown. Local outlet stores carry name-brand clothing, housewares and gifts. At the **Tanger Outlet Center**, you'll find Brooks Brothers, Calvin Klein, Coach, Polo, J. Crew, Kenneth Cole and more. ~ 311 Stanley K. Tanger Boulevard, Lancaster; 717-392-7260; www.tangeroutlet.com.

The **Rockvale Square Outlets** are a favorite with locals, with stores such as Bass Shoes, Jones New York, Levi's, Pottery Barn and Reed & Barton in a compact area. ~ Routes 30 and 896, Lancaster; 717-293-9595; www.rockvalesquareoutlets.com.

Farther afield are the outlets and shops of Reading. The **Reading Outlet Center** is one of the nation's first outlet malls. ~ 801 9th Street, Reading; 610-373-5495. **VG Outlet Village** has a collection of hundreds of stores, including Coach, Pier 1, Gap, Wrangler and Vanity Fair, in 450,000 square feet of retail space. ~ 801 Hill Avenue, Reading; 610-378-0408, 800-772-8336.

The **Weathervane Museum Store** at the Landis Valley Museum should be a destination for shoppers, regardless of whether they pass through the exhibits at the historic village. This store is a showcase of German and Pennsylvania Dutch craftsmanship, carrying quilts, pottery, folk art, weavings and carvings. ~ 2451 Kissel Hill Road; 717-291-1888; www.landisvalleymuseum.org.

◀ *HIDDEN*

Lancaster has its share of entertainment extravaganzas and Christian-themed theater. For information on these shows, contact the **Pennsylvania Dutch Convention & Visitors Bureau**. ~ 501 Greenfield Road, Lancaster; 717-299-8901.

NIGHTLIFE

The **Fulton Opera House** was built in 1852 and is on the National Register of Historic Places for its architecture as well as its role in American history as a roadhouse and Vaudeville stage. Mark Twain lectured here in 1872. Other luminaries to have appeared include Buffalo Bill Cody and Wild Bill Hickok, Sarah Bernhardt, W. C. Fields, Al Jolson and Helen Hayes. Today the opera house stages numerous presentations, including symphony, opera and Broadway shows like *The Music Man*. ~ 12 North Prince Street; Lancaster; 717-397-7425.

The 1600-seat **American Music Theatre** stages big-name concerts and musicals in an intimate venue. Taking the stage in 2006 are Emmylou Harris, Debbie Reynolds, Arlo Guthrie, George Jones and more. From big band to doo-wop to jazz, if it's American music, it's been played on this stage. ~ 2425 Lincoln Highway; 717-397-7700, 800-648-4102; www.americanmusictheatre.com.

The **Dutch Apple Dinner Theatre** presents Broadway favorites and comedy shows along with a buffet dinner. Past productions include *Annie*, *Camelot* and *1776*. ~ 510 Centerville Road, Lancaster; 717-898-1900.

The **Lancaster Barnstormers** minor league baseball team plays at Clipper Magazine Stadium in Lancaster from April through October. Several players from this new team have signed with minor league affiliates of Major League teams, and the team also has a few former Major League players. ~ 650 North Prince Street, Lancaster; 717-509-3633; www.lancasterbarnstormers.com.

On the grounds of the Mount Hope Winery, the **Pennsylvania Renaissance Festival** celebrates days of yore in a re-created Elizabethan village. Activities include jousting demonstrations, shows, dining, drinking and all-around merriment. Those who attend in costume receive a discount off their ticket price. Open weekends from August through October. ~ Mount Hope Estate and Winery, Cornwall; 717-665-7021; www.parenfaire.com.

Amish Heartland

While Amish and Mennonite communities are scattered throughout the county, much of their activity is centered on the bustling little villages of Bird-In-Hand and Intercourse. These cute boroughs are among the county's busiest, with such attractions as farmer's markets, furniture stores and quilt shops.

SIGHTS

As you travel east on Route 340 to the towns of **Bird-In-Hand** and **Intercourse,** note the Amish farms along the roadways. Stray off the main thoroughfare, and you're likely to see Amish women hanging their laundry in the morning or plowing their fields in the afternoons (yes, the women plow, too).

A number of commercial enterprises in the area of Bird-In-Hand seek to relate the Amish "experience" to visitors. The first

AUTHOR FAVORITE

To get a better understanding of the Amish, Mennonite and Brethren movements without the schlock, the **People's Place** shows a three-screen documentary called *Who Are the Amish?* An interactive museum explains the differences between the sects and includes activities, such as "dress-up" for children. The organization runs a bookstore as well, and across the street, the excellent People's Place Quilt Museum showcases pre-1940s antique quilts, and a craft shop sells Amish-made wares. Closed Sunday. Admission. ~ 3513 Old Philadelphia Pike, Intercourse; 717-768-7171.

is called, aptly, the **Amish Experience F/X Theatre**, a multimedia presentation that tells the tale of the Amish and of a teen facing decisions regarding religion and lifestyle. The **Amish Country Homestead** is the re-created farmhouse from the movie, and bus tours of the county are available on-site. Admission. ~ Plain and Fancy Farm, 3121 Old Philadelphia Pike, Bird-In-Hand; 717-768-8400.

The **Amish Farm and House** is a tour through a 19th-century home re-created as an Old Order Amish farmstead. The attraction features animals, a waterwheel, a kiln and barns. Admission. ~ 2395 Lincoln Highway, Lancaster; 717-394-6185; www.amish farmandhouse.com.

Finally, near Strasburg, is the **Amish Village**, a re-creation of an Amish settlement built by Amish craftsmen that includes a one-room schoolhouse, blacksmith shop, store and smokehouse. Closed November through March. Admission. ~ Route 896, one mile south of Route 340, Strasburg; 717-687-8511.

Another popular activity in the bustling tourist areas is guided buggy rides. You can enjoy Lancaster's roads from an Old Order Amish point of view, enjoying the county's backroads as costumed guides explain the Amish. Riding on the busy roadways can be a hair-raising experience, reminding everyone in Lancaster County to slow down. Carriage rides are offered by **Aaron and Jessica's Buggy Rides**, an Amish and Mennonite-owned operation running out of Plain & Fancy Farm. Closed Sunday. ~ Old Philadelphia Pike, Bird-In-Hand; 717-768-8828. **Abe's Buggy Rides** is located right on the main thoroughfare between Bird-In-Hand and Intercourse. ~ 2596 Old Philadelphia Pike, Bird-In-Hand; 717-392-1794. **Ed's Buggy Rides** can be found south of the busy tourist drag. ~ Route 896, Strasburg; 717-687-0360.

Given the pacifist nature of the Pennsylvania Dutch, it's odd to find the **American Military Edged Weaponry Museum** here, but military history buffs will appreciate this interesting collection of swords, bayonets, Bowie knives and K-Bars. The facility also displays recruiting posters and military art, and other weapons, including a Browning Automatic Rifle and Thompson machine gun. Closed Sunday and from December through April. ~ 3562 Old Philadelphia Pike, Intercourse; 717-768-7185.

◄ HIDDEN

For a spectacular view high over the Pennsylvania heartland, **U.S. Hot Air Balloon Team** runs balloon rides out of a small airport in Smoketown, east of Lancaster on Route 340. The outfit operates rides twice daily May through October, in the mornings and at sunset. Once you've landed, you're treated to snacks and a delightful champagne toast. Balloon trips are expensive, but

◄ HIDDEN

Text continued on page 212.

The Plain People

The Amish, with their simple clothes and traditions that buck what most consider to be progress, never cease to fascinate the modern world. In Lancaster County, you'll meet the "Old Order Amish"—those who grow beards, wear hats and refuse to use buttons. But you'll also find other old German sects, including Mennonites, Moravians, the Brethren and Lutherans, who remain active in this region.

The Pennsylvania Dutch people, or, more accurately, *Deutsch* (German), began settling in this region starting in the early 1700s. Menno Simons, a Catholic priest from Switzerland, broke from the church during the Reformation and started a religion based on nonviolence, separation of church and state, adult baptism and freedom of religion. Followers were called Mennonites. One of those followers, Hans Herr, traveled with several families to Lancaster County, drawn by William Penn's promise of religious tolerance in his new home.

In 1693, a Swiss Mennonite, Jacob Amman, broke from the Mennonites because he felt they were straying from their strict traditions. Amman's followers became known as the Old Order Amish. The Brethren, a conservative Protestant group that also believed in adult baptism, settled in Lancaster to escape persecution in Europe.

These groups differ in their interpretations of their religion, their use of technology, their dress, their acceptance of the outside world, their language and their forms of worship. For example, many Mennonite children attend public schools, and they worship in churches. Old Order Amish have their own schools and worship in their own homes.

Today, roughly 150,000 Old Order Amish live in 22 states in the U.S. and in Ontario, Canada. The largest concentration of Old Order Amish lives in Holmes County, Ohio, but Lancaster is second in population. The Amish live and work on Lancaster farms, growing tobacco, corn, hay and soybeans. Many supplement their farm incomes by selling homemade furniture, crafts, quilts and food products.

The Amish speak several different languages—a form of German at home, High German for worship, and English. Their English often is based on the original sentence structure found in German, so sometimes, their phrases may sound reversed, as in "Make the door closed" or "Have a wonderful good day."

The Amish learn much from their families—religion, societal duties, manners and work ethics. They attend school in one-room schoolhouses until the eighth grade. They learn enough to run a farm and a business, and they're often major participants in family businesses and house chores by the time they're 16. When they turn 16, they embark on *rumspringa*, a ritual where they're allowed to leave their religion and rules to explore the English (modern) world. The Amish believe that only after experiencing what is out there can they be baptized of their own free will as adults. The Amish are free to choose their own spouses, and they marry in November or early December at the end of harvest. Amish couples rarely divorce; their faith encourages the importance of family above all other matters.

Clothing distinguishes the members of the Pennsylvania Dutch community from most Brethren and Lutherans, who have fully assimilated into modern dress. Conservative Mennonite women wear simple dresses and white head caps. Old Order Amish women and girls wear modest, solid-colored dresses with hems to halfway below their knees. They wear aprons and capes fastened with snaps or pins—never buttons, which are considered too "fancy." Amish women don't cut their hair. They wear it in a bun and cover it with a prayer cap. Single women wear a black prayer covering.

The men wear dark-colored suits, straight coats without lapels, suspenders, solid-colored shirts, black socks and broad-brimmed hats. Their shirts have buttons, but their coats and vests have hook-and-eye closures. When Amish men marry, they grow beards, but never mustaches—the mustache is a symbol of militarism and a reminder of the persecution their people suffered in the 16th and 17th centuries in Europe.

The Amish live largely without electricity, although some groups allow for limited use to power farm tools. They believe that tapping into electricity will bring them further into the English world, drawing away from their faith and families, their two main priorities. They don't drive automobiles because they believe that everyday access to rapid transportation would affect family life by allowing them to travel far from home. The horse and carriage limits the distance they can travel. (Although they don't drive, the Amish will take rides or hire cars if needed.)

The Ordnung, a set of rules for expected behavior, govern Amish life. The basic tenets of the Ordnung are the same throughout Amish groups. One set of Ordnung governs religion and worship, the other lifestyle; there are variations to the lifestyle rules. Some Amish groups permit their members to keep a telephone at the edge of their property for use in emergencies; others allow their members to drive colored carriages. Another quirky rule is that carriages and tractors cannot have rubber tires.

For more information on the Amish, read *Amish Society* by John Hostetler, an American sociologist and Temple University professor who was born into an Amish family and dedicated his life to studying the Plain People. Hostetler died in 2001.

the views are unbeatable. Admission. ~ 311 Airport Drive, Smoketown; 800-763-5987; www.ushotairballoon.com.

LODGING   The **Bird-In-Hand Family Inn** is a good value for those traveling with small children. A family-run establishment, the property offers a number of amenities, including one outdoor and two indoor pools, tennis courts, a mini-golf course and a petting zoo. Rooms are spacious and very clean. The Bird-In-Hand Family Restaurant offers Pennsylvania Dutch food as a smorgasbord or à la carte, and there's an ice cream parlor on-site. ~ 2740 Old Philadelphia Pike, Bird-In-Hand; 717-768-8271, 800-537-2535; www.bird-in-hand.com/familyinn. BUDGET TO MODERATE.

DINING   For massive amounts of Pennsylvania Dutch food served family-style, the **Bird-In-Hand Family Restaurant** piles up the platters with popular favorites. This is the place to go if you have hungry teens. Besides the fried chicken, greens, hams, noodles and pies, there's a soup-and-salad bar and scads of desserts from one of the best bakeries in town. ~ 2760 Old Philadelphia Pike, Bird-In-Hand; 717-768-8266; www.bird-in-hand.com/restaurants. MODERATE.

For authentic Pennsylvania Dutch fare and a glimpse into country life, check out a local farm auction or benefit sale—you can find out about them in the local paper or by watching for road signs.

The **Stoltzfus Farm Restaurant** is located in a former Amish farmhouse near Intercourse. Specialties include ham, buttered noodles, pickled vegetables and sausages prepared locally. The place is all-you-can-eat and includes dessert choices such as traditional shoofly and apple crumb pie as well as cakes and cookies. Closed Sunday and from December through March; limited hours in April and November. ~ Route 772, Intercourse; 717-768-8156. MODERATE.

SHOPPING   In Bird-In-Hand and Intercourse along Route 340 (Old Philadelphia Pike), you'll find a slew of craft stores, antique reproductions and quilt shops. The crowds are here too, especially on weekends. The selection here also includes baskets; primitive country home decor; furniture, including Windsor chairs and farm tables; gifts; dolls and folk art. Stores that are run by the Amish or Mennonites are closed Sundays.

The **Old Country Store** at the People's Place has a nice selection of quilts and other items and a helpful staff. ~ 3513 Old Philadelphia Pike, Intercourse; 717-768-7171.

Many quilters travel to New Holland, northeast of Lancaster, to **Witmer Quilt Shop**, to see Emma Witmer's selection of more than 100 patterns. Closed Sunday. ~ 1070–76 West Main Street, New Holland; 717-656-9526.

Southeast of Lancaster and south of the Amish Heartland lies Strasburg, a small rural crossroads town that
sprang up as a rowdy frontier village. When the railroad was built through Lancaster County, Strasburg was passed
by. But innovative Strasburgers decided to connect their own single track to the main line, and today, these rails are among
Lancaster County's biggest attractions, drawing thousands to the
short-line rail and neighboring museums. There's not much to
Paradise except its idyllic name. This rural area near Strasburg is
home to a number of bed and breakfasts, scenic farms, markets
and a few tourist attractions. The scenic Pequea Creek runs
through the area.

Strasburg Area

The **Strasburg Railroad** runs roundtrips from a 1915 train station to the village of Paradise. Passengers ride in plush rail cars
as Victorian travelers did in the golden days of railroading. The
trains have dining cars that feature full menus, or you can buy a
box lunch and eat a picnic at a wayside stop, Groff's Grove. The
railroad runs special holiday trains and a Thomas the Tank
Engine train on certain weekends. Closed January to mid-
February. Open daily mid-April through October; open weekends mid-February to mid-April and November to mid-
December. Special holiday times Christmas week. Admission. ~
Route 741, east of Strasburg; 717-687-7522; www.strasburgrail
road.com.

SIGHTS

The extraordinary **Railroad Museum of Pennsylvania**, across
the highway from the Strasburg Railroad, features more than 40
locomotives, locomotive parts and coaches on five tracks in a
giant, glass-roofed exhibit hall. The collection includes several
steam locomotives, electric engines and diesel trains, as well as
exhibits on train history and memorabilia. A new simulator allows visitors to see what it's like to drive one of these steel be-
hemoths. Hint—it's hard to stop. Closed Monday from November through April. Admission. ~ Route 741, east of Strasburg;
717-687-8628.

Around the corner from the Railroad Museum is the **National Toy Train Museum**, displaying antique and new model
trains in a 13,000-square-foot facility modeled after the Victorian station in Perris, California. The museum features five main
tracks, each of different gauge, and guests can operate portions
with the touch of a button. Other artifacts on display include
cars, accessories and engines. Open May through October and
Christmas week; open weekends in April and from November to
mid-December. Admission. ~ Paradise Lane, Strasburg; 717-687-
8976; www.nttmuseum.org.

For a unique perspective of Lancaster County and Pennsylvania Dutch country, the **Choo Choo Barn** has a 1700-square-

foot model of the region with toy O-gauge trains. This collection began as a Groff family tradition of collecting trains at Christmas, starting with the 1945 purchase of a train to go under the tree. The collection soon grew to fill the Groffs' basement, and neighbors came over for special holiday exhibits. The vast collection went commercial in the 1960s, and today, it includes many Lancaster landmarks, including Plain and Fancy Farm, the train stations, an Amish barn-raising, a parade and a blazing house fire. Closed January through March. Admission. ~ Route 741, Strasburg; 717-687-7911; www.choochoobarn.com.

Northeast of Strasburg lies Paradise, a collection of homes, farms and at least one attraction—a place where it's paradise all year for Christmas lovers. The **National Christmas Center** is a walk-through attraction that features exhibits about Christmas around the world, as well as displays about the first Christmas, Pennsylvania celebrations and the story of Santa Claus. The presentation of nativities reminds patrons why they celebrate the holiday. Closed January through April, weekdays in May and Christmas Day. Admission. ~ 3427 Lincoln Highway, Paradise; 717-442-7950; www.nationalchristmascenter.com.

LODGING   The **Netherlands Inn and Spa**, the former Historic Strasburg Inn, sits on 18 acres in the middle of Amish farmland, a re-creation of a building that once stood in Strasburg. Brick trails meander through fields, inviting guests to stroll or bike through the surrounding countryside. The 110 rooms offer a variety of options, including suites with jacuzzi tubs, family suites, deluxe and standard rooms. The contemporary rooms feature fluffy duvets, simple yet elegant furnishings, and folk art accents in shades of red, white, blue and beige. Guests can relax at the Spa Orange, which offers massages, facial therapies and more, borrow a bicycle or swim in a heated pool. The Bistro restaurant offers New American fare. ~ 1 Historic Drive, Strasburg; 717-687-7691, 800-872-0201; www.netherlandsinn.com. ULTRA-DELUXE.

Lancaster County has its share of tourist traps, bearing giant statues of Amish farmers or selling furniture reproductions that may or may not have been made by Amish hands, but some-

PHOTO ETIQUETTE

It is against the religion of Old Order Amish and traditional Mennonites to have their picture taken, a rule stemming from their interpretation of the second commandment, which prohibits the creation of graven images or likenesses. Please refrain from taking their photos. Some Mennonite sects allow their photos to be taken, but it's best to ask first.

times, kitsch can be cool, or at least fun for a weekend. The **Red**   ◄ *HIDDEN*
Caboose Motel, near the Strasburg Railroad, is a complex of 39
cabooses turned into motel rooms. This campy lodge includes
suites for families and a honeymoon car; some rooms have king-
sized beds. Furnishings are simple—many rooms have faux-
wood paneling—but it's all fun. A Victorian dining car operates
as the motel restaurant, and there's a petting zoo. The motel is
next door to the Toy Train Museum and across a field from the
Strasburg Railroad tracks. ~ Route 741, Strasburg; 717-687-
5000, 888-687-5005. MODERATE.

The **Neffdale Farm** is a working dairy that doubles as an inn,
with six rooms that are simply furnished in two different houses
on the property. The beauty of this place lies in its simplicity; the
farm is surrounded by acres of cornfields and pasture. There are
calves and other animals to feed and chores to be done, and
guests are invited to help out. The cows, however, don't have to
be milked—that's done by machine. If you've ever dreamed of
living on a farm, this is the place to take a test-drive. Breakfast
is not included in your room rate, but you'll save a bundle on
lodging. ~ 610 Strasburg Road, Paradise; 717-687-7837. BUDGET.

Another working farm, **Rayba Acres** invites you to milk their
cows *and* feed the chickens *and* sweep the barns. Rooms are
available in two houses, a newer home with four bedrooms and
an 1863 farmhouse with six bedrooms (four share bathrooms).
The rooms resemble motel facilities, with two queen-sized beds,
chairs, tables and nightstands, yet rather than look over a parking lot, you see barns and pastureland. There are gazebos and
common areas for relaxing. Breakfast is not included. ~ 183
Black Horse Road, Paradise; 717-687-6729. BUDGET.

For a quiet country getaway, the **Frogtown Acres Bed and**   ◄ *HIDDEN*
Breakfast has four rooms in a refurbished carriage house in the
heart of Amish country. In fact, the Amish neighbors—friends of
the proprietors—are likely to come hang out in the evenings, if
they don't have anything else to do. The rooms, several with multiple beds tucked into alcoves, are appropriate for families and
are decorated with Amish quilts and country furnishings. A full
breakfast of fruit, bread dishes, sausages or scrapple is served at
the farm table. Innkeepers Gloria and Joe Crenshaw are known
for their friendly service and great humor. ~ 44 Frogtown Road,
Paradise; 717-768-7684, 888-649-2333; www.frogtownacres.
com. MODERATE.

The **Bistro** at the Netherlands Inn and Spa is a full-service restau-   **DINING**
rant and lounge that offers both indoor tables in an airy, casual
atmosphere or outdoor dining overlooking rolling countryside.
The menu features several interesting takes on local farm favorites, including a grilled pork chop braised in burgundy (an

Amish no-no) and pan-seared crusted cod with squash succotash. The lobster strudel is a popular appetizer, as are the grilled poached pears. For dessert, try the scrumptious pear-cherry crisp or apple strudel. Despite the upscale menu and setting, the Bistro is family friendly. ~ One Historic Drive, Strasburg; 717-687-7691; www.netherlandsinn.com. MODERATE TO DELUXE.

Take a trip back in time by stopping at the Strasburg Railroad Station and supping aboard the nation's only operating wooden dining car. During daytime trips, the **Lee E. Brenner Dining Car** serves up hot and cold sandwiches and soups, including the locally popular chicken-corn soup. Dinner is a more formal affair, with white-clothed tables and Queen Anne chairs in a paneled dining room. Diners select one of three entrées, either prime rib, stuffed baked fish or chicken cordon bleu, from a fixed-price menu. Occasionally on summer evenings, the chefs put together a Pennsylvania Dutch menu of baked ham, roast turkey, sweet potatoes, creamed corn and shoofly pie. Reservations are required for the dinner train. Closed weekdays from mid-February to mid-April and November to mid-December. Closed January to mid-February. ~ Route 741, east of Strasburg; 717-687-6486. DELUXE.

Also at the Strasburg Railroad Station is the **Sweet & Treats Shop**. In addition to fudge and pies, you can buy lunch and eat at the station, or pick up boxed sandwiches to enjoy a picnic at Groff's Grove, a stop on the railroad. The lunch menu for station eating features hamburgers, chicken salad sandwiches, hot dogs, barbecue, soup and more. Boxed lunches consist of sandwiches, applesauce, cookies and a drink. ~ Route 741, east of Strasburg; 717-687-7522. BUDGET.

SHOPPING If you're in the market for Victorian furniture, tools, road signs or taxidermy, check out **Old Mill Emporium**, if only to see the full-sized stuffed lion, elk or boar's head on display and for sale. The store has a wide selection of Victorian settees, chairs and curios, as well as 1940s-era Colonial reproductions. Closed Tuesday from April through November; closed Tuesday through Thursday in winter. ~ 215 Georgetown Road, Strasburg; 717-687-6978.

▼▼▼▼▼▼▼▼▼▼▼▼▼▼▼▼▼▼▼
Northern Lancaster County In northern Lancaster County lie the small towns of Ephrata, Lititz, Churchtown, Blue Ball and Adamstown. Many of these towns began as settlements for religious movements, and they boast a wealth of individual historic sites and destinations. The roads between these towns began with wagon ruts; today, they are mostly two-lane country roads shared by tourists, locals and Amish carriages.

Ephrata is a small borough with a vibrant city center and Main Street of businesses and shops. The town grew up around the establishment of the Ephrata Cloister, a monastic religious sect founded in 1732 by German immigrant Conrad Beissel.

The **Ephrata Cloister** is a serene grouping of 12 Medieval-style buildings that once housed a radical offshoot of the Brethren. Roughly 80 celibate members—men and women—lived here from 1735 to the late 1700s, supported by 200 families, who lived nearby and were also members of Beissel's faction. The last celibate member died in 1813. Self-guided and guided tours of the Cloister are available; visitors can only see the main meeting house and the Sisters' House by tour. Be sure to check out the Solitary House while on tour—you can test out a typical "bed" used by members, a 15-inch wide wooden bench with a wooden block pillow. Closed Monday in January and February. Admission for guided tour. ~ 632 West Main Street, Ephrata; 717-733-6600 ext. 3001; www.ephratacloister.org.

Less than a mile west of the Ephrata Cloister on Route 272 is a Wawa Food Market—a Pennsylvania-based chain that sells fuel, snacks and hoagies. If the weather is nice, buy lunch at Wawa and picnic on the lovely cloister grounds.

The **Green Dragon Farmers Market and Auction** takes place on Fridays in Ephrata, an experience similar to a county fair every week. Locals, Plain People and visitors alike attend to watch agriculture and livestock auctions and browse the vending stalls. More than 400 vendors hawk meats, cheeses, produce, baked goods, ready-to-eat food and crafts. ~ 955 North State Street, Ephrata; 717-738-1117; www.greendragonmarket.com.

Lititz is a charming town to shop and enjoy the historic stone homes, churches and parks that appear to have changed little since the borough was founded in the mid 1700s. Settled by Moravians, Lititz grew as a church village and was named for the town in Germany where the denomination was founded in the 15th century. Lititz has several historic buildings, including a 1787 Moravian Church and the home of General John Sutter, founder of Sacramento, California. The beautiful campus of **Linden Hall,** the nation's oldest girls' boarding school, was built by Moravians to house the church's unmarried female members. It began accepting non-Moravians in 1794, although Lititz remained a closed community of Moravians until the mid-1800s. ~ 212 Main Street, Lititz.

If you're wondering why the soft pretzel is a trademark food in the region, you can find out at **The Pretzel House,** *the* first pretzel bakery in the Western Hemisphere. The house was the residence of baker Julius Sturgis, who allegedly got the recipe from a wanderer in 1850. The house is refinished in historic style and is a fine example of Federal architecture, but the real fun begins when you get to roll out your dough and shape your own pretzel. Closed Sunday. Admission. ~ 219 East Main Street, Lititz; 717-626-4354.

Pretzels aren't the only treat made in Lititz; the **Wilbur Chocolate Company** is a favorite destination for locals who enjoy the factory's homemade fudge and sweets. The company runs a Candy Americana Museum and Store telling the history of confections. Best of all, they give away samples! Closed Sunday. ~ 48 North Broad Street, Lititz; 888-294-5287.

Adamstown is a year-round antiques destination, but sales in this small city just four miles north of Ephrata shift into overdrive on Sundays when dealers, browsers and locals flock to several antique co-ops that are only open on the Sabbath. The two largest indoor antique malls are Stoudt's Black Angus and Renninger's, selling American country, fine furniture, French and English antiques, toys, estate jewelry, china, glassware and more. **Shupp's Grove**, an outdoor flea market that began Adamstown's march to fame as "Antiques Capital USA," is where you'll find some real deals from April through October, weather permitting. See "Shopping" below for more details.

Stoudt's is a brewery, antique mall and so much more, but most know the name for the company's award-winning beers. The first micro-brewery in Pennsylvania, Stoudt's produces a range of regular and seasonal beers, and it plays host to numerous events throughout the year, including micro-brewery festivals, Oktoberfest, weekend tastings and more. Free tours given Saturday at 3 p.m. and Sunday at 1 p.m. ~ Route 272, Adamstown; 717-484-4385; www.stoudtsbeer.com.

Fans of sci-fi will be amused by the **Toy Robot Museum**, a collection of more than 1000 robots and robot-themed toys, including several classic pinball machines. Open Friday through Sunday; during the week, shop hours vary. Admission. ~ Shops at Stoudtburg Village, Route 272, adjacent to Stoudt's Black Angus Antique Mall, Adamstown; 717-484-0809.

LODGING

Off the beaten path is Churchtown, a small country village with two fine bed and breakfasts and several excellent antique stores. The **Churchtown Inn** is a 1735 stone home decorated in Victorian furnishings, and featuring eight rooms with private baths, two formal parlors, a cozy den and glass breakfast room with wide views of neighboring farms. Rooms feature fireplaces or Franklin stoves, seating areas, televisions and beds dressed in colorful quilts. Breakfast is a sit-down affair; many guests are repeat customers who return for the ambience and the four-course meal. ~ Main Street, Churchtown; 717-445-7794, 800-637-4446. MODERATE.

HIDDEN ▶

The **Inn at Twin Linden** is a stunning mid-19th-century home of white brick and black shutters, with a graceful porch beckoning you to sit forever. The eight rooms are traditional yet have a crisp, contemporary flair, with canopy or antique beds, Franklin stoves, country tables and wing chairs. The lovely Palladian Suite, dressed in calming shades of tan and cream, is romantic with a skylight and a large semi-circular window overlooking farmland. The common rooms are early American. A gourmet breakfast is served in the garden-view dining room, and dinner is available on Saturday evenings. ~ 2092 Main Street, Churchtown; 717-445-7619; www.innat twinlinden.com. DELUXE TO ULTRA-DELUXE.

Legend has it that the pretzel was originally given as a reward to children in Europe for saying their prayers. The crossed dough symbolizes arms folded across the breast.

The **Historic Smithton Inn** is right on Ephrata's Main Street for good reason; it was a stagecoach stop built in 1763. The distinct stone inn has been restored and furnished completely with handmade items, from the beds to the architectural details, including the door latches. Owner Dorothy Graybill has taken great care to provide for her guests. Extras include featherbeds, luxury linens and nightshirts. The rooms feature four-poster or canopy beds, and most have fireplaces. The grounds boast Graybill's award-winning dahlias, which bloom in the summer. A full breakfast is served. ~ 900 West Main Street, Ephrata; 717-733-6094. MODERATE TO DELUXE.

The **Alden House** is a unique Federal-style home with some Victorian touches. It's on the main road in Lititz, near quaint shops and historic homes, and a street away from the town's beautiful 1787 Moravian church. This 1850 home has two suites and three rooms, some with a canopy or antique bed and some with fireplaces. Two have their own porch entrance. The upstairs Parlor Suite has a canopy bed, private bath and dressing room up a small flight of stairs. A full breakfast of fruit, eggs or a sweet offering such as pancakes or french toast is served in the dining room or on the porch if weather is nice. ~ 62 East Main Street, Lititz; 717-627-3363; www.aldenhouse.com. MODERATE.

◀ HIDDEN

The **General Sutter Inn** is a historic facility that has served as an inn for more than 240 years. It is named for the man who founded Sacramento in 1839; General Sutter lived in Lititz after leaving California. The hotel is decorated in Victorian finery, and the verandas are lovely places to linger, with fountains and windows allowing guests to watch the passersby. The rooms feature Victorian antique beds, dressers and chairs. There are several on-site restaurants, including the upscale 1764 Restaurant, the more casual Sutter Café, and Pearl's Bar and Tavern, one of the few places in northern Lancaster County where you can buy an alcoholic beverage. ~ 14 East Main Street, Lititz; 717-626-2115; www.generalsutterinn.com. MODERATE.

Within blocks of Adamstown's "Antique Mile" are the **Inns at Adamstown**, a pair of hotels—the Adamstown Inn and

Amethyst Inn—set in two homes that date to the early to mid-1800s. The Amethyst Inn is an Italianate Victorian, sporting a coat of aubergine paint with teal trim. Its seven rooms differ in decorating style; the Jade Room is Victorian with a sunny bay window; the Ruby Suite has contemporary furnishings and two gas fireplaces. The Adamstown Inn has four guest rooms. The Regar Room is handsomely done in stripes and rich reds. ~ 62 West Main Street, Adamstown; 717-484-0800, 800-594-4808. MODERATE.

DINING

The **Restaurant at Doneckers**, run by Le Bec-Fin alumni Greg Gable, is a former neighborhood grocery store transformed with European art and French antiques. Gable fuses French style with American classic dishes, creating entrées like a surf and turf of veal and lobster, spice-rubbed ribeye and monkfish *au poivre*. A chef's tasting menu pairs Gable's picks with wines selected by the sommelier. ~ 333 North State Street, Ephrata; 717-738-9501; www.doneckers.com. ULTRA-DELUXE.

HIDDEN ▶

The humble town of Ephrata hosts another fine eatery, **Lily's on Main**, an art deco–style café hidden on the second floor of an office complex. With wide windows, Lily's has lovely views of quaint Ephrata. Tables are set with white linens, and each has a candle and a single lily. The menu features a variety of choices, from trusted light favorites like chicken *quesadillas* and Cobb salads, to more ambitious meals like pan-roasted duck and calf's liver. The house signature dish is meatloaf, but not the bread-and-ketchup kind your mother made. This is a grilled combination of ground beef, pork, veal and mushrooms, all served with garlic mashed potatoes. ~ 124 East Main Street, Ephrata; 717-738-2711. MODERATE.

The simple yet comfortable **Sutter Café** in the General Sutter Inn can jump-start your day with eggs benedict or eggs florentine, fresh fruit, sinful cinnamon buns and strong coffee. With its stained oak wainscoting, creamy walls and Mission-style buffets that complement the brick fireplace, this is also a nice spot for lunch during a busy day of sightseeing and shopping in Lititz. The soups, salads and stews are fresh, and the café has a selection of coffees and desserts for a midday treat. Closed Monday evenings. ~ 14 East Main Street, Lititz; 717-626-2115; www.generalsutterinn. MODERATE.

HIDDEN ▶

Something different is cooking each month at the **Nav Jiwan International Tea Room**, a restaurant tucked in the back of Ten Thousand Villages home handicrafts, just outside Ephrata. The Tea Room is a misnomer; Nav Jiwan serves international fare for lunch and is open until 8 p.m. on Friday. The restaurant rotates its offerings to reflect the diversity of the craftsmen who sell wares at Ten Thousand Villages. Countries whose cuisine is featured include India, Thailand, South Africa, Pakistan and Vietnam. ~ 704 Main Street, Akron; 717-859-8100. BUDGET.

For a meal and ale that hits the spot after a full day of antique shopping, **Stoudt's Black Angus** serves satisfying steaks, prime rib and German specialties in a Victorian-style restaurant, located conveniently near Stoudt's vast antique mall. Stoudt's microbrewed beers are also made in the same complex. The brewery whips up seasonal offerings such as an Oktoberfest lager, a fruity summer ale and a winter amber ale. ~ Route 272, Adamstown; 717-484-4385; www.stoudtsbeer.com. DELUXE TO ULTRA-DELUXE.

Farmer's markets are held in many of Lancaster's northern towns during the week; the variety of goods available here is enormous and includes fine and country antiques, crafts, foodstuffs, quilts, fabrics, reproduction furniture, canned goods, farm-fresh produce, and Pennsylvania Dutch meats and cheeses. On Sunday, the population of Adamstown swells temporarily as browsers and dealers from all over the East Coast flock to Adamstown and the surrounding areas for Sunday-only antique shopping.

SHOPPING

In Churchtown, the **Village Barn** is an antique co-op of at least 30 dealers who have arranged their wares beautifully in an old barn. Staff is friendly and knowledgeable of the area. ~ 2058 Main Street, Churchtown; 717-445-2276

Near Ephrata, shoppers can purchase beautiful handmade housewares and gifts and ease their social conscience at **Ten Thousand Villages**, a store operated by the Mennonites to benefit artisans in Third World countries. This shop carries hand-knotted Persian rugs made in Pakistan, baskets from Africa, fabrics from India and Thailand, and pottery from Vietnam. All handiwork is done by adults in these countries; they receive wages and put the profits they earn back into their businesses or toward expanding the program. Prices are reasonable and non-negotiable. ~ 704 Main Street, Akron; 717-859-8100; www.tenthousand villages.com.

◄ HIDDEN

AUTHOR FAVORITE

Fine 18th-century antiques can be found at **Churchtown Antiques**. Proprietors Daniel and JoLyn Vence have a discriminating selection of chairs, mirrors, candle stands, tilt-top tables and chests, which they sell out of a beautiful 1767 farmhouse and former general store. Closed Sunday through Tuesday. ~ 2083 Main Street, Churchtown; 717-445-4969; www.churchtownantiques.com.

The road from Adamstown to Denver is a main thoroughfare through antique country. Some stores operate during the week, but many are only open weekends.

Stoudt's Black Angus Antique Mall has more than 500 permanent dealers selling fine and folk art, furniture, rugs, quilts, lighting and collectibles. Open Sunday. ~ Route 272, Adamstown; 717-484-4385

The **Shops at Stoudtburg Village** is an eclectic collection of old, new and unique. More than 20 storefronts sell antiques, custom crafts, jewelry, handmade gifts, flowers and dried flower arrangements. ~ Route 272, adjacent to Stoudt's Black Angus Antique Mall, Adamstown; 717-484-4389; www.stoudtburgvillage.com.

Renninger's Antique and Collectors Market is a Sunday-only opportunity as well, with 375 indoor dealers and nearly 400 outdoors spring through fall. Dealers sell art, furniture, hardware, glass, linens and more. ~ 2500 North Reading Road, Denver; 717-336-2177; www.renningers.com.

In nice weather, dealers, browsers and buyers flock to **Shupp's Grove**, the area's oldest outdoor antique market. You'll find nearly every type of collectible here, including military paraphernalia, housewares, farm implements, furniture, silverware and more. Open Saturday and Sunday from April through October. ~ Route 897 South, Adamstown; 717-484-4115.

▼▼▼▼▼▼▼▼▼▼▼▼▼▼▼▼▼
Southern and Western Lancaster County

To escape the shopping and gawking crowds that seem to flock around central and northern Lancaster County, slip off to the southern and western reaches, where you'll find the homes of Old Order Amish as well as scenic roads, rolling fields of tobacco and corn, and none of the trappings of tourism. There are no malls, no traffic, no convenience stores, just farms, woodland and the Susquehanna River.

SIGHTS
South of Lancaster off Route 222 is the **Hans Herr House**, the oldest example of Medieval-style architecture in the New World. This stocky German sandstone structure served as a Mennonite meeting house and was built in 1719. The grounds, including a barn, tobacco house and several other farmsteads, are maintained and operated by the Lancaster Mennonite Historical Society, which gives tours and sponsors the exhibits about the history of the Mennonites. Closed Sunday and from December through March. Admission. ~ 1849 Hans Herr Drive, Willow Street; 717-464-4438; www.hansherr.org.

Continue south on Route 222 and you'll come to a bend in the road, a small creek and the **birthplace of inventor Robert**

Fulton, born November 14, 1765. Fulton not only invented the steamboat, he also created a dual-propulsion submarine and torpedoes. The stone house, small herb garden and grounds are open on weekends during the summer, but if you're here any other time of year, walk around and enjoy the scenic acreage; the sycamore shading the doorway is thought to be at least 150 years old. Admission. ~ 1932 Route 222, Quarryville; 717-548-2679.

The town of **Columbia** lies west of Lancaster on Route 462. An industrial town that grew near a well-planned canal system on the Susquehanna, it was briefly considered as a sight for the United States capital. Today, it is a city with a population of roughly 10,000, a scenic rest of beautiful bridges and Tudor and Victorian homes.

Each of the restaurants at Bube's Brewery holds special events or has live music: the Catacombs, 40 feet underground, hosts medieval feasts on Sundays, and Alois has live jazz on weekends.

Wrights Ferry Mansion, in Columbia, is a Georgian-style manor home built in 1738 by Quaker Susan Wright, who also contributed to the development of the town. The home is known for its excellent collection of early Pennsylvania furniture, including Queen Anne–style Philadelphia chairs and an elegant Philadelphia poster bed. The house is considered to have been an Underground Railroad way station; the shackles in the attic may have belonged to a runaway. Closed Monday, Thursday and Sunday, and from November through April. Admission. ~ 38 South 2nd Street, Columbia; 717-684-4325.

The **National Watch and Clock Museum** features more than 12,000 timepieces and artifacts related to counting the hours. Highlights include the magnificent Engle Clock, an "apostolic clock" that features 48 biblical figures, three towers and two organ movements, and a lovely silver and turquoise Tiffany globe clock that once rotated on its base. The whimsical cuckoo collection features clocks shaped like cats, birds and the U.S. capitol. Closed Sunday and Monday from January through March, and Monday from April through December. Admission. ~ 514 Poplar Street, Columbia; 717-684-8261; www.nawcc. org/museum.

Nearly half the town of **Marietta,** a river town north of Columbia, is marked as a National Historic District, with beautiful Queen Anne–style Victorian homes, some log cabins and Federal-style homes. It sprang up as an industrial city where the Pennsylvania Railroad crossed the Susquehanna. This restored town features myriad examples of architecture, from log cabins to elaborate Queen Anne Victorians. The downtown area is a perfect spot for lunch and light shopping at several antique shops and galleries.

DINING   Bube's Brewery is beloved by locals, an original brew house that's a National Historic Landmark. Three restaurants are housed under one roof in this former 19th-century brewery. The casual **Bottling Works** whips up light fare. A former cellar, the **Catacombs** features candlelit dinners of hearty fare such as French onion soup and crab-stuffed lobster as well as waiters in medieval attire. **Alois** (closed Monday; 717-653-2057), a French restaurant, serves a seven-course traditional meal, starting with cocktails in the Victorian parlor of the former Central Hotel, which is part of the brewery complex. ~ 102 North Market Street, Mount Joy; 717-653-2056; www.bubesbrewery.com. The Bottling Works and Catacombs are MODERATE; Alois is DELUXE.

PARKS   **SUSQUEHANNOCK STATE PARK** 🏃 A state park that's preserved mainly as a nature area, Susquehannock, on the Susquehanna River, offers spectacular views of the Conowingo Reservoir and the Susquehanna River. From Hawk Point Overlook, you can see several islands in the river; a few are bald eagle habitats. If you have binoculars with you, you'll be likely to spot turkey vultures, osprey and eagles. From Wissler's Run Overlook, examine the tops of the power line towers for osprey nests; in spring, you'll often be able to see baby birds, especially as summer draws near and the birds are large enough to be spotted in their nests. The .55-mile Overlook Trail will get you to both these spots. Facilities include picnic tables, restrooms and softball fields. ~ 1880 Park Drive, Drumore; 717-432-5011.

HOLTWOOD ENVIRONMENTAL PRESERVE 🏃 🚤 🚤 🚣 A Pennsylvania Power & Light–run environmental preserve, Holtwood spans the Susquehanna River in Lancaster and York counties, offering these areas access to land abutting PPL's hydroelectric plants. The preserve has more than 200 campsites, 150 of which have access to dumping station, camp store, showers and flush toilets. The area also has more than 35 miles of hiking trails, including 15 miles of the rugged, stunning 61-mile Conestoga Trail. Lake Aldred is a popular motorboat destination, with ramps and a sand beach for day use. Also here are an Indian museum and a preserved lock on what used to be the Susquehanna and Tidewater Canal. Those fortunate enough to

HIDDEN ▶   be visiting in April (weather permitting) should go to **Shenk's Ferry Wildflower Preserve**. The display of Virginia bluebells is one of the East Coast's finest. Amenities include restrooms and boat ramps. ~ 9 New Village Road, Holtwood; 800-354-8383; www.pplweb.com/holtwood.

▲ There are 55 tent sites and 30 travel trailer sites near Pequea Creek, with lavatories, hot showers, a general store and laundry facilities. All facilities are open April through October.

In the winter months, camping is permitted with only vault restrooms open. Fees vary.

MUDDY RUN RECREATION PARK 🏃 ⛴ 🛶 Muddy Run, also at Holtwood, is managed by the Philadelphia Electric Company. It is one of the area's top places for outdoor recreation, with miles of hiking trails and campsites along a large lake. The 2.7-mile hike around the lake is rugged yet doable for a family with preschool children. You'll find a playground as well as boat rentals. Other facilities include an education and nature center, restrooms and picnic tables, as well as softball fields. ~ 172 Bethesda Church Road West, Holtwood; 717-284-4325.

> Holtwood Environmental Preserve is a hydro-electric power plant, using a system of dams to generate electricity. Hikers should leave the riverbed areas if an alarm sounds.

CHICKIES ROCK COUNTY PARK 🏃 The highlight of this county-run park is Chickies Rock, an outcropping that rises 200 feet above the Susquehanna. From here, you can see Marietta and the farmland of Lancaster and York counties. Trails in the area also take hikers past ruins of iron furnaces, farmhouses and other historic sites. There are picnic facilities, restrooms and play areas. ~ Route 441, north of Columbia; 717-299-8215.

Outdoor Adventures

FISHING

Lancaster County's numerous lakes, streams and rivers provide ample opportunity to catch large and smallmouth bass, trout, pickerel and more. **Muddy Run Reservoir** is a popular spot for families to hook largemouth bass. To snag smallmouth bass, consider fishing just south of the city of Lancaster on the Conestoga River. The county also has several designated trout streams. Fishing licenses are required for anyone over 16 years old. Licenses can be obtained at the Lancaster County treasurer's office and sporting good stores.

The **Pennsylvania Boat and Fish Commission** has information and maps about Lancaster area streams, lakes and rivers on its website. ~ 50 North Duke Street; 717-299-8222; www.fish.state.pa.us.

Evening Rise Flyfishing Outfitters can help fishermen find local spots for casting. They sell supplies as well. ~ 1953 Fruitville Pike, Lancaster; 717-509-3636.

GOLF

Lancaster County has one 18-hole public golf course, **Overlook**, a relatively easy course with a number of par-5 holes. ~ 2040 Lititz Pike, Lancaster; 717-569-9551.

Willow Valley Resort has a nine-hole course that is open to the public. ~ 2416 Willow Street Pike, Lancaster; 717-464-2711, 800-444-1714; www.willowvalley.com.

The **Lancaster Host Resort** has an 18-hole championship golf course that's been played by PGA golfers. The beautiful greens abut several Amish farms, making this one of the most scenic courses in the county. ~ 2300 Lincoln Highway East, Lancaster; 717-299-5500, 800-233-0121.

TENNIS

Lancaster County operates several public tennis courts at **D.F. Buchmiller Park**, just south of the city. ~ Parks and Recreation Department, 1050 Rockford Road, Lancaster; 717-299-8215.

RIDING STABLES

If you'd like to take a horseback ride and didn't bring your horse, you'll have to travel over the Susqehanna to York County to **Plantation Estate Stables**, which offers one-and-a-half-hour trail rides on their sweet, gentle horses. Even those who've never ridden will find a match. Plantation Estate has both English and Western tack for those with a preference. ~ 405 Throne Road, Fawn Grove; 717-382-4171; www.horseloversb-b.com.

JOGGING

HIDDEN ►

Lancaster County has a couple of "rails to trails" paths that are ideal for hiking and jogging. The **Conewago Recreation Trail** is a five-mile trail in northern Lancaster County that follows the Cornwall-Lebanon rail line. It moves along a creek through farmland and woods. During winter, the trail is used by cross-country skiers. To reach it from Elizabethtown, take Route 230 West one mile. The trailhead is on the right just before the Conewago Creek Bridge. ~ Parks and Recreation Department, 1050 Rockford Road, Lancaster; 717-299-8215.

HIDDEN ►

The **Lancaster Junction Trail** is a two-mile trail on the former Reading Columbia railroad through meadows and beside Chickie's Creek. A flat, straight trail, it is ideal for hiking, running and cross-country skiing. To reach it, take Route 283 west of Lancaster, turn right on Spooky Nook Road and right onto Champ Road. Go a half-mile to the trailhead on the left. ~ Parks and Recreation Department, 1050 Rockford Road, Lancaster; 717-299-8215.

BIKING

Cyclists will enjoy peddling along Lancaster's back roads, such as Quarry Ridge Road near Strasburg and Route 772 between Lititz and Intercourse. The terrain varies from smooth, flat roadways to hilly byways and gravel trails. In the west, you can bike through rolling hills and farmland and experience scenic vistas of the Susquehanna. In the county's heart, you can coast past interesting architecture and working Amish farms. The **Lancaster County Planning Commission** has created several maps and a 20-mile bike tour of Amish Country on peaceful roads from Strasburg to Ephrata. ~ www.lancastercountyheritage.com. The **Lancaster Bike Club** sponsors a number of rides and has a list-

ing of club favorites, as well as maps. ~ www.lancasterbike
club.org.

Bike Rentals   If you didn't bring your bike, you can rent one
by the day, weekend or week at **Bike Line** in Lancaster. ~ 117
Rohrerstown Road; 717-394-8998.

All distances listed for hiking trails are roundtrip unless other-   **HIKING**
wise noted.

The longest trail system in Lancaster County is the 61-mile
Conestoga Trail, which winds its way across the county on a
north–south heading. You can hike part of it in the city of
Lancaster, heading to Rock Ford Plantation, the home of General
Edward Hand. This four-mile roundtrip portion of the trail runs
along the river and through the city's Central Park. From East
King Street, cross the Conestoga River at Witmer's Bridge. Turn
left on Conestoga Drive and follow the river. Turn left at the
bridge and cross the Conestoga on South Duke Street. Cross the
street and enter the park. Where the parking is available on the
left, turn right on the trail. Pass Indian Maiden View and turn
left, taking the side trail to Rock Ford Plantation. Central Park
also is home to a several Indian graves and burial grounds. ~
1050 Rockford Road, Lancaster; 717-299-8215.

At Susquehannock State Park, the **Overlook Trail** (.55 mile
one way) wends through beautiful scenery to Hawks Point and
Wissler's Run overlooks. In late June and early July, the **Rhodo-**   ◀ *HIDDEN*
dendron Trail blooms in pinks, rosy whites and pale lavenders.
This steep trail leads through wild rhodos and past an area of de-
forestation, where diseased hemlocks were removed.

For more challenging terrain, head to Holtwood Environmental Preserve and the trail network that runs through Kelly's
Run Natural Area, part of the preserve. The natural area is on
the southeast shore of the lower Susquehanna River. One **loop
trail** (6 miles) reaches 500 feet above the waterway.

Chickies Rock County Park in the western part of the county
maintains a trail system that includes the **Chickies Rock
Overlook trail** (1 mile). This flat trail leads to a scenic overlook
that offers views of neighboring York County and the nearby
borough of Marietta.

There are essentially three main thoroughfares through
Lancaster County. **Route 30** runs from Philadelphia's   **Transportation**
Main Line through the city of Lancaster and westward
to York. Running north to south is **Route 222**, which links   **CAR**
Adamstown and points north, including Reading, with Lancaster
and points south, including Maryland. **Route 322** links the
county's northern villages. In the far northern reaches, the
Pennsylvania Turnpike crosses the county, with at least three

exits in the region. For more maps and information, inquire at the Pennsylvania Dutch Country Visitors Center. ~ 501 Greenfield Road, Lancaster; 717-299-8901, 800-723-8824; www.pa dutchcountry.com.

AIR

US Airways services **Lancaster Airport**, located north of Lancaster on Route 501 in Lititz; private flights are welcome as well. ~ Lancaster Airport Authority, 500 Airport Road, Lititz; 717-569-1221.

The nearest full-service airports are the **Philadelphia International Airport** (see Chapter One for more information), about 65 miles away; the **Harrisburg International Airport**, 38 miles away, and the **Lehigh Valley International Airport**, 65 miles away.

TRAIN

Amtrak runs train service directly to Lancaster. ~ 53 McGovern Avenue, Lancaster; 800-872-7245; www.amtrak.com.

BUS

Greyhound also provides service to Lancaster. ~ 53 McGovern Avenue; 717-397-4861, 800-231-2222; www.greyhound.com.

CAR RENTALS

Several major car rental agencies have offices in Lancaster; a few are based out of the airport and Lancaster, including **Alamo Rent A Car** (800-327-9633), **Avis Rent A Car** (800-831-2847), **Enterprise Rent A Car** (800-325-8007), **Dollar Rent A Car** (800-800-4000), **Hertz Rent A Car** (800-654-3131) and **National Car Rental** (717-227-7368).

NINE

Brandywine Valley

The historic Brandywine Valley covers the border of southeastern Pennsylvania into Delaware, spreading through the tidal marshes and suburbs of Wilmington. Known for its rural scenery, formal gardens, prized collections of decorative arts and museums, it is a favorite weekend destination for Philadelphians. The valley has much to offer in terms of sightseeing, including the expansive Longwood Gardens; the world-famous Winterthur Museum in Delaware, and the beautiful, historic Revolutionary War battlefield of Brandywine at Chadds Ford. Just outside its reaches lies Valley Forge National Historical Park, one of the nation's most famous historic parks, which attracts not only history buffs but local residents, for its excellent hiking trails, picnic grounds and scenery.

The Brandywine area is packed with restaurants, cozy B&Bs and shops. Its quaint towns of West Chester and Chadds Ford have captured the hearts of many, including three generations of Wyeths—American realist artists who made their home at Chadds Ford and immortalized its scenery in their works. Today, along U.S. 1, development is rampant, and the region has its share of strip malls and suburban neighborhoods. Yet just off the main streets, much of the region remains as it was more than two centuries ago, a vast expanse of farmland and small towns linked by winding country roads. The region's landscape is embroidered with historic structures and homes, including 15 covered bridges and numerous gristmills and barns.

Flanking the Brandywine River—or Brandywine Creek, as it's often called—the valley was settled initially as farmland. Other settlers, mainly Quakers, arrived and established businesses to serve travelers heading west. During the Revolution, George Washington's army was defeated soundly by the British on September 11, 1777, along the banks of the Brandywine. Later, a new generation of Europeans moved in; the DuPont de Nemours family relocated to Brandywine from France following the French Revolution. The DuPonts established a number of gunpowder mills along the river, factories that profited considerably during expansion and grew into the vast chemical and textile corporation that continues to carry the family name. The DuPonts, who established what amounted to fiefdom in the Wilmington area, left an indelible mark on the region. Many of Wilmington's well-known sites either bear the name DuPont or were owned by the family, including the manor homes of Winterthur, the Nemours Mansion and Gardens, and the Hagley Museum.

SIGHTS   To get a sense of the Brandywine region and its heritage, it's best to start in one of its two large towns and move outward. This section explores the area beginning in scenic West Chester in order to remain in Pennsylvania and work southward. You could start your tour at the famous attractions in Wilmington and move northward, depending on your itinerary.

West Chester, a settlement since 1692, has served as the county seat of Chester since 1786. It's a charming small town featuring more than 3000 structures dating to the Colonial period, and its downtown is listed on the National Register of Historic Places. Besides examples of Greek-revival architecture, West Chester also boasts a selection of Victorian-style homes and businesses. West Chester is considered the heart of cosmopolite in Chester, with numerous restaurants, antique shops, galleries and bars.

Outside West Chester lies a must-see for fans of Diamonique jewelry: QVC, the $3.4 billion-per-year-in-television-sales corporation. An hour-long studio tour takes visitors past the company's five state-of-the-art studios and explains the inner workings of this television retail giant. QVC takes more than a 100 million phone calls a year and ships 70 million packages. Visitors can call ahead if they want to be part of a live audience. The tour is geared for those aged six and older. An on-site store sells QVC merchandise. Admission. ~ 1200 QVC Drive, West Chester; 800-600-9900; www.qvctours.com.

If home shopping doesn't interest you, perhaps the great collection of more than 50 aircraft at the **American Helicopter Museum** will start your motor. The museum honors the rotor blade industry, which traces some of its roots to southeastern Pennsylvania. Exhibits at the museum include civilian and military craft, including a Bell H13D Sioux, immortalized as an evacuation helicopter by the television series *M*A*S*H*; a Coast Guard HH-52 Sea Guardian, the service's last amphibious helicopter; and a prototype V-22 Osprey, the tiltrotor craft currently being fielded by the Marine Corps. There are helicopters for children to explore as well as a toddler learning area. Family helicopter rides are offered the third Saturday of the month for a fee. Admission. ~ 1200 American Boulevard, West Chester; 610-436-9600; www.helicoptermuseum.org.

HIDDEN ►

Text continued on page 234.

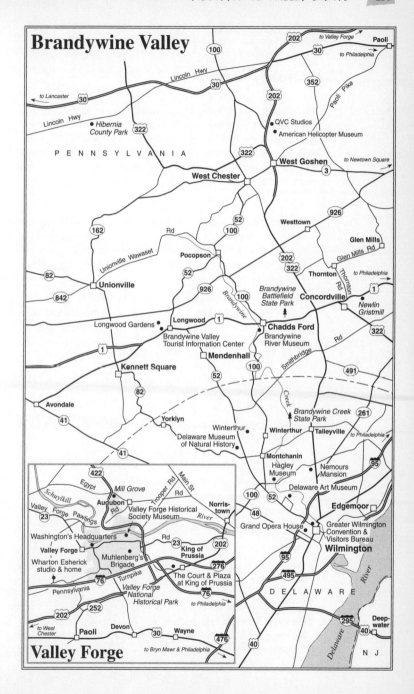

Three-day Weekend

19th-century Escape

Many Brandywine Valley attractions date to before the Revolutionary War, and you'll easily find many fine examples of Federal and Colonial architecture and other Colonial sites as you drive through the region. This tour will take you back 200 years, to the establishment of mills and commerce in the region, through the Civil War and into the Gilded Age as the DuPonts emerged as captains of industry.

Day 1
- Start your day by waking at a Brandywine area B&B, like, say, the **1800 Tory Inne** (page 240) or the 1815 wing of **Sweetwater Farm Bed and Breakfast** (page 240). Head to the **Brandywine River Museum** (page 234) to view the vast collection, set in a 19th-century gristmill.

- Head to Kennett Square. Visit the **Kennett Underground Railroad Center** (page 235) to learn about the area's rich Quaker and abolitionist history. Pick up a map of "railroad stops" and tour them by car, or enjoy the exhibits at the KURC and stroll the streets of Kennett Square—you can arrange a walking tour of the town's architectural highlights, which include many 19th-century Victorian, Queen Anne and Four Square homes.

- Catch lunch at the 1836 **Kennett Square Inn** (page 243).

- Afterward, explore Pierre DuPont's botanical wonders at **Longwood Gardens** (page 235).

- Return to your inn for afternoon tea and to rest before dinner.

- For fine dining, try the **Dilworthtown Inn** (page 241), one of the area's most popular dining destinations. For more-casual fare and live music, consider making reservations at **Vincent's** (page 242), a lively bistro set in a Victorian row house.

Day 2
- Breakfast at **Hank's Place** (page 242). This local diner is definitely not 19th century, but you'll mingle with the locals here.

- Head toward Wilmington to tour **Winterthur** (page 236).

- Consider having a late brunch at the Hotel DuPont's **Green Room** (page 243). The lavish setting and fine service will make you feel like a DuPont. Last seating is at 2 p.m. For a less stuffy dining experience, grab sandwiches or brunch from Winterthur's **Garden Cafeteria** (page 244) or **Cappuccino Café** (page 244).

- Visit the **Hagley Museum and Library** (page 236) in the afternoon, especially if the weather is nice. If the weather is poor, consider visiting the **Delaware Art Museum** (page 237).

- For dinner, relax and enjoy a meal and adult beverage at **Iron Hill Brewery** (page 243) on the waterfront in Wilmington. Housed in a former warehouse, the restaurant seats 300 guests and serves a variety of homebrews.

Nine miles south of West Chester stands the quaint hamlet of **Chadds Ford,** famous for its battlefields and scenic beauty. Among the homes at Chadds Ford is the 1725 residence of John Chads, a ferry operator who ran a tavern and way station at a shallow crossing—ford—in the Brandywine River.

Brandywine Battlefield State Park is the site of Washington's defeat early in the Revolution, a loss that allowed the British to march into Philadelphia and send the Second Continental Congress fleeing to Lancaster. Today, visitors can tour a stone home that served as Washington's headquarters as well as a smaller Quaker house that quartered the Marquis de Lafayette. The museum and visitors center contains a collection of Colonial items and Lafayette memorabilia, as well as historical displays. Each year, in conjunction with the event's anniversary, the park hosts a spectacular reenactment featuring costumed actors, demonstrations of encampments and military drills, and a craft fair. ~ Route 1 at Chadds Ford; 610-459-3342.

Nearby, the **Brandywine River Museum** houses a renowned collection of American art in a 19th-century gristmill. In a lovely setting of exposed beams, rough-hewn floors and plaster walls, the museum's collection shines with the works of Chadds Ford residents N. C. Wyeth and Andrew Wyeth, as well as Andrew's son Jamie. N. C. Wyeth is best known for his illustrations of such classic works as *The Last of the Mohicans* and *Treasure Island.* Andrew Wyeth's works, which have become known to the masses through successful print sales, include *Christina's World* and *Master Bedroom.* And Jamie Wyeth, who at the age of 18 had works displayed at the Wilmington Society of Art, has painted memorable oils of various subjects, ranging from pigs to dancer Rudolf Nureyev. Others featured in the museum's collection include Winslow Homer, Maxfield Parrish, Charles Addams and Theodor Geisel (Dr. Seuss). Tours of the N. C. Wyeth house and studio are available Wednesday through Sunday for an extra fee. ~ Route 1 at Chadds Ford; 610-388-2700; www.brandywine museum.org.

Chaddsford Winery ranks among the finest of Pennsylvania's vintners, consistently winning awards for its dry reds as well as a few whites. The winery's tasting room is located in a renovated 17th-century barn and its main house sits nestled in the arbors, a great spot for enjoying vino and cheese. The winery hosts a blues festival on Memorial Day and jazz on Labor Day, as well as Friday-night concerts in the summer. ~ 632 Baltimore Pike, Chadds Ford; 610-388-6221; www.chaddsford.com.

Just west of Chadds Ford is **Kennett Square,** known to Philadelphia diners by the presence of "Kennett Square mushrooms" listed on nearly any menu in the city. This Victorian town and its environs produce more than half the country's mushroom crop each year, and the tasty fungus remains the biggest cash crop in Pennsylvania. Kennett Square is rich with Victorian buildings and its downtown area features a number of interesting art galleries, gift shops and handmade jewelry stores. Most are open late the first Friday of the month.

Near Kennett Square is the one of the United States' grandest European-style botanical gardens, the 1050-acre **Longwood Gardens**. Pierre DuPont's masterpiece began in 1906; today Longwood features 11,000 types of plants in 20 manicured gardens and 20 heated conservatories and indoor spaces. Among the biggest attractions in these lush environs are DuPont's magnificent fountains, some of which shoot up to 130 feet in the air (fountain shows are held during the summer and holidays). Though spring is Longwood's finest season, when dogwood, azaleas, redbud and rhododendrons are in bloom, nearly any time of the year is good for visiting, since the indoor spaces often are decorated lavishly and feature flowers, bonsai, orchids, water gardens and rose beds. Special events include Christmas light displays; an orchid show; and Fountains and Fireworks, a musical water-and-lights extravaganza on certain summer weekends. In 2006, Longwood will open its ballroom and music room and will christen a new children's area containing fountains, trails and hidden surprises. Admission. ~ Route 1, Kennett Square; 610-388-1000; www.longwoodgardens.org.

At age six, Pierre DuPont was captivated by the water pumps and flowers at Horticulture Hall during Philadelphia's 1876 Centennial Exposition. This passion evolved into his creation of one of the nation's best botanical gardens.

Southern Chester County was a major thoroughfare for the Underground Railroad, and this rich past is explored at the **Kennett Underground Railroad Center**. This small museum features maps and displays about the region's 20-plus hideaways and stops as well as examples of hidden rooms. In summer, the center sponsors driving tours to key sites and farms on the Railroad. Open weekends or by appointment; call for hours. Admission. ~ 505 South Broad Street, Kennett Square; 610-347-2237; www.undergroundrr.kennett.net.

◄ HIDDEN

A few of Brandywine's key destinations can be seen in a day, but to explore the region more intensely, you should consider spending a weekend or more. For help planning your trip, the **Brandywine Conference and Visitors Bureau** publishes a free visitors guide with information on attractions, dining, lodging and events. ~ 1 Beaver Valley Road, Chadds Ford; 610-565-3679, 800-343-3983; www.brandywinecountry.org.

TheBrandywine.com is an online guide maintained by Chadds Ford resident Seth Fox. You can also call or e-mail for information. ~ 610-388-6841; e-mail hello@thebrandywine.com.

Chester County sponsors the **Brandywine Valley Tourist Information Center**, which also publishes guides on area attractions and businesses ~ Route 1 north of Kennett Square; 610-388-2900, 800-228-9933; www.brandywinevalley.com.

An industrial city with a rich history of commerce and development, **Wilmington, Delaware**, lies 29 miles southwest of Philadelphia. A city of roughly 73,000 residents, Wilmington was founded in 1638 as a Swedish settlement and became a boomtown during the Civil War. Today, it is home to several major banks and financial institutions, and of course, the DuPont Corporation. The downtown area is blessed with fine examples of various architectural styles, from Federal to art deco. Among the best known buildings are the **Hotel DuPont**, an Italian Renaissance–style hotel of a grand era, featuring opulent interior spaces, great halls and a full-sized theater; and the French Renaissance–style **Grand Opera House**, a working theater built in 1871 by the Delaware Most Worshipful Grand Lodge of Ancient Free and Accepted Masons.

The **Greater Wilmington Convention and Visitors Bureau** also offers in-depth information on the Delaware portion of the valley. ~ 100 West 10th Street, Wilmington, DE; 302-652-4088; www.visitwilmingtonde.com.

Just outside Wilmington you'll find one of America's great estates, **Winterthur**, acclaimed for its vast collection of decorative arts. Winterthur has 175 rooms, numerous museum galleries and 982 acres of open land, including a 60-acre naturalist garden. On display at this former home of Henry Francis DuPont are some of his family's incredible collections of china, silver, paintings and furniture dating from the mid-17th to mid-19th centuries. The 96,582-square-foot house—built in 1837 by Jacques Antoine Bidermann, a DuPont investor, and his wife, Evelina, a daughter of original settler E. I. DuPont—has been expanded over the years to nine stories. Highlights of the historic art and artifacts housed at Winterthur include silver tankards made by Paul Revere, paintings by Gilbert Stuart and Charles Willson Peale, and Chinese porcelain made for George Washington. The gardens, open for walking tours or seen by a guided tram tour, include acres of bulbs, eight acres of azaleas and rhododendrons, a reflecting pool and a tree that is thought to have lived at the time of William Penn. Children enjoy the Enchanted Woods, a three-acre garden with a Faerie Cottage, tea room and tree house. Admission. ~ Route 1 at Route 52, Winterthur, DE; 800-448-3883; www.winterthur.org.

The restored 19th-century village, powder mill and home at the **Hagley Museum and Library** give visitors insight into the

> The house at Winterthur, Henry Francis DuPont's sprawling estate, boasts 50 fireplaces.

early days of the DuPonts. Constructed on the site of the original powder mill built by E. I. DuPont, the museum encompasses 230 acres and maintains exhibits on DuPont company history, the story of the family, the gunpowder mills and Eleutherian Mills, a magnificent Georgian mansion that was the first DuPont home in the country. Museum admission includes access to the home, the grounds and a restored French garden. Open daily mid-March through December; open weekdays for one guided tour daily from January to mid-March. ~ 298 Buck Road East, Wilmington, DE; 302-658-2400; www.hagley.lib.de.us.

The **Nemours Mansion** was the country home of Alfred I. DuPont, a 47,000-square-foot Louis XVIth–style French chateau named for the French village from which the DuPont family emigrated to the United States. The home contains an array of antiques from around the world, including furniture, tapestries, rugs, lighting and decorative arts. Highlights include a Louis XVI clock and a crystal chandelier thought to have been owned by the Marquis de Lafayette. Nemours is undergoing an extensive renovation that is expected to be complete in 2007. Children under 12 not admitted. Closed January through April. Admission. ~ 1600 Rockland Road, Wilmington, DE; 302-651-6912, 800-651-6912; www.nemoursmansion.org.

Having undergone a recent $30 million renovation and expansion, the **Delaware Art Museum** is a 100,000-square-foot showcase of the visual arts, featuring 20,000 works in 17 galleries. Highlights of the collection include the works of American artists Benjamin West, Frederic Church and Winslow Homer. Sculptor George Segal and local artist Andrew Wyeth feature prominently as well. The museum also holds an impressive collection of early English art, including paintings by Dante Gabriel Rossetti and Edward Burne-Jones. Planned exhibitions include Andrew Wyeth's early works and a compilation of African-American portraiture. Closed Monday. Admission. ~ 2301 Kentmere Parkway, Wilmington, DE; 302-571-9590; www.delart.org.

Best known for its seashell collection and bird clutches, the **Delaware Museum of Natural History**—the state's only museum of this type—has more than two million mollusk specimens. Its bird egg collection is the second largest in North America, with more than 36,000 examples. Exhibits also include dinosaur bones, fossils and mineral collections. The hands-on Discovery Room is especially popular with children, offering such activities as animal talks, pretend play and scientific experiments. ~ 4840 Kennett Pike, Wilmington, DE; 302-658-9111; www.delmnh.org.

LODGING

For the most part, you'll find nationally recognized chain hotels and motels in Wilmington, along the U.S. 1 corridor and near the

Text continued on page 240.

Valley Forge

The cold, heartless winter of 1777 to 1778 marked a turning point in the American Revolution—the transformation of a ragtag group of soldiers into a professional fighting force led by George Washington. The story of **Valley Forge** is taught in every U.S. history course, a tale of hardship, hunger and suffering. But Valley Forge is also where, once provisions, supplies and new troops arrived, soldiers trained and learned tactics, marched and drilled and established protocols for supply, advance and, eventually, victory. The story of this encampment's contribution to history is related at **Valley Forge National Historical Park**, a 3600-acre preserve of ruins and reconstructed buildings, forts and historic sites administered by the National Park Service. There are numerous other attractions in the neighborhoods surrounding Valley Forge, including Mill Grove, the home of John James Audubon, the Wharton Escherick Museum and Philadelphia's biggest shopping mall, the Court and Plaza of King of Prussia.

Valley Forge National Historical Park is the site of the famous winter encampment, a destination for history buffs and area outdoor enthusiasts, who enjoy the park's 23 miles of hiking trails and walks, picnic areas and waterways. A tour of Valley Forge should begin at the visitors center, where you can watch an 18-minute orientation film and pick up a map for a self-guided automobile tour (or ambitious six- to ten-mile hike). Highlights include reconstructed log cabins that served as home for soldiers led by General Peter Muhlenberg; Artillery Park, a repository for hundreds of cannon; Washington's quarters; and the beautiful 18th-century farmhouse that overlooks the parade grounds and served as quarters for General James Varnu. More than 2500 soldiers died of disease and hunger during their encampment of Valley Forge, but the park has surprisingly few graves or markers. According to historians, most of the ill were transported to area hospitals where they perished.

A six-mile loop, popular with hikers and cyclists, wends through the park, passing most historic sites. Traffic on the park's main thoroughfare is at its worst during peak summer hours and on sunny weekends. Admission. ~ 1400 North Outerline Drive (Route 23 and Route 263), King of Prussia; 610-783-1000; www.nps.gov/vafo.

The distinctive mountaintop retreat and studio of American craftsman **Wharton Esherick** lies southwest of Valley Forge National Historical Park and is open by appointment for tours. Known for his artistic furniture and flowing woodcarvings, Esherick, the "Dean of American Craftsmen," contributed greatly to the craft art movement, creating furniture, sculpture and household goods designed around inspirational shapes and figures Esherick saw in wood. His most famous work is part of his Malvern, Pennsylvania, home: a freeform, red oak, spiral staircase that reaches three stories. It was displayed in 1958 at the New York Museum of Contemporary Art. Open by appointment only. Admission. ~ 1520 Horseshoe Trail Road; Malvern; 610-644-5822; www.levins.com/esherick.html.

John James Audubon's home for two years, **Mill Grove**, is thought to be the inspiration for many of Audubon's earliest works and wildlife studies. The 1762 home was purchased by Audubon's father in 1789, and Audubon occupied it in the early 1800s, attempting to run a lead mine on-site while also conducting his first bird-banding experiments in this country. The home features a number of Audubon's works and taxidermy, and is set within a 175-acre sanctuary of meadows, woods, waterways, and hiking and nature trails. Closed Monday. Admission. ~ Audubon and Pawlings roads, Audubon; 610-666-5593.

busy towns of King of Prussia and Media. If you seek a hotel with luxurious appointments and amenities, consider staying in downtown Wilmington. Country inns or B&Bs can be found in small towns or along isolated country roads.

HIDDEN ►

Set in a former general store and post office, the decidedly British **1800 Tory Inne** draws patrons for both its theme and hospitality. The inn's three rooms are named for famous British generals, and although the building wasn't actually constructed when they marched through the area, the rooms have been renovated and decorated with Colonial flair, including poster beds and Williamsburg reproduction bedding. Innkeeper Linda Waterhouse-Koski is of British descent, a fact made obvious by the rich breakfasts she serves, which include scones and bangers, bacon or other breakfast meat. ~ 734 North Chester Road, West Chester; 610-431-2788; www.toryinne.com. DELUXE.

The cozy and warm **Brandywine River Hotel** is ideally situated across from the Brandywine River Museum and the historic battlefield. Boasting a beautiful stone hearth and seating area in the lobby, and a sunny breakfast room, this 40-room hotel feels more like a guesthouse than a mid-sized hotel. The staff is courteous and friendly, able to guide you through your stay. Rooms are decorated with cherry furniture, floral and striped bedding and rich jewel tones. Amenities include a small table set in every room, hairdryers, high-speed internet access and satellite television. Some rooms have jacuzzi-style tubs and fireplaces. A continental breakfast is included in the room rate, as is afternoon tea. The hotel lobby has a handy little cash bar for beer and wine purchases in the evenings. ~ Route 1 and Route 100, Chadds Ford; 610-388-1200, 800-274-9644; www.brandywineriverhotel.com. DELUXE.

AUTHOR FAVORITE

The gorgeous **Sweetwater Farm Bed and Breakfast** is set on 50 acres of rolling Brandywine Valley countryside east of Chadds Ford. This large stone manor home built in 1734 features a selection of room options, from cozy Colonial rooms in the 1734 portion to opulent rooms with canopy beds and 12-foot ceilings in the 1815 wing. Families traveling with children are welcome to stay in one of five cottages, including a renovated carriage house and greenhouse. The rich Lafayette room features a canopy bed, fireplace, comfortable wing chairs and views of adjacent pastures and cornfields. A hearty breakfast is served in the formal dining room or by the kitchen hearth, depending on occupancy. Be sure to set aside a few hours to sit and enjoy the scenery from the porch. ~ Sweetwater Road, Glen Mills; 610-459-4711, 800-793-3892; www.sweetwaterfarm bb.com. DELUXE.

The **Pennsbury Inn** sits on a busy thoroughfare, but its thick, 18-inch stone walls buffer guests from the outside world, creating a sense of simple beauty and relaxation. The inn features seven bedrooms, each with private baths and decorated with antique beds, Colonial bedding or quilts, wallpaper and artwork. An upstairs attic room is popular with couples, featuring exposed beams, an electric fireplace and large Palladian window overlooking the garden. Common rooms include a garden room with walk-in fireplace, a music room and a library with cherry built-ins. The hearty three-course breakfast includes eggs, a meat dish and fresh fruit. ~ 883 Baltimore Pike, Chadds Ford; 610-388-1435; www.pennsburyinn.com. DELUXE.

The **Hilton Garden Inn** is a 93-room hotel located less than a mile from Longwood Gardens. A clean, comfortable hotel with indoor pool, fitness rooms and internet access in the rooms, the Hilton Garden is a favorite for business travelers and families. Rooms are simply decorated, with light cherry contemporary furniture, floral and striped bedding in vibrant colors and microwaves. There's a breakfast café on-site as well. ~ 815 East Baltimore Pike, Kennett Square; 610-444-9100. MODERATE.

The guest registry at the luxurious, historic **Hotel DuPont** has included aviators, movie stars, monarchs, U.S. presidents and baseball royalty—Amelia Earhart, Prince Rainier, Katharine Hepburn, Elizabeth Taylor, John F. Kennedy and Joe DiMaggio, to name a few. The hotel was built to rival the finest European lodgings; Pierre S. DuPont planned a 150-room hotel with dining room, rathskellar, men's café, ballroom and club room. Just months after opening in 1913, a theater—larger than all but three New York stages—was added. Today, the hotel has grown to 206 rooms and 10 suites (although all rooms have their own seating area). Rooms are decorated in neutral colors and feature mahogany furniture, including large columns that hide the TV set; and luxurious marble baths with soaker tubs and separate showers. The hotel has a restaurant on-site, shops and 24-hour room service. ~ 11th and Market streets, Wilmington, DE; 302-594-3100, 800-441-9019; www.dupont.com/hotel. ULTRA-DELUXE.

DINING

The region boasts a variety of bistros and restaurants, many featuring locally grown produce and game.

Rich in Colonial atmosphere, the **Dilworthtown Inn** is a favorite destination for locals, who enjoy supping in a 1754 tavern that hosted the victorious—and pillaging—British after the Battle of Brandywine. The inn features 15 cozy rooms with deep windowsills and plaster walls. Some have large walk-in stone fireplaces. Tables are set with white linens and candles, creating a cozy, romantic atmosphere. Entrées include such Continental favorites as châteaubriand, roast rack of lamb and filet mignon *au* *poivre*, served with a spicy pepper sauce and sautéed Kennett Square mushrooms. The inn also boasts an impressive selection of more than 800 wines. ~ 1390 Old Wilmington Pike, West Chester; 610-399-1390; www.dilworthtown.com. ULTRA-DELUXE.

In a lovely setting that overlooks the Brandywine River, **Simon Pearce on the Brandywine** mixes the experience of dining with the art of glassblowing—the restaurant is set in an on-site workshop, similar to Pearce's first dining establishment, at the Mill in Quechee, Vermont. Nearly every table in the airy, contemporary dining room overlooks the creek and is decorated with samples of the company's glass art. The seasonal menu features inventive, New American fare. Entrée choices include jumbo lump crab cakes with roasted asparagus, chive saffron sauce, or roasted pork loin with parsnip potato purée. ~ 1333 Lenape Road, West Chester; 610-793-0948. ULTRA-DELUXE

In the late 1700s through 1821, the Dilworthtown Inn operated under several names: Sign of the Pennsylvania Farmer, The Black Horse Tavern, Sign of The Rising Sun, and Cross Keys.

Set in a restored Victorian home in the heart of West Chester, **Vincent's** has been a popular destination for romantic evenings as well as fun nights out on the town since the 1980s. The menu changes with the seasons, but you'll find a variety of veal dishes, steaks, pastas and other delights. The ravioli is always a tasty surprise, sometimes filled with salmon or arugula and sun-dried tomatoes. The restaurant has both indoor and outdoor seating in good weather, and during the week, you might be serenaded by a wandering fiddler. Vincent's also is a local haunt for good jazz. ~ 10 East Gay Street, West Chester; 610-696-4262; www.vincentsjazz.com. DELUXE.

Need a quick pick-me-up? Pop into **Brew HaHa** for an authentic Italian espresso or cappuccino. The panini, with fresh tomatoes, mesclun and fresh mozzarella tastes like a slice of Tuscany. ~ 9 West Gay Street, West Chester; 610-429-9335. BUDGET.

HIDDEN ►

A hidden surprise in Newtown Square, east of West Chester, **Roux 3** is a contemporary restaurant with an adventurous menu—more Philadelphia Center City bistro than suburban strip mall eatery. The modern atmosphere is *très* chic, with burnt oranges, gold and rich chocolate brown circular booths and banquettes lit by suspended discs. The New American fare includes several delightful fusion choices—fried calamari with a Thai-inspired dip and chicken spring rolls. Fish, chicken and seafood dishes make up the bulk of the menu, which is rounded out by an array of dessert choices, including homemade ice creams and sorbets. ~ 4755 West Chester Pike, Newtown Square; 610-356-9500; www.roux3.com. DELUXE.

Hank's Place isn't fancy, but it's a great place to grab a sandwich and mingle with locals, who come mainly for the incredible eggs benedict and blueberry pancakes at breakfast. The restaurant overlooks the Brandywine River and offers good comfort food, including chicken pot pie. The lines are out the door on weekends; go early or during the week to avoid the crowds. No credit cards accepted. ~ Route 1 and Creek Road; Chadds Ford; 610-388-7061. BUDGET.

A historic commercial building located at the heart of Pennsylvania's mushroom capital, the **Kennett Square Inn** was constructed in 1835 and restored in 1976 as an early American tavern in 1976. Hardwood floors and cozy cherry tables create a rich atmosphere. The menu, as expected, is heavy on the mushrooms, with stuff, fried, sautéed and grilled varieties available as appetizers. Lunch features hearty sandwiches, salads and soups. Dinner selections are Continental, with dishes such as veal Oscar, pan-fried duck with mixed berries, and New Zealand spring lamb with baked oysters. ~ 201 East State Street, Kennett Square; 601-444-5687; www.kennettinn.com. DELUXE TO ULTRA-DELUXE.

Catherine's is a local favorite BYO, specializing in new dishes   ◀ HIDDEN
with a Southwestern kick. Set in a former general store, the romantic setting includes hurricane lanterns on the floor and fine table settings. Interesting meal combos include a Caesar salad jazzed with chipotle peppers and blackened tuna with raspberry jalapeño coulis. ~ 1701 West Doe Run Road, Unionville; 610-347-2227. DELUXE.

For a special celebration or memorable dinner, the historic **Green Room** in the Hotel DuPont is Wilmington's ultimate destination dining room, with rich oak paneling, opulent draperies and Versace china. Topping the appetizer list is cocoa-dusted scallop seared in vanilla oil and served with sweet potato purée, a tantalizing juxtaposition of sweet and salty. An international selection of seafood highlights the rest of the menu: perch from Lake Victoria in Africa, mahimahi from the Gulf of Mexico and organic salmon from Ireland. Even the meats have a pedigree: the rack of lamb is from Australia and the venison hails from New Zealand. Lunch is a throwback to the days of tennis whites, with club sandwiches and steak *frites*. The crab-and-fontina sandwich, made using the hotel's cherished old recipe, is wonderful, as are the Old Bay potato chips served with it. ~ 11th and Market streets, Wilmington, DE; 800-441-9019. ULTRA-DELUXE.

Between the delicious beer and the "shared plate" offerings on the menu, it's hard to get to the entrées at **Iron Hill Brewery**. The appetizer menu, which is where you'll find the "shared plates," complements the beer and is tailored perfectly for eating and drinking with friends. The selection includes delicious spicy, smoked pork quesadillas and cheesesteak egg rolls you won't find anywhere else. Entrées are popular basics such as ahi tuna and baby back ribs, with some light offerings (a crab and shrimp cake with sweet corn and pepper relish). ~ 710 South Madison

Street, Wilmington, DE; 302-472-2739; www.ironhillbrewery. com. There's also a West Chester location at 3 West Gay Street; 610-738-9600. DELUXE.

Winterthur provides two places to sate grumbling tummies. The **Garden Cafeteria** is a favorite destination for Sunday brunch or afternoon tea; at lunch, enjoy fresh-made hearty sandwiches, hot entrées and snacks seated inside or out. For a quick breakfast or a morning cup of coffee before touring the estate, or for tea afterward, stop at the **Cappuccino Café**, which opens at 8 a.m. The café also serves snacks, soups and sandwiches. ~ Route 1 at Route 52, Winterthur, DE; 800-448-3883; www.winterthur.org. BUDGET TO MODERATE.

SHOPPING Quaint and scenic West Chester has one of the finest shopping districts in the Brandywine region, featuring galleries, antique stores and specialty shops. Special events include evening hours on Gay Street the first Friday of the month and a growers market on Saturday mornings May to October. **Baldwin's Book Barn** is a five-story treasure trove of rare and used books, maps and prints. Baldwin's vast collection lures visitors in, and the 1822 stone barn setting keeps them there to enjoy the rare volumes among the stacks. (A first edition of *The Great Gatsby* was recently found in a pile to be sorted.) ~ 865 Lenape Road, West Chester; 610-696-0816.

HIDDEN ► With the demise of the Mushroom Museum in Kennett Square, the **Mushroom Cap** is the best place to learn about the area's largest cash crop—and buy the little fungi, cookbooks, gift baskets, and specialty sauces and condiments. The store runs a ten-minute video on the history and cultivation of mushrooms. That unique smell in the air? Don't frown, locals say it's the smell of money. ~ 114 West State Street, Kennett Square; 610-444-8484; www.themushroomcap.com.

The shopping mall at King of Prussia is the largest on the East Coast. **The Court and Plaza of King of Prussia** feature eight department stores, including Neiman Marcus, Nordstrom, Lord and Taylor and Macy's. There are also 40 restaurants and nearly 400 individual shops, ranging from mid-budget such as the Gap and Express, to high-end stores like Burberry and Louis Vuitton. ~ 160 North Gulph Road (Route 202 and Mall Boulevard), King of Prussia; 610-265-5727; www.kingofprussiamall.com.

NIGHTLIFE Everyone should have a favorite Irish pub, and for many West Chester 20- and 30-somethings, that spot is **Kildare's**, a popular place to drink pints, sing, frolic and eat authentic Irish fare. Although there are several Kildare's pubs in the Philadelphia area, this is the original, with an authentic Irish pub interior—built in Ireland and shipped piece by piece for installation. The

menu features stacked sandwiches, fish and chips, and *boxtys*—
potato pancakes stuffed with various fillings. Kildare's has 12
ales on tap, including Guinness (of course) and, surprisingly,
Stella Artois. ~ 18–22 Gay Street, West Chester; 610-431-0770;
www.kildarespub.com.

Fans of microbrewed beer will like **Iron Hill Brewery**, which
attracts a young, loud college crowd as the evening advances. The
menu is savory and aimed toward complementing the beer selection. The Jamaican jerk porterhouse is particularly tasty. Some
reviewers have said the beer doesn't deliver, but I found the Lode-
stone Lager delicious. (Note, however, that my faves are Bass and
Yeungling—not too adventurous.) The Iron Hill has six locations; the two most popular are the West Chester location on
trendy West Gay Street, and in Wilmington, in a refurbished
warehouse. ~ 3 West Gay Street, West Chester, 610-738-9600;
and 710 South Madison Street, Wilmington, DE, 302-472-2739;
www.ironhillbrewery.com.

For culture and the arts, West Chester University frequently
hosts cultural events. The **Brandywine Ballet Theatre** is a professional company that stages three full-scale productions a year
as well as smaller summer performances and workshops. Housed
at the Emilie K. Asplundh Concert Hall on campus, the ballet has
staged productions of *Cinderella*, *The Nutcracker* and *Dracula*.
~ 317 Westtown Road, Suite 5, West Chester; 610-696-2711;
www.brandywineballet.com.

Wilmington also boasts a number of stages and performing
arts venues, with the finest being its **Grand Opera House**. The
opera house hosts a classic film series as well as concerts and stage
productions. Past performers include singer-songwriter Shawn
Colvin, violinist Itzhak Perlman and former Monkee Davy Jones.
~ 818 North Market Street, Wilmington, DE; 302-652-5577, 800-
374-7263; www.grandopera.org.

The **DuPont Theatre** at the Hotel DuPont is Wilmington's
venue for traveling Broadway musical troupes and regional concerts. Past productions include *Rent*, *Chicago* and *Thoroughly
Modern Millie*. The theater has been in operation since 1913 and

WEST CHESTER JAZZ JOINT

Four nights a week, someone is playing at **Vincent's**, perhaps a sultry saxo-
phonist on Tuesday, a hot-jazz trio on Thursday or a mournful blues band
on Friday. There's a full bar and plenty of seating in this restored Victorian
home. Live music Tuesday, Thursday, Friday and Saturday. On Wednesday,
diners are serenaded by a strolling violinist. ~ 10 East Gay Street,
West Chester; 610-696-4262; www.vincentsjazz.com.

is set in one of Wilmington's most magnificent hotels. ~ Hotel DuPont, Wilmington, DE; 302-656-4401, 800-338-0881; www.duponttheatre.org.

PARKS **VALLEY FORGE NATIONAL HISTORICAL PARK** 🏃 🚲 🛶 🛶
Historic Valley Forge is a favorite outdoor destination for residents of Southeastern Pennsylvania, with 23 miles of trails, including six of paved multipurpose trails. There are numerous scenic picnic venues in the park, including a spring house and grove near the former quarters of General James Varnu which overlook the parade fields. There's also a popular stream for trout fishing. This park is a year-round destination; in the winter; cross-country skiers take to the trails. The park service offers ranger-led hikes and nature excursions as well. Facilities here include a welcome center, restrooms, picnic tables, a gift shop and a chapel. ~ 1400 North Outerline Drive (Route 23 and Route 263), King of Prussia; 610-783-1000; www.nps.gov/vafo.

> Before the Brandywine River received its ear-pleasing name, it was called the "Fishkill" by the Swedish settlers, meaning "river of fish."

BRANDYWINE CREEK STATE PARK 🏃 🛶 Across the Brandywine in Delaware lies Brandywine Creek State Park, a 933-acre preserve that once housed a DuPont family dairy farm. The park marks the region where the hilly Piedmont flattens into tidewater, so it features a mix of rolling woods and pasturelands as well as freshwater wetlands. An interpretive nature center provides an overview of the region's flora and fauna and includes an observation deck for birding. The park has 14 miles of hiking trails and a main cycling trail. The park's ranger-led canoe trips are a well-kept regional secret; for $14, you can spend an afternoon seeing the area from the creek and learn about this fragile environment from a park ranger. The state park holds Civil War re-enactments in the spring. Amenities include a disc golf course, restrooms and a nature center. ~ Adams Dam Road, State Routes 100 and 92, Wilmington, DE; 302-655-5740.

HIDDEN ▶ **NEWLIN GRISTMILL** 🏃 🚲 🛶 Pennsylvania's only working gristmill, the Newlin mill was built in 1704. It remained in operation, grinding wheat, corn, oats, buckwheat and rye until 1941, and it still works today, although it's no longer used as a commercial enterprise. The park encompasses 150 acres, including nature trails, fishing ponds, streams, picnic areas, restrooms, a playground and a baseball diamond. On weekends from March through October, fishermen can try their luck at the mill's trout ponds for a fee. You can bring your own pole or borrow one, and any trout caught must be kept. ~ 219 South Cheyney Road, Glen Mills; 610-459-2359; www.newlingristmill.org.

HIBERNIA COUNTY PARK 🏃 🚴 ⛵ 🚣   The 800-acre Hiber-   ◀ *HIDDEN*
nia County Park encompasses woodlands and meadows, creeks,
wetlands and scenic pastureland. Home to Hibernia Mansion, an
18th-century ironmonger's home, Hibernia offers numerous opportunities for outdoor recreation, including playgrounds, picnic
facilities and a children's pond. Hayrides are offered April
through November. ~ 1 Park Road, Wagontown; 610-383-3812.

▲ Camping at 39 primitive sites is allowed on weekends
from the first weekend of trout season (usually mid-April)
through the last weekend of October; $11 per night.

The Brandywine region contains numerous   ▼▼▼▼▼▼▼▼▼▼▼▼▼▼
creeks, waterways and rivers abundant with   **Outdoor Adventures**
freshwater fish, including largemouth and
smallmouth bass, walleye, pike, panfish, trout and muskellunge.   **FISHING**
Fishing licenses are required for those 16 and older in both
Pennsylvania and Delaware. For information and fishing supplies, check out **French Creek Outfitters**, which carries a complete line of hunting, fishing and outdoor recreation gear. ~ 270
Schuylkill Road, Phoenixville; 610-933-7200; www.frenchcreek
outfitters.com.

In winter, ice fishing is a popular sport in the region, although
there are few places in the city to try this sport. **Marsh Creek
State Park** in Chester County has popular reservoirs and ponds
for ice fishing. ~ 675 Park Road, Downingtown; 610-458-5119.

The Brandywine River is a gentle, meandering waterway that **KAYAKING &**
flows through miles of pasturelands, parks and small towns.   **CANOEING**
From April through September, several outfitters in Chester
County offer canoe and inner-tube trips down the Brandywine.
The **Northbrook Canoe Company** rents canoes, kayaks and inner-   ◀ *HIDDEN*
tubes for enjoying this pristine waterway and scenic country.
Nonguided canoe trips range from one-hour to full-day, taking
adventurers past Chadds Ford and under historic covered bridges.
Kayaks also can be rented for up to one day, and the company
also offers two- and three-hour tubing adventures. Northbrook
runs a small snack shack for those who are hungry before or
after their trips. Rentals are available all week May through
September and weekends only in October. ~ 1810 Beagle Road,
West Chester; 610-793-2279, 800-898-2279; members.aol.com/
railsriver/index.html.

Wilderness Canoe Trips also rents canoes, kayaks and inner-
tubes for use on the Brandywine River. The outfitters run a Wilmington, Delaware, store and drive customers to and from drop-
off sites along the river. The company has canoes, single and
tandem kayaks available for as few as two hours and up to a day.

Inner-tube trips are roughly two hours. ~ 2111 Concord Pike, Wilmington, DE; 302-654-2227; www.wildernesscanoetrips.com.

Brandywine Outfitters, Inc., offers scenic tours of the region by canoe. One of the most popular tours includes a catered lunch. You also can simply rent a canoe for a few hours. ~ 2096 Strasburg Road, Coatesville; 800-226-6378.

Valley Forge Hidden River Canoe, Tube and Rafting offers one-hour to full-day trips, roughly 25 miles from Center City. ~ Route 724 and Main Street, Monocacy; 610-582-5800.

GOLF

At the **Golf Course at Glen Mills** you can play a round and feel benevolent at the same time; this course is maintained and operated by the students of Glen Mills School, a 180-year-old institution for troubled youth. The course is a training facility for students in turf management and golf operations, and revenues go toward scholarships. ~ 221 Glen Mills Road, Glen Mills; 610-558-2142; www.glenmillsgolf.com.

The **Tattersall Golf Club** features an 18-hole public course designed by Rees Jones. The top-rated course is scenic, if not hilly, and the club has two PGA professionals on hand for instruction and guidance. ~ 1520 Tattersall Way, West Chester; 610-738-4410.

Loch Nairn is a public facility located five miles south of Longwood Gardens. This 18-hole course is set among beautiful wetlands, streams, a lake and woods. All this scenery makes for some challenging play, however. The clubhouse features a 19th Hole with full bar and outdoor dining overlooking the course. ~ Off Route 1 at the Toughkenamon exit; 610-268-2234; www.lngolf.com.

RIDING STABLES

To enjoy the region from atop a horse, **Gateway Stables** offers half-hour and hour-long trail rides, even for those with little or no experience. A knowledgeable guide and well-mannered horses will lead you through the scenic region. Western and English tack available. ~ 949 Merrybell Lane, Kennett Square; 610-444-1255; www.gatewaystables.com.

CAMPING IN STYLE

The **Philadelphia–West Chester KOA** offers RV sites, tent camping and cabins along the Brandywine River. There are a number of amenities for campers, including free wireless internet as well as van tours to Philadelphia and Lancaster County. Closed November through March. ~ 1659 Embreeville Road, Coatesville; 610-486-0447, 800-562-1726; www.koa.com.

You can't ride the horses, but you can visit and fawn over the more than 100 equines at **Ryerss Farm** near Phoenixville, the nation's oldest nonprofit that cares for aged and abused horses. This remarkable facility was established for "ill, aged or injured animals" and originally took in retired horses from Philadelphia's firehouses. Visiting hours are 10:30 a.m. to 3:30 p.m. in winter; 10 a.m. to 3:30 p.m. any other time of the year. Call first for directions. ~ 1710 Ridge Road, Pottstown; 866-469-0507; www.ryerss.com.

◄ HIDDEN

County parks and recreation areas have numerous hiking, walking and running trails. The **Struble Trail**, located at Route 282 and Norwood Road in Downingtown, just west of West Chester, is a popular rails-to-trails, flat three-mile run that follows the Brandywine River. Plans are in place to extend the trail for 16 miles, but the current setup is particularly popular with joggers.

JOGGING

The Brandywine Valley has numerous roadways, trails and wooded paths for cycling, although (as in many areas with curvy two-lane roads) drivers often go too fast and pay too little attention to cyclists. Still, there are excellent cycling trails, including the ever-popular byways at Valley Forge and Brandywine Creek State Park.

BIKING

In Valley Forge, the 6-mile **loop trail** is popular with road cyclists and hikers, a relatively easy, paved path around the camp's most historic areas. Mountain bikers prefer Brandywine Creek, which has several woody trails that meander around this 900-acre park. For maps of specified mountain bike trails, stop by Brandywine Creek's nature center. If an intense mountain biking experience is what you're after, the **Horseshoe Trail** should not be missed. This 140-mile stretch between Valley Forge and the Appalachian Trail winds over parkland, on roads and through French Creek State Park.

Bike Rentals   **Bike Line** in Wilmington carries a selection of mountain bikes, road cycles and hybrids for rent. ~ 2900 North Concord Pike, Wilmington, DE; 302-479-9438. If you travel with your own bike and seek supplies and information, Bike Line's location in West Chester can help. ~ 909 Paoli Pike, West Chester; 610-436-8984.

All distances listed for hiking trails are roundtrip unless otherwise noted. The **Rocky Run Trail** (2 miles) at Brandywine Creek State Park wends through pine forests and meadows. This moderately strenuous hike features a scenic view and crisscrosses a small creek, making it an ideal activity in warm weather. The trailhead is at Thompson Bridge parking lot.

HIKING

Valley Forge National Historical Park is a beautiful, historic place to hike. Try to avoid the **loop trail** (6 miles) during the summer, when it gets crowded with walkers, joggers and bikers. But at other times, and farther afoot from the visitors center, the pathway is peaceful and scenic. Running from Valley Forge to the Appalachian Trail is the **Horseshoe Trail**, a 140-mile, multiuse trail that wends through woodlands, fields and over bridges. The **River Trail** (3 miles) skirts the Schuylkill River north of the main historic area—a less-traveled footpath that's perfect for viewing the area's flora and fauna. It connects to the **Schuylkill River Trail** (11.5 miles), which travels into Philadelphia. Park at Pawling Parking area.

In Hibernia County Park, consider hiking the **Forest Hill trail** (1.14 miles), which traverses three footbridges and winds along gentle slops and up one steep bank.

▼ ▼ ▼ ▼ ▼ ▼ ▼ ▼ ▼ ▼ ▼ ▼
Transportation

CAR

To reach the southern Brandywine region by car, you can take **Route 1** south from Philadelphia. To get to West Chester and the Chadds Ford area, take **Route 76 West** toward King of Prussia and Valley Forge. Exit onto Route 202 at Exit 328A and continue to Paoli Pike; follow Paoli Pike into West Chester.

AIR

The nearest large airport is **Philadelphia International Airport**, roughly 25 miles from major sites in the Brandywine Valley. For information, see "Transportation" in Chapter One.

TRAIN

Amtrak trains service Philadelphia's 30th Street Station and Wilmington station. ~ 215-824-1600; www.amtrak.com. SEPTA's R2 commuter train also runs to Wilmington. ~ 215-580-7800; www.septa.org.

BUS

Greyhound runs bus service to King of Prussia from both Philadelphia and Wilmington, although you'll need a car or must rely on taxi service to explore the backroads and country byways. ~ 215-931-4075, 800-231-2222; www.greyhound.com.

Index

Lodging Index

Dining Index

HIDDEN GUIDES

Adventure travel or a relaxing vacation?—"Hidden" guidebooks are the only travel books in the business to provide detailed information on both. Aimed at environmentally aware travelers, our motto is "Where Vacations Meet Adventures." These books combine details on unique hotels, restaurants and sightseeing with information on camping, sports and hiking for the outdoor enthusiast.

PARADISE FAMILY GUIDES

Ideal for families traveling with kids of any age—toddlers to teenagers—Paradise Family Guides offer a blend of travel information unlike any other guides to the Hawaiian islands. With vacation ideas and tropical adventures that are sure to satisfy both action-hungry youngsters and relaxation-seeking parents, these guides meet the specific needs of each and every family member.

Ulysses Press books are available at bookstores everywhere. If any of the following titles are unavailable at your local bookstore, ask the bookseller to order them.

You can also order books directly from Ulysses Press
P.O. Box 3440, Berkeley, CA 94703
800-377-2542 or 510-601-8301
fax: 510-601-8307
www.ulyssespress.com
e-mail: ulysses@ulyssespress.com